BRAND AID

An Easy Reference Guide to Solving Your Toughest Branding Problems and Strengthening Your Marketing Position

Brad VanAuken

AMACOM

American Management Association

New York • Atlanta • Brussels • Buenos Aires • Chicago • London • Mexico City
San Francisco • Shanghai • Tokyo • Toronto • Washington, D.C.

This publication is designed to provide accurate and authoritative information in regard to the subject matter covered. It is sold with the understanding that the publisher is not engaged in rendering legal, accounting, or other professional service. If legal advice or other expert assistance is required, the services of a competent professional person should be sought.

Library of Congress Cataloging-in-Publication Data

VanAuken, Brad.
    Brand aid : an easy reference guide to solving your toughest branding problems and strengthening your market position / Brad VanAuken.
        p.   cm.
    Includes bibliographical references and index.
    ISBN-10: 0-8144-0681-5
    ISBN-13: 978-0-8144-0681-6
    1. Brand name products—Management.   2. Brand name products—Marketing—Management.   3. Trademarks—Design.   I. Title.

HD69.B7 V36   2001
658.8'27—dc21

                                        2003001112

Printing number

15 14 13 12

Contents

Foreword

A FEW YEARS back, the topic of branding began to surface on the radar screens of senior executives. Managers everywhere began to grow in their appreciation for brands as they began to recognize the impact the brand has on overall business performance. Brands became recognized and promoted as assets for the corporation and the language of branding became required vernacular for anyone involved in business.

With this recognition of the importance of the brand came a flurry of industry conferences, published white papers, academic books, and business articles on the subject. Everywhere you turned, it seemed that someone was talking about branding. It was in this environment that I first met Brad VanAuken. We were both working inside major corporations and tasked with the complex challenge of managing our brands in dynamic business environments. While both of us found the plethora of material written on the subject intriguing, we agreed that much of it only began to scratch the surface in addressing the broad range of issues we were facing in managing our brands.

There can be little argument that strong brands enable organizations to prosper. But how do you get there? After all, strong brands do not just happen. Rather, they result when a series of cross-organizational fundamentals, designed against a common strategy, come together in alignment and are delivered through every business process and point of contact the organization has with its customers. Successfully managing a brand goes beyond understanding the fundamentals of the branding process—it also requires formally applying and establishing them within the organization.

In practice, brand management involves solving complex issues: How do you go about obtaining the kind of information that will allow you to position your brand in the marketplace? How do you build a unique relationship with your customer when competition is fierce? How do you communicate and translate your strategy consistently throughout the range of interactions your customers will have with your brand? How do you stand out with your brand in the market when you're working with limited resources? And how do you get every part of the organization to live the promise of the brand?

These are the questions and challenges brand managers face in their day-to-day responsibilities. And it is for this reason that *Brand Aid* is so important.

If you are a brand and marketing professional chartered with managing brands inside your organization, *Brand Aid* is an essential resource for you. Based on extensive research and Brad's first-hand experience, *Brand Aid* is a comprehensive guide unlike any other on the market today. It walks you through the complex range of topics facing brand managers and is organized in an easy-to-understand, quick-reference style. It is ideal for practitioners looking to understand the various components involved in the brand management process and especially tailored to those looking to directly apply what they have learned.

The robust set of tools incorporated throughout the book will prove immediately useful. The comprehensive checklists included at the conclusion of most chapters will help you assess your own organization's brand health and directly apply what you've learned to your own brand building challenges. Importantly, the checklists also enable you to prioritize elements that may need immediate attention and will subsequently help guide you in both short and long-term decision making

Brad provides a comprehensive overview of the brand management process. This overview, unique in its comprehensive design, helps articulate how the various components of branding come together and work as part of an overall system. Understanding this system is critical for those charged with managing brands within organizations because it helps outline the linkages and processes which must be developed to establish and maintain brand management as a discipline within an organization.

If you are chartered to increase the value of your brand, I know you will find *Brand Aid* an important companion in your quest. I am confident it will prove to be an essential reference tool for you and one to which you will return time and again. Read it. Write in it. Keep it on your desk. And most importantly—apply what you learn to your own brand building activities and watch the value of your brand and business bottom line increase.

Amy Kelm
Worldwide Consumer
Marketing Manager
Hewlett-Packard

Acknowledgments

As I HAVE discovered, although writing a book is a somewhat daunting task, it is not an entirely solitary one. Lance D'Amico, Julianne Hanes, and Jeff Kuzmich provided valuable input and feedback related to their areas of expertise. Lance Teitsworth squeezed time out of his busy schedule to help me with an illustration. David Thiel provided helpful additions to the "Brand Building on the Internet" chapter. I am indebted to my business partner, Dan Vandenberg, for his contributions to the "Brand Research" and "Brand Equity Measurement" chapters. I am particularly grateful to Amy Kelm for agreeing to write the Foreword, and to Susan Stim and Niels Buessem for their invaluable help in editing the book.

Some sections of this book have been published previously, and I am grateful for the permission of the copyright holders for them to be reprinted here: versions of Chapter 11, "Brand Building on the Internet," as "Brand ing.com: building and leveraging brands online," in *The Advertiser*, Oct/Nov 2000, pp. 70-76 (copyright Association of National Advertisers) and as "Branding.com: brand building on the internet," in *Admap*, issue 421 (October 2001) pp. 21-25 (copyright World Advertising Research Center); and Chapter 12, "Developing a Brand-Building Organization," as "Developing the brand building organization," in *Journal of Brand Management*, 7 (4) (March 2001) pp. 281-90 (copyright Henry Stewart Publications).

This book is the composite of years of experience coupled with extensive research. I am grateful to all of those individuals and organizations whose expertise and research findings have made this a more useful book. I have attempted to cite every source as precisely as possible. If I have made an oversight, please let me know and I will rectify the situation in the next edition.

Brad VanAuken

Introduction

THE BRAND INCREASINGLY is becoming the key source of differentiation that guides customer purchase choice. It is the focal point around which an organization defines how it will uniquely deliver value to the customer for a profit—effectively embodying the "heart and soul" of that organization. The brand's promise is delivered through its products, services, and consumer communication—the total customer relationship and experience. If the brand is well conceived and consistently delivered through all business processes and customer contacts, the organization will grow and prosper.

Not too long ago, marketers at consumer product companies seemed to be the only ones interested in talking about brand management and branding. But, these days, all kinds of organizations are recognizing the importance of branding. In the past few years, museums, universities, restaurants, churches, and individuals have approached me to help them build their brands. And now, it seems as though even the average person on the street is talking about brands.

Why has this marketing discipline become so popular? In an age of increasing product commoditization and choice, the brand is an easy way for people to break through the clutter. It helps them simplify certain choices in their lives. And brands are increasingly fulfilling peoples' needs for affiliation and identification—needs that traditional institutions are struggling to meet as well as they used to.

Senior management interest in brands has soared for a variety of reasons:

✔ Studies have shown that more and more categories are moving toward commoditization as companies (a) use increasingly sophisticated customer research to understand and address customer needs, and (b) are able quickly to determine and emulate the best practices of their competitors. A strong brand can help combat category commoditization and the resulting downward pressures on price.

✔ Manufacturers want to obtain increased leverage vis-à-vis retailers (this is a relationship the manufacturer can own with the consumer).

✔ Brands provide a flexible platform for growth (beyond current categories).

✔ Recent deregulation in several industries (notably, the utilities) has resulted in a need for differentiation.

✔ There is increased competition for consumer dollars.

✔ The emergence of the Internet has changed commerce.

Branding also becomes a critical issue for businesses that are spun off from the parent company (such as AT&T's Bell Labs, now Lucent Technologies) and as more and more companies merge or acquire one another. The brand identity of the new combined enterprise becomes critical.

Organizations have discovered that brands are perhaps their most important assets (along with their people) for a number of reasons. There is increasing evidence and consensus that strong brands deliver the following benefits to organizations:

✔ Increased revenues and market share

✔ Decreased price sensitivity

✔ Increased customer loyalty

✔ Additional leverage with retailers (for manufacturers)

✔ Increased profitability

✔ Increased stock price and shareholder value

✔ Increased clarity of vision

✔ Increased ability to mobilize an organization's people and focus its activities

✔ Increased ability to expand into new product and service categories

✔ Increased ability to attract and retain high quality employees

If brand management is new to you or your organization, you most likely need a quick but comprehensive overview of the key elements necessary for successful brand building. (I certainly would have found this very helpful a few years ago when I assumed the role of director of brand management and marketing for Hallmark Cards.) So, with this in mind, I have written this book using what I've learned from a wide variety of sources—books, seminars, consultants, industry benchmarking studies, my own consulting on this subject, and, most importantly, hands-on experience establishing brand management functions and brand-building cultures at Hallmark Cards and at Element K, a leading online learning company.

I wrote this book to be a thorough but pithy quick reference guide to all of the most important aspects of brand management and marketing. I have included every concept, template, formula, worksheet, research finding, "rule of thumb," checklist, and assessment tool that I have found to be useful in building strong brands throughout my twenty years as a marketing practitioner. Feel free to read the book a chapter at a time or to zero in on the topics that are of greatest interest to you.

Most chapters contain a brand management checklist at the end of the chapter. Use this checklist to identify the areas where your brand practices are strong and where they may be weak. Also use it to identify brand management activities and approaches that are new to you. The checklist takes the form of questions. The more questions to which you can answer yes, the better you are doing. After answering all the questions, it should be obvious which areas of brand practice require your attention. If you have answered no to a question, it should be clear what the associated action step should be. If it is not clear, you should at least be able to identify the general area in which you need help and the type of resources that may be of help to you.

Appendix B and the Web site www.brandforward.com contain information about online resources to help you further explore topics in much greater detail than can be covered in this book. Also, the boxed "Did You Know?" items scattered throughout the book feature interesting facts, rules of thumb, and other handy information you may find useful as you manage your brand.

Did You Know?

✔ In December of 1993, Charles Cobb purchased the PanAm trademark for $1.32 billion.

✔ Disney paid more than five times book value for Capital Cities/ABC. (*Source*: Don E. Schultz and Anders Gronstedt, "Making Marcom an Investment: Market-driven accounting system splits spending into business-building and brand-building activities," *Marketing Management,* Fall 1997, p. 45.)

✔ In 1988, Phillip Morris Co. acquired Kraft Foods for $12.9 billion, $11.6 billion over book value.

Book Overview

The book's first section, Part One, is an introduction to brand management, and it assumes no prior knowledge of brand management. Part 1 ends with *an overview of the brand management process*—to help put the rest of the book in perspective. The remainder of the book roughly follows this brand management process. Part Two covers brand design. Brand management must start here—with a thorough *understanding of the target consumer*. Included in this section is a chapter on the all-important topic of internal brand building, including defining the brand essence, promise, personality, and positioning.

Part Three focuses on building the brand, and it begins by showing the reader how to create brand insistence using BrandForward's model for *creating consumer brand insistence* in detail. This model is based on extensive research across multiple product and service categories, and it demonstrates that five common elements drive consumers to insist upon a particular brand: awareness, accessibility, value, relevant differentiation, and emotional connection. There is also an entire chapter devoted to *brand building on the Internet*, which presents thirty techniques that effectively build brands online.

Part Four covers the "R" in brand "ROI"—leveraging the brand for increased revenues and profits through *brand extension and by leveraging the brand globally*. Part Five addresses *brand metrics*, covering the spectrum of *brand research* (from logo recognition and recall to brand extension), and providing a detailed look at *brand equity measurement*. Part Six covers two miscellaneous brand management topics: the relationship of brand management issues to organization age and size, and legal issues in brand management. The final section, Part Seven, serves as a *brand management summary*. It includes a chapter that outlines twenty-two of the most common brand problems organizations encounter in managing their brands. A final chapter features twenty keys to success in brand building, including over seventy of the most important considerations in managing, building, and leveraging strong brands.

The first of the book's three appendixes explains the value of a brand *audit*. It outlines the components of a brand audit, offers suggestions on what to look for when selecting an outside brand auditor, and discusses the cost and duration of brands audits. Through a brand audit, an organization can assess the strengths, weaknesses, opportunities, and threats of its brand and it brand management practices.

Appendix B is an annotated listing of about forty online resources on various aspects of brand management and advertising.

Finally, congratulate yourself on how much you now know about brand management by taking the Brand Management Quiz in Appendix C, which touches upon key brand management and marketing concepts.

For an additional fifty pages of information on brand management topics, for hypertext links to thousands of online brand management and marketing resources that are not included in this book, and for citations of over 140 books, papers, and articles that I referenced to write this book, go to www.brandforward.com.

PART ONE

INTRODUCTION TO BRAND MANAGEMENT

CHAPTER 1

The Importance of Brands

PEOPLE OFTEN ASK me, "What is brand equity?" There are many ways to answer this. Some say it's everything associated with the brand that adds to or subtracts from the value it provides to a product or service. Others emphasize the financial value of the brand asset. Still others stress the consumer loyalty or price premium generated by brand equity. Some even talk about the permission and flexibility a brand gives an organization to extend into new product and service categories. While all of these are very important parts of brand equity, I think the following story best illustrates what brand equity is.

Imagine you are having lunch with a long-time and very good friend. Several times throughout the lunch, she makes disparaging and sarcastic remarks that make you feel bad. You think to yourself, "This just isn't like her. She must be having a bad day." You meet with her again a week or two later, and again she acts ornery and negative. You think to yourself, "Something must be going on in her life that she's really struggling with. Maybe she is having difficulties with her job or her health or her marriage or her children." You may even ask her if everything is all right. She snaps back, "Of course it is."

Your interaction with her continues in this vein over the next couple of months. You continue to try to be supportive, but she's definitely getting on your nerves. After many meetings and much interaction, you finally decide that she's a changed person and someone with whom you prefer to spend less and less time. You may get to this point after a few months, or perhaps even after a year or more. She doesn't change, and eventually the relationship peters out.

Now consider for a moment that the person you first had lunch with is the same person as before, with one exception: She is a total stranger to you. You haven't met her previously and she is not your dear friend. I would guess that after enduring many caustic comments and being insulted a few times at that lunch, your first impression wouldn't be very positive. In fact, you'd probably be inclined not to get together with that person again. You'd probably walk away from that lunch thinking, "What a miserable person. I hope I don't run into her again."

In both of these scenarios it is the same person behaving the same way in the same situation. Yet in the first scenario, you are very quick to forgive the behavior. In fact, you feel a lot of concern toward her. In the second scenario, you can't wait for the lunch to be over and you hope never to see the person again.

In the first scenario, the person was a long-time good friend. She had a lot of equity with you. In the second scenario, she had no equity at all. You see, if people or brands have a lot of equity—that is, if you know, like, and trust them —you will "cut them a lot of slack" even if they repeatedly fail to meet your expectations. If a person, product, service, or organization has no equity with you, no emotional connection, and no trust, then you are much less inclined to forgive unmet expectations.

Did You Know?

- ✔ "Familiarity (exposure and/or use) leads to liking." (*Source*: Andrew Ehrenberg, Neil Barnard, and John Scriven, "Differentiation or Salience." *Journal of Advertising Research,* November–December 1997, p. 9.)

- ✔ Declining brands tend to lose buyers while the brands' loyalty and purchase rates stay stable among remaining buyers. (*Source*: Andrew Ehrenberg, "Description and Prescription," *Journal of Advertising Research,* November–December 1997, p. 19.)

- ✔ In most product categories, price is the primary purchase incentive for no more than 15 percent to 35 percent of all customers. (*Source*: Kevin J. Clancy, "At what profit price?" *Brandweek,* Vol. 38, Issue 25, June 23, 1997, pp. 24–28.)

Brand equity creates a relationship and a strong bond that grows over time. It is often so strong that it compensates for performance flaws, such as an out-of-stock situation, poor customer service, a product that falls apart, inconvenient store hours, or a higher-than-average-price. In the end, you want to deliver good quality and good value, innovation, relevant differentiation, convenience, and accessibility with your brand. However, we must never forget that building brand equity is like building a close friendship. It requires a consistent relationship over time, trust, and an emotional connection.

CHAPTER 2

Understanding the Language of Branding

IT IS IMPORTANT to establish a common brand management vocabulary in your organization. Establishing this common vocabulary will ensure that people can communicate with fewer misunderstandings. More importantly, it will help communicate and reinforce key brand management principles.

I worked with organizations in which different managers used different terms to describe positioning the brand. Terms ranged from "essence" and "promise" to "position" and "unique value proposition." This caused great confusion. I worked with other organizations that struggled with the differences among master brand, family brand, parent brand, umbrella brand, corporate brand, brand, subbrand, endorsed brand, product brand, etc. The aim is to agree on one set of terms and to simplify the brand architecture.

Brand

The American Marketing Association describes a brand as a "name, term, sign, symbol or design, or a combination of them intended to identify the goods and services of one seller or group of sellers and to differentiate them from those of competition."

More importantly, *a brand is the source of a promise to the consumer.* It promises relevant differentiated benefits. Everything an organization does should be focused on enhancing delivery against its brand's promise.

Combining a few different definitions, a brand is the name and symbols that identify:

✔ The source of a relationship with the consumer
✔ The source of a promise to the consumer
✔ The unique source of products and services

✔ The single concept that you own inside the mind of the prospect (per brand management experts Al Ries and Laura Ries, in their new book *The 22 Immutable Laws of BRANDING*)

✔ The sum total of each customer's experience with your organization

Brand Equity

Brand equity is the commercial value of all associations and expectations (positive and negative) that people have of an organization and its products

---

Tip

For those nonprofit organizations who are loathe to use the word "brand" (because of its corporate or business overtone/connotation) but who still want to actively manage their brands internally and externally, consider using the word "promise" in place of "brand." For instance, talk about *managing our promise, delivering upon our promise,* or *[name's] promise is.*

---

and services due to all experiences of, communications with, and perceptions of the brand over time. This value can be measured in several ways: as the economic value of the brand asset itself, as the price premium (to the end consumer or the trade) that the brand commands, as the long-term consumer loyalty the brand evokes, or as the market share gains it results in, among many others. From an economist's perspective, brand equity is the power of the brand to shift the consumer demand curve of a product or service (to achieve a price premium or a market share gain).

To use a metaphor, brand equity is like a pond. People may not know how long the pond has been around or when it first filled with water, but they know that it supports life, from fish and frogs to ducks and deer. It also may be a source of recreation, irrigation, and possibly even human drinking water. Clearly it is a valuable resource. But many people take the pond for granted. It seems as if nothing can diminish its supply of water, but yet we sometimes notice that it rises with the spring rains or lowers after a long drought or excessive overuse for irrigation.

Similarly, brand equity is a reservoir of goodwill. Brand-building activities consistently pursued over time will ensure that the reservoir remains full. Neglecting those activities or taking actions that might deplete those reserves will reduce the reservoir, imperceptibly at first, but soon all too noticeably until it is too late and all that is left is mud.

This illustrates one of the most difficult problems in brand management. Brand equity is critically important to a company's success, yet because of its reservoir-like nature, it is often taken for granted, overly drawn upon, and not adequately replenished, especially in times of crisis or to meet short-term needs.

Brand Image

Brand image is the totality of perceptions resulting from all experience with and knowledge of the brand. It is how consumers perceive the brand.

Brand Associations

Brand associations are anything a consumer associates with the brand in his or her mind. As David Aaker, "guru" of brand management, points out, these associations could be organizational, product related, symbolic, or personified. If there is a strong brand connection with a specific retail outlet, the associations could also be based on the retail experience.

Other brand equity components that are not listed in this chapter but which are covered in detail in Chapters 8 and 18 include awareness, accessibility, value, relevant differentiation, emotional connection, preference, usage, loyalty, and vitality.

Brand Positioning

Brand positioning is the way the brand is perceived within a given competitive set in the consumer's mind. Ideally, it is a function of the brand's promise and how the brand compares to other choices with regard to quality, innovation, perceived leadership, value, prestige, trust, safety, reliability, performance, convenience, concern for customers, social responsibility, technological superiority, etc. Relevant differentiation is the most important aspect of brand positioning.

One could argue that the brand essence, promise, and personality are all a part of the brand positioning. Given that, brand positioning is very similar to what I refer to as brand design in Chapter 3.

Brand positioning elements can be intentional and crafted by the marketer, for instance, as written in the brand positioning statement. The brand essence, promise, and personality can also exist "in the mind of the consumer." Ideally, what exists in the mind of the consumer is congruent with the intended brand positioning, or if not, hopefully the brand management team is actively managing the brand so that congruence will occur.

Brand Essence

This is the *heart and soul of a brand*—a brand's fundamental nature or quality. Usually stated in two to three words, a brand's essence is the one constant across product categories and throughout the world. Some examples are:

Nike: *Authentic Athletic Performance*

Hallmark: *Caring Shared*

Disney: *Fun Family Entertainment*

Disneyworld: *Magical Fun*

Starbucks: *Rewarding Everyday Moments*

The Nature Conservancy: *Saving Great Places*

Typically, it is rare for an organization's brand essence and slogan to be the same. For instance, Nike's essence—"Authentic Athletic Performance"—was translated to the following two slogans: "Just do it!" and "I can." But, "Saving Great Places" more directly translates to its slogan "Saving the Last Great Places on Earth."

Kevin Keller, brand expert and author of the popular brand book, *Strategic Brand Management*, has coined the term "brand mantra," which is very closely related to brand essence. The "mantra" concept reinforces the role of brand essence in internal communication. According to Keller:

▶

[Brand mantra should] define the category of business for the brand and set brand boundaries. It should also clarify what is unique about the brand. It should be memorable. As a result it should be short, crisp and vivid in meaning. Ideally, the brand mantra would also stake out ground that is personally meaningful and relevant to as many employees as possible.

Brand Promise

To be successfully positioned in the market place, a brand must promise differentiated benefits that are relevant and compelling to the consumer. The benefits can be functional, experiential, emotional or self-expressive. A brand promise is often stated as:

▶

Only [brand name] delivers [benefit] in [product or service category]. Sometimes, with corporate brands, it is stated as: [Brand name] is the (trusted/quality/innovative) leader in [benefit] in the [product or service category].

To be believable, brand promises require compelling proof points (and what advertising professionals call "reasons to believe") in support of the brand's promise. A brand promise must:

- ✔ Address important consumer needs
- ✔ Leverage your organization's strengths
- ✔ Give you a competitive advantage through differentiation
- ✔ Inspire, energize, and mobilize your people
- ✔ Drive every organizational decision, system, action, and process
- ✔ Manifest itself in your organization's products and services

As Kristin Zhivago, respected marketing consultant and editor of the "Marketing Technology" newsletter, puts it in the July/August 1994 double issue of her newsletter:

► **The simple truth** about branding—a brand is not an icon, a slogan, or a mission statement. It is a promise—a promise your company can keep. First you find out, using research, what promises your customers want companies like yours to make and keep, using the products, processes and people in your company. Then you look at your competition and decide which promise would give you the best competitive advantage. This is the promise you make and keep in every marketing activity, every action, every corporate decision, every customer interaction. You promote it internally and externally. The promise drives budgets and stops arguments. If everyone in the company knows what the promise is, and knows that they will be rewarded or punished depending on the personal commitment to the promise, politics and personal turf issues start to disappear.

Visually, the brand promise should drive, or at least be congruent with, each of the five star points shown in Figure 2-1.

Brand Personality

Brand personality refers to adjectives that describe the brand (such as fun, kind, sexy, safe, sincere, sophisticated, cheerful, old fashioned, reliable, progressive, etc.). How consumers perceive a brand's personality is often discovered through qualitative research by asking people to describe the brand as if it were a person or an animal.

FIGURE 2-1. BRAND PROMISE.

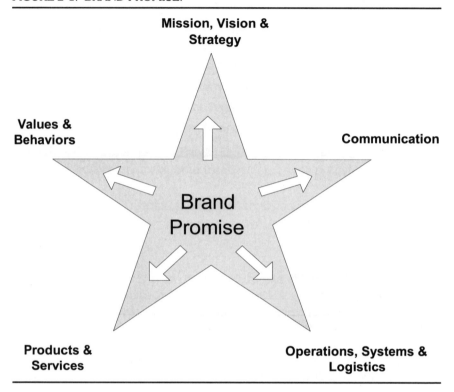

Brand Identity

Brand identity is a combination of visual, auditory, and other sensory components that create recognition, represent the brand promise, provide differentiation, create communications synergy, and are proprietary.[1] Some define brand identity more broadly to include almost everything in a brand's design, including essence, promise, personality, and positioning. The more specific definition used in this book reflects the most common usage of the term, especially as used by firms focused on the creation of brand identity standards and systems.

Names and nomenclature, logotypes, symbols and other graphic devices, distinctive shapes and colors, brand voice and visual style, sounds, jingles and other mnemonic devices, typography, theme lines or slogans, and characters that are uniquely associated with a brand are all components of a brand's identity.[2] Textures, scents, flavors, and other sensory elements also can be components of a brand's identity.

Brand Portfolio

Brand portfolio is the mix of brands and subbrands owned by an organization. This portfolio should be actively managed to ensure effective, efficient brand management. For example, Procter & Gamble and Unilever both have a large portfolio of brands; General Motors manages Buick, Cadillac, Dodge, and other brands; Hallmark manages the Hallmark, Shoebox, and Crayola brands among others; Darden restaurant group manages the Olive Garden, Red Lobster, and Bahama Breeze brands.

Brand Architecture (or Brand Structure)

Think of brand architecture as a brand's family tree or its hierarchy. It is how an organization organizes the various named entities within its portfolio, and how they relate to each other. Ideally, the brand architecture is simple, with no more than two levels: brand and subbrands. In fact, brand/subbrand is the type of architecture most often used. It takes many forms, mostly based upon the type of name used for the subbrands. Some organizations add a third level: named products. But, any more than two levels can be confusing.

The four general types of architecture are:

1. Master brand
2. Brand/subbrand
3. Endorsed brand
4. Separate (stand-alone or independent) brands

Brand architecture addresses the following:

- Number of separately named entities
- Criteria for becoming a separately named entity
- Levels of relationships between separately named entities
- Naming and other brand identity conventions for each level
- Nature of the relationships between the named entities at different levels

Corporate Brand

Corporate brand is the brand bearing the company name. It is always the highest in a brand hierarchy. Examples are Ford, Hewlett-Packard, IBM, General Motors, 3M, and Kodak.

Master Brand

Master brand is the dominant, highest level brand in a brand hierarchy. Typically, it is also the *only* brand in the system. Historically, many corporate brands were also master brands. Today, there are few master brands left.

Parent Brand

Parent brand is a brand that is extended into more than one product category. It may or may not be the same as the corporate brand. Examples are Ford and Honda.

Parent brands offer the following advantages:

- ✔ Less expensive new product launches
- ✔ Trust/assurance
- ✔ Marketing economies of scale

Subbrand

A subbrand is a new brand that is combined with a parent or corporate brand in the brand identity system. The subbrand can make the parent brand more vital and relevant to a new consumer segment or within a new product category. Examples are Taurus and Accord.

Endorsed Brand

Endorsed brand is the primary name the consumer is intended to use to refer to a product. It is a brand that is endorsed by the parent or corporate brand in the brand identity system. The parent brand is also identified with the product; however, the endorsed brand is given much greater visual weight than the parent brand. In this situation, the corporate or parent brand lends credibility or assurance to the endorsed brand without overpowering it with its own associations. An example is Shoebox, a tiny division of Hallmark.

Trade Dress

Trade dress refers to aesthetic elements that provide legal protection for a brand's identity. For example, Coca-Cola's bottle shape is a part of its trade dress, as are Absolute vodka's bottle shape and Harley-Davidson's engine sound.

Brand Extension

Brand extension means applying the existing brand to new products, services, or consumer segments. If this is done by combining the existing brand with a new brand, the new brand is called a subbrand. If executed properly, brand extensions can broaden and clarify the meaning of the brand. If executed improperly, they can dilute or confuse the meaning of the brand. Examples are Crayola (from crayons to markers and pens) and Jell-o (from gelatin to pudding).

Marketing Plan

A marketing plan is a request for funds in return for a promised level of incremental revenues, unit sales, market share or profits.[3] One can develop marketing plans for products, services, market segments, or brands. The critical components of a marketing plan includes the following:

- ✔ **Summary.**
- ✔ **Objectives** (attract new consumers, create new uses, increase share of requirements, incent trial, encourage repeat purchase, encourage add-on purchase, increase awareness, increase loyalty, change value perception, increase emotional bond, extend into new product and service categories, etc.).
- ✔ **Situation Analysis.**
  - ✔ Market Analysis
  - ✔ Competitive Context
  - ✔ Customer Profile (segments, needs, attitudes, behaviors, insights, etc.)
- ✔ **Strategies and Tactics** (touching upon all key marketing components that will be used: product, packaging, pricing, distribution, advertising, publicity, sales promotion, selling, etc.; be specific).
- ✔ **Operations Considerations** (impact on plant capacity, need for new assets, etc.).
- ✔ **Financial Projections.**
  - ✔ Pro forma profit and loss statements, balance sheets, cash flows, etc.
  - ✔ Funds required to execute plan
- ✔ **Supporting Customer Research** (qualitative research, concept testing, volumetric modeling, market test results, etc.).
- ✔ **Risks and Contingency Plans.**

Brand Plan

A brand plan is similar to a marketing plan. Its objectives focus primarily on changing or improving brand equity components, like those listed below. Increased market share is a frequently specified brand objective.

- ✓ Brand awareness
- ✓ Brand accessibility
- ✓ Brand value
- ✓ Brand relevant differentiation
- ✓ Brand emotional connection
- ✓ Brand vitality
- ✓ Brand loyalty
- ✓ Brand personality
- ✓ Other brand associations

Notes

1. Definition courtesy of Lister Butler Consulting, New York.
2. Courtesy of Lister Butler Consulting, New York.
3. Source: "What are the key issues to be covered in my marketing plan?" http://www.uwa.com/marketing/consultants/mrktplan.htm 8/7/01.

CHAPTER 3

Brand Management Process: An Overview

THE BRAND MANAGEMENT process starts with a deep understanding of consumers and competitors. You will need to fully understand the consumer benefit structure by segment, including which benefits are cost-of-entry and which are differentiating. In-depth qualitative consumer research will help uncover this information. You will also need to know which benefits each competitor delivers in consumers' minds. Ultimately, you will need to know which benefits are important, personally relevant, unique and differentiating, purchase motivating, and appropriate for your brand. You also need to know that consumer benefits can be functional, emotional, experiential, or self-expressive. Once you know all this, you can begin to design your brand.

Designing Your Brand

In brand positioning or design, there are four components to be addressed:

1. *Target Audience.* Define the target customer.
2. *Brand Essence.* Articulate the "heart and soul" of the brand.
3. *Brand Promise.* Develop the relevant differentiating benefits the brand promises to deliver to its target audience.
4. *Brand Personality.* Describe the brand as if it were a person.

After addressing these four components, you need to define your brand's competitive frame of reference and map out how your brand is positioned against competitors (Exhibit 3-1 is an example of a brand positioning statement). Although this may sound like a linear process, it is actually iterative and even organic. In the end, though, you will have determined each of the elements of your brand's design.

The diagram shown in Figure 3-1 provides an overview of the brand management process.

EXHIBIT 3-1. BRAND POSITIONING STATEMENT OF THE NATURE
CONSERVANCY.

THE NATURE CONSERVANCY

Target Audience:

1. Affluent people who are concerned about environmental conservation
2. Opinion leaders

Brand Essence:

Saving Great Places

Brand Promise:

Only The Nature Conservancy has the expertise and resources to work
in creative partnership with local communities in the United States and
internationally with exceptional range and agility to conserve the most
important places for future generations.

Brand Personality:

Results oriented, action oriented
Effective
Entrepreneurial
Focused
A good ally, a reliable partner
Possessing integrity
Businesslike, professional
Hard working, persistent, tireless, dedicated
Positive, constructive, nonconfrontational
Science-driven

Once the brand is designed, this design must drive all of your consumer
communication, all your other marketing elements, and your organization's
design, particularly the company culture. It must also drive what Michael Porter, Harvard Business School professor and thought leader, calls the "customer value chain." ("Value chain" is the concept that each activity an
organization undertakes should lead to added value to its target consumers.
If it doesn't, it should be reevaluated and possibly eliminated.)

The brand design should be directly translated into and supported by the
brand identity standards and systems. This ensures that the brand design is
realized at each point of contact with the consumer, resulting in a total brand
experience. If done right, a brand and the experience it delivers transcend the
brand's products and services. In essence, you are selling the brand experience more than anything else.

FIGURE 3-1. BRAND MANAGEMENT PROCESS.

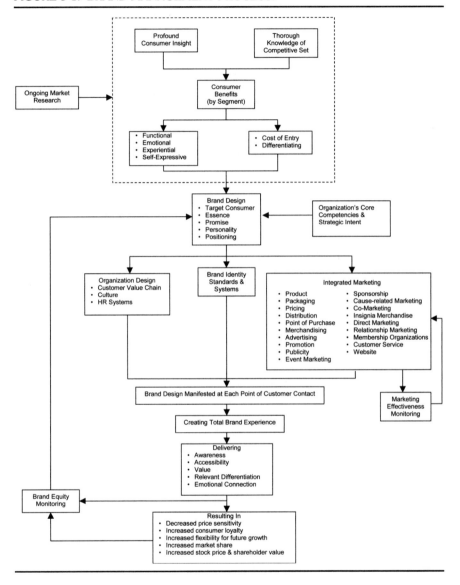

All of this should deliver awareness, relevant differentiation, value, accessibility, and emotional connection—the key components in creating brand insistence.

Ultimately, strong brand equity should result in price premiums, decreased price sensitivity, increased consumer loyalty, increased flexibility for future growth, increased market share, and increased shareholder value.

The Most Important Tasks of a Brand Management Function

✔ **Develop and execute brand plans, including brand marketing plans**

✔ **Build brand awareness**

✔ **Position the brand for sustainable competitive advantage**

✔ **Transform the organization's leadership team into brand champions**

✔ **Transform all employees into brand champions**

✔ **Measure and actively manage your brand's equity**

✔ **Actively manage the brand's identity, including enforcement of its guidelines and standards**

✔ **Legally protect the brand**

✔ **Always keep the brand customer focused**

✔ **Design and implement plans to create emotional connection between your brand and its customers**

✔ **Develop and execute brand loyalty programs**

▨ Research that Supports the Brand Management Process

There are many types of research that aid in the brand management process. Some are ongoing, while others are only conducted periodically or as needed. Ongoing research includes brand equity, marketing effectiveness, and competitive monitoring, among other categories of research.

Monitoring Brand Equity

Brand equity monitoring should highlight changes in consumers' attitudes, preferences, and behavior regarding your brand. It should also perform a diagnostic role, providing insights into why those changes are occurring.

Monitoring Marketing Effectiveness

Marketing effectiveness monitoring takes many forms—from simple advertising copy testing to using an ongoing system to identify the relative effectiveness of each element in your marketing mix, including estimates of return on marketing investment. It can be even more detailed, including analysis of effectiveness against different marketing objectives, such as customer retention, share of requirements, category buying rate, in-store capture, and conversion rates.

Competitive Monitoring

Competitive monitoring can take many forms, from diary panel studies and market tours to product preference testing and POS (point of sale) data analysis—chain specific data or from AC Nielsen (Scan Track) or IRI (DataServer, FasTrac, and InfoScan).

One-time or periodic research includes attitude and usage studies, in-depth qualitative consumer research, focus groups, conjoint analysis, Perception Analyzer testing, recognition and recall tests, concept testing, benefit testing, test markets, etc.

Brand Extension

A brand is an asset, and to provide strong shareholder value, assets must be leveraged. Brand extension is the primary way of doing that. Brand extension can be a powerful way to optimize the performance of your brand, but it also can be a complicated endeavor. Brand extension, including its benefits and risks, will be discussed in detail in Chapter 15.

PART TWO

DESIGNING THE BRAND

C H A P T E R 4

Understanding the Consumer

ORGANIZATIONS EXIST FOR one purpose—to meet human needs. Thriving organizations do that exceedingly well. Venerated organizations have managed to meet evolving human needs over a long period of time. All of an organization's revenues and profits result from one thing—customers who are willing to pay money for products and services that meet their needs. Therefore, any brand management initiative, any marketing initiative, and indeed any business or organizational initiative must start with a solid understanding of the customer.

Defining the Target Customer

Focus is an important part of a brand's success. Brands focus on a target customer and often narrow their focus to a particular customer need segment. As mentioned in Chapter 3, customer targeting is the first step in brand design. Everything else emanates from that. So let us start with how to identify your brand's target customers.

Look for customers who meet the following criteria:

✔ They have an important need, and your brand meets that need.

✔ Your brand has the potential to be preferred by them.

✔ There is something about your brand that they admire.

✔ They have the potential to provide your organization with ample revenues and profits over the long run.

✔ Your organization can grow by building a long-term relationship with and increasingly fulfilling the evolving needs of these customers.

At a minimum, you should identify and understand the following target customer attributes:

✔ Demographics
✔ Lifestyle
✔ Needs/desires
✔ Hopes/aspirations
✔ Fears/concerns
✔ Product purchase behavior
✔ Product usage behavior

The Power of Focus

The power of brands lies in focus. Very few, if any, brands can be all things to all people within a product or service category. That is why segmentation

---

Did You Know?

That through carefully researched consumer insight, John Deere was able to significantly increase sales of its lawn tractors. Most men really admired the brand but believed that it was "too much for them." They could never justify buying it for themselves. Here's the insight. When their wives were made aware that 8 out of 10 men would prefer a John Deere lawn tractor if given the option, sales significantly increased. The way in was through the gift giver. (*Source*: Barry Krause, President of Publicis & Hal Riney Chicago in his presentation "Advertising Agency's View on Corporate Branding" at the American Management Association's "Corporate Branding: Leveraging Your Company's Key Intangible Asset" conference in San Francisco, February 24, 1999.)

---

is important. Ideally, a brand or subbrand focuses only on the customer segment that it can best serve. It becomes an expert provider of products and services to that segment. I am a firm believer that in today's business environment, the most robust brands will be those that:

✔ Focus on one customer group
✔ Become intimate with that group
✔ Strive to meet more and more needs of that group
✔ Cocreate products and services with the group
✔ Epitomize what that group stands for

Although we most often think of brands targeting specific customer groups, different brands can also target different needs for the same people.

For instance, different needs are driving your purchase decision in each of the following situations, and you are very likely to consider a different set of restaurants (or brand) for each:

- ✓ Catching a quick bite to eat on your way to work in the morning
- ✓ Taking your children out to eat
- ✓ Celebrating a special occasion with a loved one
- ✓ Staying on your diet and losing weight

▓ Techniques to Better Understand the Customer

Understanding your customer is a never-ending process. Here are some simple ways to do so:

- ✓ Conduct ongoing customer research, from focus groups and depth interviews to anthropological and other quantitative research techniques (see Chapter 17 on brand research).
- ✓ Conduct customer satisfaction surveys.
- ✓ Maintain and monitor customer service/support mechanisms (help lines, e-mail support, etc.).
- ✓ Establish and monitor discussion boards and chat rooms devoted to different customer groups/segments.
- ✓ Establish and consult with customer advisory boards.
- ✓ Establish customer membership organizations. Participate in and monitor their events. (Harley-Davidson executives are masters at this. They attend—and ride in—HOG (Harley Owners Group) rallies, talk with their customers at those rallies, observe new product accessories, and debrief after every HOG rally back at the office for new product ideas and other action items.)
- ✓ Have key executives/managers participate in sales calls.
- ✓ Have key executives/managers occasionally rotate through front-line customer service positions.
- ✓ Hire employees who are also passionate customers. (There is one danger with this approach. Even if you are a passionate brand customer, don't assume that all other customers are just like you.)

Because of their extensive market research, people who develop new products (marketers and marketing researchers) often understand the market (including deep customer insights) better than anyone else in the organization. Seek them out to gain a better understanding of your brand's customers and their needs.

Environmental Scanning

For most businesses, environmental scanning can also be very helpful in staying abreast of the latest customer, industry, and societal trends. "Environmental scanning" is a fancy term for the following process:

- ✔ Reading a broad cross-section of books and publications of relevance to your business
- ✔ Monitoring any other relevant media
- ✔ Keeping very close track of the emerging trends by counting the number of times certain ideas, needs, or concepts are referenced
- ✔ Seeking better to understand emerging ideas, needs or concepts—those that are steadily increasing in frequency and intensity

Market Segmentation

Market segmentation is often necessary to effectively meet the needs of different customer groups. Different segments will value different aspects of your products, services, and brands differently. You should have a good understanding of the following dimensions of each market segment:

- ✔ Its overall size and its growth rate
- ✔ Its price sensitivity
- ✔ The benefits that are most and least important to it
- ✔ How well it is served by existing products and brands
- ✔ How brand loyal it is
- ✔ How it selects and purchases the product
- ✔ How accessible it is
- ✔ The distribution methods it prefers
- ✔ How it uses the product
- ✔ Its product usage/replacement rate
- ✔ Its longevity and projected evolution over time

Markets can be segmented in the following ways:

- ✔ *Product Usage Segmentation.*
- ✔ *Purchase Behavior Segmentation.* In many industries, four groups that often emerge to one degree or another are:

1. Brand-loyal consumers

2. Convenience-driven consumers

3. Price-driven consumers

4. Consumers who enjoy seeking out new brands and products within the category

✓ *Benefit Segmentation.*

✓ *Price Segmentation.* Price segmentation will yield higher overall revenues and profits if designed properly. Airlines have made a science out of price segmentation. First class travelers pay more. Business travelers with tight schedules will be less price sensitive. Tourists with fixed budgets, flexible schedules, and a long planning horizon will look for lower fares. Some people will only travel taking advantage of last minute seat-filling bargain prices. Other last-minute travelers have no choice and behaviorally (but probably not attitudinally) are virtually price insensitive. Seats are less expensive on slower days (Saturdays, December 25th, etc.).

✓ *Lifestage Segmentation.* Consult: Stanford Research Institute's VALS™ 2 (values and lifestyles) at www.sri.com, Yankelovich MONITOR® at www.yankelovich.com, and the University of Michigan's LOV (list of values).

✓ *Cohort Group Segmentation* (people who were born at approximately the same time and who have experienced the same events at the same lifestages).

✓ *Psychographic Segmentation* (segmenting people based upon their values, attitudes, and lifestyles).

✓ *Geographic Segmentation.*

✓ *Geodemographic Segmentation* (segmenting people based upon their location—typically zip or postal code—and demographics, such as age, income, etc.). Consult: Claritas' PRISM and MicroVision at www. velocity.claritas.com and CACI's ACORN®, www.demographics.caci.com.

As the list above illustrates, consumers can be segmented on many dimensions. The trick is to arrive at a segmentation scheme that relates to differences in purchase motivations and behaviors. Different brands are designed to appeal to different needs with unique points of difference. It is important to understand the consumers to whom your brand will mean the most and who will have the highest likelihood of responding to your brand messages.

Business-to-Business Customers

For B2B (business-to-business) organizations, understanding the purchase decision-making process is usually more complicated. Decisions are often made by teams or committees comprising people from different functions.

Some people initiate the purchase order or RFP (request for proposal). Others are gatekeepers, influencers, decision makers, purchasers and users. Each has a different role in the process at a different point in the process. They often focus on different product, service, and brand attributes, and they respond to different types of appeals. Also, they usually rely upon different sources for their information. An astute B2B marketer should understand how best to get to each of these individuals, what angle to emphasize in the communication, and in what verbal style to communicate (see Exhibit 4-1).

For instance, in a corporation considering e-learning (online learning) solutions, the CLO (chief learning officer) may be the primary decision maker for enterprise-wide solutions; however, many others are typically a part of the process, such as:

- ✓ The CFO (chief financial officer) may have suggested that e-learning be investigated as a cost savings measure and may have final approval of the purchase.
- ✓ General managers whose employees will be beneficiaries of the training will have their own point of view.
- ✓ The CIO (chief information officer) may have an opinion regarding the technology training components of the solution.
- ✓ The HR vice president may want to know how this fits into the organization's overall approach to human capital management.
- ✓ There may even be a group of end users set up to evaluate each of the alternatives considered.

EXHIBIT 4-1. B2B PURCHASER MOTIVATIONS.

These purchaser motivations are usually present in B2B buying situations:

Price
Perceived quality
Technical specifications
Warranties
Other service or post-sale support
Financial stability of the seller
Buyer's past experience
Organizational policies
Fear of making a mistake
Friendship
Seller's interest in buyer's business
Persuasiveness of seller

SOURCE: Gabriel M. Gelb, Gelb Consulting Group, Inc., "The Nuts and Bolts of Business-to-Business Marketing Research," as featured on CRM University Learning Center (http://www.techmar.com/ubusmktresearchbma.asp) 9/25/01.

✓ Lawyers may provide their opinion on aspects of the proposal.

✓ And, depending on the organization, the list of stakeholders in the decision-making process may be extensive.

A marketer will have to decide which audiences are the most important, how many different types of communications are necessary, and how much the brand needs to be built with each stakeholder. As resources are always finite, decisions on reach versus frequency for each audience will be necessary.

In B2B situations, once one decision maker has been identified through research, it is very useful to ask that person, "Who else in your organization is involved in the decision-making process?"

Business markets can often be segmented by Standard Industrial Classification (SIC) code. Various publications and other sources provide information by SIC code, including U.S. Industrial Outlook, U.S. Census of Manufacturers, Dunns Marketing Services, and mail houses.

In organizations with a wide variety of products and services serving multiple markets, business units are often formed around different customer groups. Another approach to serving different markets is to create the segment marketing manager role. Segment marketing managers become experts in their assigned markets through primary and secondary research and develop (and execute) integrated marketing plans (including product requirements) for their assigned markets. These people often interact in a matrix fashion with the product managers.

▊ Techniques to Retain Customers

The "lifetime value of the consumer" concept is based on the fact that it is much more cost effective to keep a good consumer than to attract a new one. For large-ticket items (e.g., automobiles) or items that require frequent purchase over time (e.g., breakfast cereals), the lifetime value of a consumer can be very high. So, encouraging young customers to buy your products and services will help your business to remain healthy over time and to create a longer lifetime value of the customer.

Techniques for keeping good consumers include the following:

✓ Database marketing

✓ Special services

✓ Product customization

✓ Personal touches

✓ Legendary service

✓ Communication that reinforces previously made purchases (especially to overcome post-purchase anxiety or doubts over large-ticket items)

✔ Programs that reward loyalty and heavy brand consumption

✔ Avoiding programs that encourage brand switching

Did You Know?

✔ **Customers share bad brand experiences with approximately twice as many people as they do good brand experiences.**

Use the checklist in Exhibit 4-2 to assess the efficacy of your brand management practices in the area covered by this chapter. The more questions to which you can answer 'yes,' the better you are doing. The checklist also provides a brief summary of the material covered in the chapter.

EXHIBIT 4-2. BRAND MANAGEMENT CHECKLIST.

UNDERSTANDING THE CONSUMER

	YES	NO
Do you conduct customer research frequently?	_____	_____
Do you use in-depth, qualitative consumer research techniques (such as laddering, hidden-issue questioning, and symbolic analysis) to better understand your consumer's needs and motivations as they relate to your brand?	_____	_____
Do you know who your customers most frequently rely upon to gather information about your products and services? Do you know which of these sources "carry the most weight" with them?	_____	_____
Do you know the process customers use to select and purchase products and services in the product/ service categories your brand serves?	_____	_____
Do you know how people are using your products and services?	_____	_____
Do you fully understand how consumers experience your product or service when using it? Do you know what emotions it evokes? Do you know how it makes them feel? Are you aware of all the sensory components of its use? Does it stimulate their thinking? Do you know what comes to their minds when using it?	_____	_____
Do you know what problems people encounter when they use your products and services?	_____	_____
Have you experienced your brand side-by-side with your consumers?	_____	_____
Do you keep track of household participation, units per household, and average price (as components of category dollar sale growth)?	_____	_____
Do you know what drives brand preference and insistence within your categories?	_____	_____
Do you know what other brands your customers considered before they bought your brand? Do you know what it was about your brand that caused them to choose it?	_____	_____

(continues)

EXHIBIT 4-2. (CONTINUED).

Do you know all the reasons why customers switch from your brand to other brands? _____ _____

When your product or service is not available (out of stock or not carried) in a certain store, do you know what portion of your brand's consumers switch brands, switch stores, or postpone their purchases? _____ _____

Do you know what consumers infer about your brand? _____ _____

Do you know how involved consumers are with your brand? Do consumers have an opinion about your brand? _____ _____

Are consumers willing to defend your brand against naysayers? _____ _____

Do you have a thorough understanding of how the market for your brand's product and services is segmented? Do you know which segments your brand best serves? Do you know which segments are likely to provide the most long-term business potential for your brand? _____ _____

Do you know which customers are the most valuable to your organization? _____ _____

For business-to-business organizations—do you understand the customer organization's decision-making process? Do you know how to reach the decision makers? _____ _____

Have you calculated the "lifetime value" of your customers? Have you done the same by consumer segment? _____ _____

Have you identified a specific set of simple questions that separate your customers into different customer need segments? _____ _____

Is your brand attractive to younger consumers? Does the average age of your brand's consumer remain constant instead of creeping up over time? _____ _____

Do you frequently monitor what people are saying about your brand in chat rooms, discussion groups and other online forums? _____ _____

Do you know how people talk about your products and services when they recommend them to others? _____ _____

Do you invite customers and potential customers to provide input to new product development? _____ _____

Do your organization's systems and databases have a unified view of who your customers are? _____ _____

Does your organization have a CRM (customer relationship management) system? Is everything driven off of one relational database? _____ _____

Does your organization capture, learn from, and evolve based on consumer complaints? Are there mechanisms in place to ensure that happens? _____ _____

Do you share customer information broadly throughout the organization? Do you post customer research and insights on an intranet or extranet site for employees? _____ _____

Understanding the Competition

WHEN A COMPANY positions its brand in a customer's mind, it is positioning that brand against other brands. It is critical to understand the strengths, weaknesses, opportunities, and threats of each of those competitors along with the industry structure itself. (In fact, wise organizations dedicate a person to understanding the competition.)

This knowledge about your competition is necessary because you want to *uniquely* "own" an important benefit in your customer's mind. Ideally, this benefit is one that your competitors have not addressed and cannot easily address in the future. Better yet, the benefit you own should be one that takes advantage of your competitors' "Achilles' heels."

At a minimum, you will want to collect the following information on each of your key competitors:

- ✔ Key business objectives, goals, and strategies
- ✔ Sales, sales growth, profitability, market share, and other key financial measures
- ✔ Brand equity including, brand awareness, usage, preference, relevant differentiation, quality, value, accessibility, vitality, personality, key associations, emotional connection, and loyalty
- ✔ Product and service offerings
- ✔ Pricing and distribution
- ✔ Major customers
- ✔ Corporate culture
- ✔ Organization charts
- ✔ Sales organization and compensation
- ✔ Share of voice/marketing budget/advertising spend

Sources of Competitive Information

Following are sources of competitive information:

- ✓ Competitor Web sites.
- ✓ Press releases. There are free online services that can send you daily e-mail messages with press releases on industries and topics of interest to you.
- ✓ Industry analyst reports.
- ✓ Financial analyst reports.
- ✓ News clipping services.
- ✓ FIND/SVP (consulting and research services) and other similar services.
- ✓ Harte-Hanks (www.harte-hanks.com), Hoovers (www.hoovers.com), One Source (www.onesource.com), and other company databases.
- ✓ Online database searching services, such as FirstSearch, ProQuest, and Lexis-Nexis Academic Universe.
- ✓ Services that track advertising spending.
- ✓ Search engines and intelligent agents.
- ✓ Online chat rooms, bulletin boards, and discussion groups.
- ✓ Trade magazines.
- ✓ Trade shows.
- ✓ Competitor direct mail campaigns. Add a friend or relative to their lists.
- ✓ Your field sales force. Responding to the information they send will encourage them to send more.
- ✓ Ex-employees from competitors' firms. They may be under your employ now, or they can be identified from job search databases.
- ✓ Current customers. Many will pass on competitive communications they receive.
- ✓ Primary and secondary research (qualitative and quantitative, including brand equity studies). Make sure to investigate syndicated studies. Syndicated studies are typically published by large research firms such as AC Nielsen, Harris Interactive, Forrester Research, etc. An example is IntelliQuest's Computer Industry Media Study.
- ✓ Self-purchase and use of competitors' products (become one of their customers). Your management team should buy and use competitive products—an excellent way better to understand your competitors' customer experiences.

✓ Market tours. If in retail, visit stores that carry your competitors' products and talk with the sales associates about their products and services and what the companies are like to work with.

✓ Competitive intelligence firms.

This chapter has focused on how to better understand your brand's competition. Use the checklist in Exhibit 5-1 to assess the efficacy of your brand management practices in the area covered by this chapter. The more questions to which you can answer "yes," the better you are doing. The checklist also provides a brief summary of the material covered in the chapter.

EXHIBIT 5-1. BRAND MANAGEMENT CHECKLIST.

UNDERSTANDING THE COMPETITION

	YES	NO
Have you identified your brand's primary competitors for each market segment in which your brand operates?	___	___
Have you conducted a careful analysis of each of your competitors' strengths, weaknesses, opportunities and threats? Do you know where your competitors are most vulnerable?	___	___
Do you thoroughly understand each of your competitors' brand equities?	___	___
Do you know how loyal your competitors' customers are? Do you know which of their customers are less loyal than others? Do you know why?	___	___
Is there someone responsible for competitive intelligence in your organization?	___	___
Does your management team buy and use competitive products?	___	___
Does someone in your organization track competitor news and announcements on a daily basis?	___	___
Do you share competitive information broadly throughout the organization?	___	___

CHAPTER 6

Brand Design

IF A BRAND is the personification of an organization or that organization's products and services, it must have a personality and an identity. There are three major components of brand design on which you must focus once you have identified the target customer: (1) brand essence, (2) brand promise and (3) brand personality. Let's begin with brand essence.

Brand Essence

Brand essence is the timeless quality that the brand possesses. It is a brand's "heart and soul." The essence is usually articulated in the following three-word format: *adjective, adjective, noun*. For instance Nike's essence is "authentic athletic performance," Post-it's is "fast, friendly communication," and Disney's is "fun family entertainment."

Brand Essence Exercise

When I conduct brand-positioning workshops for organizations, I always warm the participants up with an exercise that demonstrates what brand essence is. I divide the group into teams of three to four people. Each team is given five minutes to define the essence of a well-known personality. (Some people I frequently use are Madonna, Arnold Schwarzenegger, Bill Clinton, John Ashcroft, Marilyn Manson, Abraham Lincoln, Albert Einstein, Adolf Hitler, Mother Theresa, Wolfgang Amadeus Mozart, and Nelson Mandela.) While there is much discussion and debate, most groups are able to agree on an essence within five minutes. The essences are always distinct for each personality assigned. (Well, almost always. In one workshop, one group defined Madonna's essence as "audacious sexual chameleon." Another group that had been assigned Bill Clinton indicated that they had arrived at the same essence for him. They must have been copying the adjacent group's notes!)

Most of the essences that teams craft "ring true" with the larger group of participants in a given workshop and are fairly consistent across workshops in different organizations. The exercise reinforces the power of having a strong and well-known essence and personality.

Occasionally, brand essences take a slightly different form. Hallmark's essence is "caring shared," The Nature Conservancy's is "saving great places," and Ritz Carlton's is "ladies and gentlemen serving ladies and gentlemen."

Exhibit 6-1 defines what a brand essence is and what it is not.

Xerox's brand essence is "The Document Company,"[1] which could be one source of their recent problems. It is a very limiting product/business description (especially in the digital age), not an extendable timeless quality.

Brand Promise

The brand promise is the most important part of a brand's design. A brand must promise a relevant, compelling, and differentiated benefit to the target customer. (People often confuse benefits with attributes and features. The

EXHIBIT 6-1. BRAND ESSENCE.

A Brand Essence Is . . .	A Brand Essence is Not . . .
The "heart and soul" of the brand.	A name.
Elegant in its economy of words. Take one word away and it loses its meaning.	An advertising theme line or slogan (The Nature Conservancy's essence being a notable exception).
A constant, timeless and enduring. It will not change over time, across geographies or in different situations.	A brand promise.
Aspirational, yet concrete enough to be meaningful and useful. [For instance, Hallmark's essence is "caring shared," not "greeting cards" (a product category description that lacks the aspirational quality), or "enriching people's lives" (aspirational but not concrete enough to be useful).]	
Extendable	A product or service (category) description.

brand must promise a benefit, not an attribute or feature.) The benefit may be functional, emotional, experiential, or self-expressive (Who am I? What do I value? What are my convictions? With whom do I associate? To what do I aspire?). Nonfunctional benefits are the most desirable, however, as they appeal to people on a visceral level and are the least vulnerable to competitive copying. The benefit must focus on points of difference, not points of parity.

The ideal benefit has the following three qualities (see Figure 6-1):

1. It is extremely important to the target consumer.
2. Your organization is uniquely suited to delivering it.
3. Competitors are not currently addressing it (nor is it easy for them to address it in the future).

In their book, *Creating Brand Loyalty: The Management of Power Positioning and Really Great Advertising*, Richard Czerniawski and Michael Maloney indicate that the most powerful benefits tap into people's deeply held beliefs, exploit your competitors' vulnerabilities or overcome previous concerns people had about your brand, its product/service category or its usage.[2] From my experience, the most powerful benefits give people hope that they can overcome or transcend their anxieties, fears, problems, or concerns.

FIGURE 6-1. CRAFTING THE MOST POWERFUL BRAND BENEFIT.

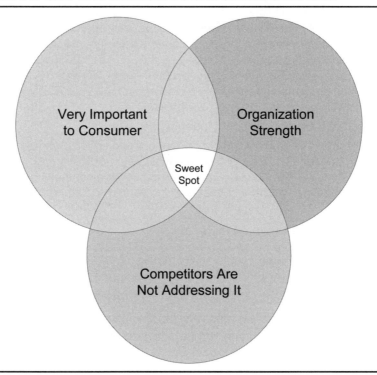

Competitive Copying

The easiest thing for a competitor to copy is a price reduction or discount. Almost as easy to copy are advertised (or otherwise communicated) product and service features. The least easy to copy are consumer benefits that are based on proprietary consumer research or behind-the-scene systems, logistics, or customer service training. For instance, if front-line service employees are trained to internalize the brand promise and are empowered to deliver it in whatever way makes sense given the situation, that is much less easy for a competitor to observe and copy. The way a company interacts with different consumers differently through database marketing is also less visible (and often highly effective).

By following these steps, you should be able to identify the optimal brand benefit:

✔ Review previous product and brand research.
✔ Conduct qualitative research (focus groups, one-on-one interviews, etc.) to better understand the target customer's attitudes, values, needs, desires, fears and concerns, especially as they relate to your brand's product/service category. Within this research step, you can develop short benefit statements and run them by the target customer iteratively to get a feeling for which are the most compelling ones.
✔ Compile a list of twenty to forty possible benefits.
✔ Do research that quantifies the importance of each of the possible benefits to your target customer together with that customer's perceptions of how your brand and each of its competitors deliver against those benefits (to identify the most important benefits which your brand could "own").

Competitive Frame of Reference

Often, exploring different competitive frames of reference will help you choose the most powerful brand benefit. Here are some questions to help you determine your brand's optimal frame of reference:

✔ Within what product/service category does our brand operate?
✔ Within which product and service categories do our customers give us "permission" to operate today? Do they give us more permission than we give ourselves?

- ✓ Does our brand stand for something broader than its products and services? Does that give it permission to enter new product and service categories?
- ✓ What compromises do we make with our customers that we take for granted but that might cause our customers to pursue alternative solutions to meet their needs?
- ✓ What could another company give our customers that would cause them to become disloyal to our brand?
- ✓ Could another brand within our category credibly insert its name into our brand's promise/positioning statement?
- ✓ What are the most likely substitute products for our product?
- ✓ What could neutralize our point of difference?
- ✓ What could make our point of difference obsolete?
- ✓ What could "kill" our category?

Consider, for example, the various frames of reference from which Coca-Cola could choose, from most narrow to most broad (see Exhibit 6-2).

Now consider how Hallmark's "differentiating benefits" might vary for each of the frames of reference listed in Exhibit 6-3?

And, interestingly, Cirque du Soleil did not define its competition as "other circuses," but rather as "every other show in town."[3]

Find out how choosing alternative frames of reference will alter competitive sets, products and services and points of difference. Broadening your brand's frame of reference can help you:

EXHIBIT 6-2. FRAMES OF REFERENCE FOR COCA-COLA.

Frame of Reference	Potential Competitors	Potential Point of Difference
Cola	Pepsi, RC Cola	?
Carbonated beverage (soda pop)	7 Up, Dr. Pepper	?
Soft drink	Crystal Light, Gatorade	?
Nonalcoholic beverage	Chocolate milk, root beer float	?
Beverage	Wine, beer	?
Liquid refreshment	Water, bottled water	?
Psychological refreshment	A walk in the woods, yoga, a swim	?

EXHIBIT 6-3. FRAMES OF REFERENCE FOR HALLMARK.

Frame of Reference	Potential Product Categories
Greeting cards	Greeting cards
Social expression products	Note cards, invitations, electronic greetings, enhanced e-mail
Caring and sharing	Flowers, candy, gift baskets, romantic cruises, family portraits, family scrapbooks, children's books, children's educational activities, family games, massage oil
Community building	Interpersonal relationship workshops, marriage enrichment courses, planned communities

1. Identify a strong point of difference within your current narrower frame of reference (for instance, Pepsi chose to "own" psychological refreshment as a point of difference over Coca-Cola).
2. Identify logical avenues for brand growth.
3. Identify potential substitute products and other competitive threats.

For the sake of simplicity and focus, I state a brand's promise as follows:

Only [brand] delivers [relevant differentiated benefit] to [target customer].

Use of the word "only" is very important. It forces you to choose a benefit that only your brand can deliver. Occasionally, clients will ask why they can't craft the brand promise as, "[Brand] is the best at delivering [relevant differentiated benefit] to [target customer]." The problem with this approach is that being the best may not change a customer's purchase behavior if other brands deliver against the chosen benefit to a sufficient degree.

Others also may use a form that incorporates the frame of reference, such as "Only [brand] delivers [relevant differentiating benefit] to [target customer] within the [product/service category]." Although the frame of reference exercise can be helpful in identifying potentially powerful differentiating benefits, incorporating it into the brand promise itself is not helpful.

The following are brand promises that well-known brands seem to make:

- Only Volvo delivers assurance of the safest ride to parents who are concerned about their children's well being.
- Only Harley-Davidson delivers the fantasy of complete freedom on the road and the comradeship of kindred spirits to avid cyclists.

✔ Only The Nature Conservancy has the expertise and resources to work in creative partnership with local communities in the United States and internationally with exceptional range and agility to conserve the most important places for future generations.

✔ Only the Boy Scouts of America instills values in boys, resulting in a more successful adulthood on a massive nationwide scale through a proven fun program.

A brand promise must be (and should be tested to be):

✔ Understandable

✔ Believable

✔ Unique/differentiating

✔ Compelling

✔ Admirable or endearing

Once crafted and agreed to, the brand promise should be delivered at each point of contact with the consumer. So, everyone in your organization should know your brand's promise.

Brand Personality

Each brand should choose an intended personality based upon the brand's aspirations and its customers' current perceptions of the brand. The personality is usually communicated in seven to nine adjectives describing the brand as if it were a person.

A brand's personality and values are often a function of the following:[4]

✔ The personality and values of the organization's founder (assuming he or she had a strong personality and values)

✔ The personality and values of the organization's current leader (again, assuming he or she has a strong personality and values)

✔ The personalities and values of the organization's most zealous customers/members/clients

✔ The brand's carefully crafted design/positioning

✔ Some combination of the above

Although personality attributes vary considerably by product category and brand, strong brands tend to possess particular personality attributes. They are, in general order of importance:

- ✔ Trustworthy
- ✔ Authentic
- ✔ Reliable ("I can always count on [brand]!")
- ✔ Admirable
- ✔ Appealing
- ✔ Honest
- ✔ Stands for something (specifically, something important to the customer)
- ✔ Likable
- ✔ Popular
- ✔ Unique
- ✔ Believable
- ✔ Relevant
- ✔ Delivers high-quality, well-performing products and services
- ✔ Service-oriented
- ✔ Innovative

Employees are also an important factor in communicating the brand's personality in organizations in which the organizational brand is used. This is why companies are increasingly recruiting, training, and managing their employees to manifest their brands' promises.

Repositioning a Brand

Brand repositioning is necessary when one or more of the following conditions exist:

- ✔ Your brand has a bad, confusing, or nonexistent image.
- ✔ The primary benefit your brand "owns" has evolved from a differentiating benefit to a cost-of-entry benefit. (For example, for airlines cost-of-entry benefits would be safe flight, needed routes, and required times.)
- ✔ Your organization is significantly altering its strategic direction.
- ✔ Your organization is entering new businesses and the current positioning is no longer appropriate.
- ✔ A new competitor with a superior value proposition is entering your industry.

✔ Competition has usurped your brand's position or rendered it ineffectual.

✔ Your organization has acquired a very powerful proprietary advantage that must be worked into the brand positioning.

✔ Corporate culture renewal dictates at least a revision of the brand personality.

✔ You are broadening your brand to appeal to additional consumers or consumer need segments for whom the current brand positioning won't work. (This should be a "red flag" since this action could dilute the brand's meaning, make the brand less appealing to current customers, or even alienate current customers.)

You follow the same steps and address the same brand design components when repositioning a brand as you do when first designing the brand. But, brand repositioning is more difficult than initially positioning a brand because you must first help the customer "unlearn" the current brand positioning (easier said than done). Three actions can aid in this process:

1. Carefully crafted communication
2. New products, packaging, etc., that emphasize the new positioning
3. Associations with other brands (cobranding, comarketing, ingredient branding, strategic alliances, etc.) that reinforce the new brand positioning

You should not rely upon an advertising agency, a brand consulting company, or your marketing department to craft your corporate or organizational brand's design. This exercise is so critical to your organization's success that your organization's leadership team and its marketing/brand management leaders should develop it themselves, preferably with the help and facilitation of a brand-positioning expert.

▓ Conducting a Brand Positioning Workshop

Frequently, a brand design is not embraced by the organization because the leadership team was not actively involved in the process at every step along the way. Often, outside experts will design a brand based upon separate interviews with key stakeholders. This input does not allow for disagreement, debate, discussion, or consensus building among the stakeholders. Brand positioning involves highly facilitated, well-prepared sessions in which all the key stakeholders (typically organization leaders and marketing executives) are "locked in a room" until they reach a consensus on all of the key elements of brand design: the target customer and the brand essence, promise, and personality.

CASE STUDY

Brand Positioning Case Study:
Element K

I became the vice president of marketing at Element K, a leading e-learning company, in September of 2000. Earlier that year, U.S. Equity Partners acquired ZD Education from Ziff-Davis and renamed it Element K. Element K has four business units: Element K Online (e-learning), Element K Courseware (computer training courseware publishing), Element K Journals (journal publishing), and Element K Learning Center (Rochester, N.Y.-based computer training center).

When I joined Element K, there was virtually no awareness of the brand by our target customers: corporate chief learning officers. And, we intended to take the company public after the turbulent market of late 2000 stabilized. My objective was simple: to quickly and aggressively build brand awareness and differentiation to make Element K the number one preferred e-learning brand.

The e-learning market is an increasingly crowded space with hundreds of relatively new companies vying for a greater share of the market and industry leadership. Merrill Lynch estimated the e-learning market at $3.5 billion in 2001, and forecast growth to more than $25 billion in 2003. According to International Data Corporation (IDC), the U.S. corporate market for online learning alone was projected to grow from $2.2 billion to $11.4 billion by 2003.

This growth is fueled by the many advantages that e-learning offers vis-à-vis traditional classroom training:

- ✔ There is great flexibility in where and when to train.
- ✔ People can learn at their own pace.
- ✔ E-learning is especially effective for decentralized organizations with geographically dispersed workforces.
- ✔ You can train an unlimited number of employees.
- ✔ Training is "on demand," which decreases cycle time significantly.
- ✔ All can be done for a fraction of the cost of classroom training.

Element K's e-learning solution is fully hosted on the Internet. We had large up-front fixed costs associated with developing our instructional design methodology, 800 + online courses, and a robust LMS (learning management system). But our variable costs were very low: Providing access to our e-learning solution was as simple as giving someone an ID for access to the site. The cost of adding servers was almost the only variable cost (that is, cost that increases with increased usage/volume). For this reason, we increasingly focused on delivering enterprise-wide solutions to Fortune 1000 companies and similarly large organizations in which the number of users was substantial with each sales agreement. Simply put—our business model favored large numbers of students.

Most of the companies vying for business in this segment of the e-learning space directed one of the following messages at corporate officers (CIOs, CFOs, etc.) (assuming they had any semblance of consistent messaging):

- ✔ We offer a complete, integrated solution.
- ✔ Our e-learning can improve your organization's performance. It produces good business results.
- ✔ High-profile clients are very pleased with our solution.

Every company seemed to be saying the same things, and there was way too much clutter to break through. We therefore embarked on qualitative and quantitative research to identify the key decision makers and the most powerful differentiating benefit for Element K to own. In our qualitative research (one-on-one interviews and mini-groups) we found that the primary decision maker is the senior-most executive with enterprise-wide training responsibility, often bearing the title of CLO (chief learning officer). In this research, we also explored people's needs, desires, fears, concerns, and other perceptions regarding training in general and e-learning in particular. From that, we developed thirty-three different brand benefit statements, which we reviewed with people toward the end of each session. We added, eliminated, and revised statements as with each round of feedback. In the process, we gained a major insight, which led to Element K's brand positioning: *People had an underlying concern that, despite all of its potential advantages, e-learning lacked the human touch.* In particular they were concerned that, with e-learning:

- ✔ You lose the personal attention that only an instructor can deliver
- ✔ It is harder to ask questions
- ✔ Feedback is not possible
- ✔ Students may feel isolated
- ✔ You lose peer-to-peer learning
- ✔ There is no peer pressure to attend or complete the course
- ✔ There is not enough personal attention available

Based upon insights from the qualitative research, we developed quantitative research to measure the importance of a wide variety of brand benefits to the target customer. This research also quantified each brand's perceived delivery against each benefit. In this way, we were able to identify the most important benefits and the benefits for which Element K had the biggest relative (and absolute) advantage.

While several benefits were higher in importance, all of them were benefits that would quickly become "cost of entry" benefits (such as affordable price, quality content, ease of use, etc.). E-learning with the human touch was validated to be important, but more importantly, it provided Element K with the biggest advantage. While two thirds of the respondents believed that Element K integrates the human element into e-learning, only one third and one quarter respectively believed Element K's two primary competitors did this (see Figure 6-2).

This benefit was particularly powerful for Element K to "own" for the following reasons:

✔ It addresses one of the major fears about e-learning. (Fear is a particularly powerful motivator.)

✔ Element K had a substantial advantage in this area according to the research.

✔ Element K delivered on this promise at multiple levels:

　✔ In the way the student experience was designed

　✔ In the way the training administrator experience was designed

　✔ In its comprehensive support services

　✔ In its participation management services

　✔ In the way the salespeople interact with customers (friendly, low pressure, consultative selling)

FIGURE 6-2. IDENTIFYING THE KEY BENEFIT.

% Who Agree that this Brand Integrates
the Human Element into e-Learning

✔ In the corporate culture itself. (Element K is naturally service oriented. This is sustainable as it is built into the corporate DNA.)

✔ Element K's most formidable competitor was generally known to be pushy and arrogant and only interested in "making the sale." (This was a part of their corporate culture.) This positioning would indirectly and subtly bring this weakness to mind.

✔ Element K's customers found the company to be very easy to work with. (There was extensive anecdotal evidence that Element K had won many contracts based upon this alone.)

✔ It felt "right" and was quickly embraced by every employee.

Here is what we now say about Element K:

> **Element K brings** a unique understanding of how people learn to the business of training. Our understanding comes from a twenty-year heritage of innovation in adult career learning for leading corporations. Today, you'll find it in our best-in-class e-learning solution—over 800 courses integrated with a state-of-the-art learning management system, all delivered with a human touch.

This statement is believable because of Element K's rich heritage as a company of training professionals, founded by two university professors who wanted to make adult training more interesting and interactive. As training professionals committed to multiple training modalities (including classroom instruction), Element K would want to share and address these concerns. The company is now committed to building "the human touch" into everything it does, from the way the sales force interacts with potential customers and the services offered to current customers to the enhancements made to our learning management system and the personality characteristics looked for when hiring new employees.

Brand Positioning Case Study:
Rensselaer Polytechnic Institute

CASE STUDY

Rensselaer Polytechnic Institute, founded in 1824, is the first degree-granting technological university in the English-speaking world. Rensselaer was established "for the purpose of instructing persons, who may choose to apply themselves, in the application of science to the common purposes of life." Since Rensselaer's founding, its alumni have impacted the world in many significant ways, including:

- ✔ Inventing television
- ✔ Creating the microprocessor
- ✔ Managing the Apollo project that put the first man on the moon
- ✔ Founding Texas Instruments and creating the first pocket calculator
- ✔ Creating e-mail (including using the @ symbol)
- ✔ Inventing baking powder
- ✔ Inventing the Reach toothbrush
- ✔ Building the Brooklyn Bridge
- ✔ Building the Panama Canal
- ✔ Inventing the Ferris Wheel

Yet, for all of its accomplishments, in the late 1980s and early 1990s, Rensselaer was not well positioned (to prospective students) compared to its world-renown rival, MIT, or even to schools such as Cal Tech, UC Berkeley, and Carnegie-Mellon. Many state universities (Purdue, University of Illinois at Urbana, etc.) offered exceptionally strong technical programs at significantly lower costs than private universities. Ivy League schools and other first-tier liberal arts universities were building their math, science, and engineering programs. And most states had public universities that provided respectable engineering programs. This increasingly competitive landscape left Rensselaer in a positioning "no man's land." I was on Rensselaer's alumni board of directors and national admissions committee at the time. We worked with the school to conduct research to better understand the college selection process. We interviewed students (and their parents), some of whom chose to attend Rensselaer and some of whom didn't. With each of these groups, we explored what factors were most important in their decision-making process. We also explored their perceptions of Rensselaer versus other schools. And we conducted focus groups with alumni and business people to better understand their impressions of Rensselaer.

Here is what we found: Almost everyone who knew of Rensselaer perceived it to be a first-rate technical school. Many people put it in the same class as MIT. People "in the know" were genuinely impressed with the school and the caliber of its students, its academics, and its research. But there were drawbacks:

- ✔ Rensselaer is in Troy, New York (which lacks the appeal of, say, Boston or California).

- ✔ Rensselaer is not as well known or prestigious as MIT. It does not have the same name cachet.
- ✔ Rensselaer is much more expensive than state engineering schools (though after financial aid, costs can be comparable).
- ✔ Rensselaer was known to be a "boot camp." It's been said that "you don't go there to have fun."
- ✔ The curriculum was perceived to be too narrow compared to liberal arts schools.
- ✔ The school had a lopsided male to female ratio (13 to 1 when I attended in the mid-to-late 1970s, 3 to 1 today).
- ✔ And, a significant portion of Rensselaer's students (mostly those who had used Rensselaer as a backup school to MIT and similar schools), felt inferior to students at their first choice schools.

Further, those with no connection to the school had *no* impression of the school. Awareness was also nil among the general U.S. population.

These were significant hurdles. And yet, looking at the school itself, there were also a number of very strong advantages:

- ✔ A rich history of alumni who have made major contributions to society
- ✔ A vital, engaged campus community
- ✔ A strong student leadership development program
- ✔ Innovations in entrepreneurship, with one of the first and perhaps best known business incubators and a strong student entrepreneurship program
- ✔ Award-winning innovations in educational techniques
- ✔ Thriving interdisciplinary research centers
- ✔ Certain programs that ranked among the best available in the world
- ✔ An increasingly strong reputation throughout the world. (Interestingly, the university's reputation was stronger in many other countries than it was in U.S. Midwestern states!)

Also, the university had embarked on a significant long-term commitment to enhance the student experience, addressing everything from administrative procedures, counseling, and breadth of course offerings to quality of instruction, the male-to-female ratio, and campus aesthetics. And, gauging from student surveys over time, the efforts were producing significant results.

Here are the key insights that led to Rensselaer's very powerful current positioning:

- ✔ Rensselaer's students have always been serious about their chosen fields of endeavor and their studies.

✔ Rensselaer's faculty, students, and alumni want to make a difference in the world.

✔ Rensselaer is and has been a leader in technological innovation.

✔ Rensselaer's alumni, throughout the school's history, have made major lasting contributions to society.

✔ Rensselaer was emerging as a leader in entrepreneurship, especially technological entrepreneurship.

✔ "Technological creativity" seemed to capture the essence of the school and the spirit of those associated with the school throughout its 175-year history.

✔ Rensselaer wanted its new positioning not only to capture the school's unique competitive advantages but also to inspire its students and give them confidence. (In the mid-to-late 1970s, under George Low's leadership, the school informally adopted the slogan, "Rensselaer: Where imagination can achieve the impossible." For a short time after that, the school used the slogan, "Rensselaer: For minds ahead of their time.")

So, Rensselaer's tag line, "Why not change the world?SM," was born.

Confident? *Yes.*

Aspirational? *Yes.*

Inspirational? *Yes.*

Accurately reflecting the school's strengths and those of its alumni? *Yes.*

An invitation to like-minded individuals and organizations to "come join Rensselaer in its quest"? *Yes*

Effective in recruiting an increasing number of highly qualified students? *Yes.*

Rensselaer's most recent entering freshman classes are the most qualified and talented in the last couple of decades. And each class seems to be more qualified than the prior class. As one measure, the Class of 2005 arrived on campus with average SAT scores of 1307, a leap of 25 points over that of the previous class.

And, the most important question: Are students satisfied with Rensselaer and its recently articulated positioning? Yes.

Today, Rensselaer is thriving. In early 2001, it received a gift of $360 million—the largest single gift (at that time) ever made to a university. It is building a $60 million biotechnology and interdisciplinary studies center to expand its research portfolio and a $50 million electronic media and performing arts center to showcase its world-leading electronic arts program.

Brand Positioning Case Study:
GEICO Direct Insurance

When BrandForward conducted its insurance industry brand equity study, it uncovered a few things about the insurance industry:

✔ The insurance industry is highly fragmented. While there are dozens of companies whose names consumers recognize, less than a handful receive significant unaided first mention.

✔ While there is high behavioral loyalty, there is low attitudinal loyalty.

✔ Consumers have a low emotional connection to insurance brands.

✔ Less than one in five people indicated that their insurance company "has never disappointed them." (One sign of emotional connection.)

✔ Although consumers perceive there to be differences among insurance companies, they don't perceive those differences to be significant. Price and rates are among the most important points of difference between companies, suggesting the category is commodity-like among many consumers.

✔ The following are the seven most important consumer benefits in the insurance industry. Of these benefits, consumers perceive only two of them to be addressed to any large degree:

  ✔ Paying claims fairly and promptly

  ✔ Good rates/prices

  ✔ Honest, trustworthy representatives

  ✔ Accessible, available representatives

  ✔ Knowledgeable, competent representatives

  ✔ Easy to understand policies

  ✔ Financial stability of company

✔ The following benefits have the widest variation in delivery and therefore provide the greatest opportunities for differentiation:

  ✔ Representatives who provide unbiased recommendations (all insurance categories)

✔ Good rates/prices (all categories)

✔ Knowledgeable, competent reps (life insurance)

✔ Honest, trustworthy reps (life insurance)

✔ Ability to establish a personal relationship (home and auto insurance)

✔ Strong overall reputation (financial services)

✔ The sales representative's and claims adjusters' points of contact with consumers are critical to the success of insurance company brands.

✔ The most brand preference exists in the auto insurance category (roughly a third with "no preference"), and the least exists in the financial services category (two thirds with "no preference").

✔ State Farm is the preferred brand by a wide margin (especially in home and auto insurance). It also has a wide lead in the emotional connection it has created with consumers.

✔ GEICO is an "up and coming" brand in auto insurance (see Figure 6-3).

✔ Prudential is the preferred life insurance brand.

While State Farm seems to be doing many things right, almost all of the other insurance companies seem to lack any significant brand equity. But this story is not about State Farm. It's about GEICO Direct, the up-and-coming auto insurance brand (see Figure 6-3). And, this is a very simple, short story: GEICO began to advertise its brand at a level that was the talk of the industry. And its message was very simple: "You could save 15 percent or more on car insurance!" (See Figure 6-4.)

In brand building, focus is everything, and GEICO focused on one product segment—auto insurance—and one benefit—low price. And

FIGURE 6-3. GEICO, THE UP-AND-COMING BRAND.

FIGURE 6-4. GEICO'S SIMPLE MESSAGE.

it did so again and again and again with a disciplined consistency. And its brand equity and market share are increasing at rates unknown to other insurance brands. In an industry with little brand equity or differentiation, GEICO decided to build its brand by aggressively focusing on an important brand benefit: low price. Its success was that simple. (In general, I would not recommend trying to own "low price" as a point of difference. Typically, it is not a sustainable point of difference. Nor does it usually contribute to building brand equity. For a number of reasons that are too involved for the purpose of this case study, it is working for GEICO in the insurance industry now.)

Use the checklist in Exhibit 6-4 to assess the efficacy of your brand management practices in the area covered by this chapter. The more questions to which you can answer "yes," the better you are doing. The checklist also provides a brief summary of the material covered in the chapter.

EXHIBIT 6-4. BRAND MANAGEMENT CHECKLIST.

BRAND DESIGN

	YES	NO
Have you carefully defined your target customer on the following dimensions: demographics, lifestyle, values, attitudes, product usage, and buying behavior?	____	____

(continues)

EXHIBIT 6-4. (CONTINUED).

Is this customer a good target for your brand in the following ways?
- ✔ market size, profitability, and growth rate _____ _____
- ✔ importance of your brand's promise to them _____ _____
- ✔ their alignment with your brand's values (i.e., your brand stands for something that is important to them) _____ _____
- ✔ the opportunity for add-on sales through brand extension _____ _____
- ✔ their potential loyalty to the brand _____ _____

Do you have profound insight into your consumer's values and motivations? _____ _____

Have you considered the intangible ways in which your brand adds value to the consumer? _____ _____

Are you constantly monitoring the market for changes in the following?
- ✔ customer segments _____ _____
- ✔ customer values, attitudes, and needs _____ _____
- ✔ customer shopping behaviors _____ _____
- ✔ competitive offerings _____ _____

Can you articulate your brand's competitive frame of reference? Can you describe the universe within which it operates? _____ _____

Have you mapped your brand's delivery of key category benefits against competitive brands' delivery of those same benefits? Did you overlay that with a consumer importance scale? _____ _____

Do you fully understand the following for all the categories in which your brand operates: (a) the different market segments, (b) the competitive set, and (c) which consumer benefits are "cost-of-entry" versus "differentiating"? (These alternatively may be referred to as "points-of-parity" and "points-of-difference.") _____ _____

Do you fully understand the decision-making process (rational or not) the consumer uses to purchase your brand? _____ _____

Do you know what benefits your competitors' brands own in consumers' minds? _____ _____

Do you have a clear understanding of the things competitive brands do that your brand should and would never do? _____ _____

Do you know how different consumer segments perceive your brand differently? _____ _____

Is your brand relevant to early adopters? _____ _____

Have you defined the role, target consumer, essence, promise, and personality for your brand? _____ _____

If your brand is not the leader in its category, can you identify a way to redefine, re-frame, or narrow the category so that your brand can be the leader in the redefined category? _____ _____

Do you know what the most important problem is that your brand solves for its customers? _____ _____

Do you fully understand what factors in your brand's history built it to what it is today? _____ _____

Do you have a vision or dream for your brand? Do you know what you'd like it to become well into the future? _____ _____

Do you know what story your brand tells? Can you articulate its myth? _____ _____

Is your brand vital and vivid? Does it have the ability to build legends? _____ _____

Is your brand dynamic? Does it learn, grow, mature, adapt, and improve over time? _____ _____

Do you know what your brand's timeless qualities are? _____ _____

Is your brand's essence aspirational and inspirational, yet concrete enough so that it can own a position in the consumer's mind? _____ _____

Does your brand embody certain beliefs, values, attitudes and behaviors that evoke widespread admiration and devotion? _____ _____

Do you have absolute clarity regarding what your brand stands for and how it is unique and compelling to consumers? _____ _____

Can you identify the one word your brand owns in consumers' minds? _____ _____

Do you know what consumers would miss most if your brand ceased to exist? _____ _____

(continues)

EXHIBIT 6-4. (CONTINUED).

Do you know what deeply felt human needs your brand addresses? _____ _____

Does your brand dominate the category by owning the "core" category benefit or does it lead the category by owning the benefit that best defines where the category is headed? (*Source*: DMB&B Communication presentation at a Sprint Brand Forum, May 11, 1999.) _____ _____

Does your brand stand for something very important to its customers? Does it capture their imaginations? _____ _____

Is your brand's promise believable? _____ _____

Can you readily verbalize the proof points to your brand's promise? _____ _____

Have you identified brand benefits that are invisible to your competitors (and therefore extremely difficult to imitate)? _____ _____

Have you defined your brand broadly enough for it to outlive specific product categories and provide flexibility for ongoing extension? _____ _____

Are you aware of any elements of your brand's heritage that may limit its opportunities for future growth? If so, have you devised plans to overcome those limitations without alienating current consumers? _____ _____

Has your brand struck the optimal balance between maintaining a strong heritage and reinventing itself for the future? _____ _____

Have you considered narrowing your brand's focus to clarify meaning and gain market share? _____ _____

Can you identify the opportunities you have sacrificed to maintain clarity regarding your brand's promise and positioning? _____ _____

Have you considered "pruning" businesses that are not congruent with your brand's essence and promise? _____ _____

Have you identified product or service features that are not valued by the consumer or that do not reinforce your brand's promise? Do you have plans to eliminate these? _____ _____

Have you established brand strategies that are consistent with the brand's promise—product, pricing, distribution, communications, etc.? _____ _____

Have you designed the brand portfolio, including a subbrand structure? _____ _____

Is your brand hierarchy simple enough for consumers to easily understand (preferably no more than two levels)? _____ _____

When your brand hierarchy has two or more levels, do you know which name (corporate, parent, endorsed, or subbrand?) the consumer uses to refer to each product or service offered by your organization? _____ _____

Do you have criteria to help you decide when you can use an existing brand, when a completely new brand is needed, and when a subbrand is the right choice? _____ _____

Do you find that all of your subbrands are distinctive? Are you certain that no two subbrands in your portfolio meet the same consumer needs and deliver the same benefits? _____ _____

Are your subbrand names distinct from one another so that they are not confused for one another? _____ _____

Do you use existing brands whenever possible to meet new consumer needs or to enter new product categories, offering instant assurance and maximizing communication efficiency? (Providing doing so doesn't dilute the meaning of the original brand.) _____ _____

Are you increasingly leveraging your corporate brand as a parent brand? _____ _____

Do you find you are spending most of your time creating sustainable competitive advantages (versus matching competitive moves) with your brands? _____ _____

Is your brand so well positioned that there are no acceptable substitutes for your products and services? _____ _____

Did you know that competitors can and often will reposition your brand in the process of repositioning their brands? Do you know the ways in which they are trying to reposition your brand? Are you actively doing something about this? _____ _____

(continues)

EXHIBIT 6-4. (CONTINUED).

If you are repositioning your brand, are you
implementing it in a way and at a pace so that
consumers can "digest" the changes?   _____ _____

Have you designed your brand so that it is, as Kevin
Keller says, "memorable, meaningful, transferable,
and protectable"?   _____ _____

Notes

1. David Reyes-Guerra, manager of corporate identity and product naming for
   Xerox, at IQPC's "Maximizing Brand Value through Internal Communication"
   conference in Chicago, May 24–25, 1999.

2. Richard D. Czerniawski and Michael W. Maloney, *Creating Brand Loyalty:
   The Management of Power Positioning and Really Great Advertising* (New
   York: AMACOM, 1999), pp.161.

3. Adam Morgan, *Eating the Big Fish: How Challenger Brands Can Compete
   Against Brand Leaders* (New York: John Wiley, 1999), p. 31.

4. Morgan, *Eating the Big Fish*, p. 74.

CHAPTER 7

Brand Identity Standards and Systems

WHEN MOST PEOPLE think about a brand's identity, they usually think about the name, the logo, and maybe the tag line. But the identity consists of so much more than that: It includes typestyles, colors, symbols, attitude and personality, brand voice and visual style, sounds and other mnemonic devices, characters and other spokespeople, product design, package design, and the list could go on and on. The most powerful brands have a consistent brand voice and visual style from product design and packaging to retail environment and external communication.

Companies such as Procter & Gamble have always practiced the traditional model of brand management. These companies managed a large portfolio of stand-alone brands (e.g., Bold, Bounty, Ivory, NyQuil, Pepto-Bismol, Scope, Folgers, Pringles) and marketed them as separate entities. While this was highly effective for those companies, it requires substantial marketing resources. Today, more and more manufacturing companies are discovering the power of using their corporate brand names (General Electric, IBM, 3M, Ford, etc.) to market their products. These companies have discovered that it is highly efficient to leverage the corporate brand name. The name offers quality assurance and familiarity at a minimum, as well as a coherent umbrella promise (example: 3M—innovative solutions), if executed properly.

Brand Architecture

Brand architecture, also called brand structure, is covered in greater detail in Chapter 2. Although situations vary greatly and company brand structures are much more complicated than the ideal, in general a highly efficient and effective brand structure leverages the corporate brand as the parent brand (for example, Ford Taurus, Honda Accord, and IBM ThinkPad) and includes individual subbrands targeted to different consumer need segments. This two-level structure, if executed correctly, maximizes consumer communication efficiency while clarifying the definition of the corporate brand and making it more vital to an increasingly wider group of consumer segments. Having said that, brand architecture is a highly complex issue, especially for organizations that (a) span multiple product/service categories and (b) are the result of mergers and acquisitions. Here are some important considerations in developing and revising brand architecture:

✔ Make sure that the architecture is based upon a careful analysis of key internal and external audiences and *not* on internal organization structures, egos, and the felt need for control.

✔ Be very sure to outline the role of the various levels in the brand hierarchy from the outset.

✔ Think through the extent to which the various brands will link to the parent brand:

1. By name only (endorsed, subbrand)
2. Through common design elements
3. By sharing the same essence
4. By sharing the same positioning and differentiating benefits

I tend to believe that the various brands should almost always relate to the parent brand in the first three ways but not always in the fourth, especially if the brands span a wide variety of product categories or are targeted at completely different customer segments.

Brand Naming

Brand naming is extremely important. Many of you are probably working with brands that already have been named, but in case you are not, here are a few pointers on naming brands:

✔ *People only refer to a person or product using one, or at the most, two names.* For instance, I am either Brad or Brad VanAuken. No one calls me Alan Bradley VanAuken (with the exception of my mother, who called me this when she was upset with me when I was a boy). It is just too hard to remember, too cumbersome to say, and just unnecessary. Likewise, a car is either a Taurus or a Ford Taurus. People say, "I drive a Honda" or "I drive a Honda Accord." Few say, "I drive a Honda Accord EX." People occasionally can remember three levels of names—but rarely more. Saturn is simple. Chrysler New Yorker Fifth Avenue and Oldsmobile Cutlass Sierra are less easy to remember (and can anyone remember what company makes these cars?) How is a Chrysler New Yorker Fifth

Avenue different from a Chrysler New Yorker Salon? How is an Oldsmobile Cutlass Sierra different from an Oldsmobile Cutlass Supreme or how are both of them different from an Oldsmobile Toronado or an Oldsmobile 88 Royal? It gets very confusing very quickly.

✓ *Products run into trouble when they have multiple levels of names.* For instance, Hallmark coproduced social expression software with Microsoft. Greetings Workshop was produced by Microsoft and Hallmark Connections (in some cases, this was a subset of another suite of products from Microsoft, with additional names). What did the consumer remember? What did they ask for? Did each consumer use the same name? It might have been easier to call it "Hallmark Greetings Workshop (brought to you by Microsoft)" or "Microsoft Greetings Workshop (featuring Hallmark cards)."

✓ *Coined names are preferred if you have sufficient resources to build their meaning.* Coined names (such as Xerox, Kodak, etc.) are distinct and can be designed to be easy to read, write, and pronounce. It is unlikely that any other brand will be confused with yours if yours has a coined name. Because coined names require significant communication over time to build their meaning, they are best reserved for parent brands or other brands that are extremely important to the organization and that will be around for a very long time.

✓ *Many organizations opt for associative descriptive names.* Associative descriptive names, which may be partly descriptive, usually allude to a key brand benefit. Examples include Amazon, Sir Speedy, Road Runner, Lean Cuisine, Sprint, BrandForward, Die Hard, and Aris Vision Institute. These names tend to work quite well and deliver the added benefit of immediately alluding to the brand's benefit. If you want to get into a product or business quickly with a name that helps reinforce the product's or business' primary benefit, while still maintaining some level of uniqueness, this is the preferred naming option.

Did You Know?

Suggestive brand names assist with recall of brand benefits suggested by the names but inhibit recall of other subsequently advertised brand benefits. (*Source:* Kevin Lane Keller, Susan E. Heckler, and Michael J. Houston, "The Effects of Brand Name Suggestiveness on Advertising Recall," *Journal of Marketing*, Vol. 62, January 1998, pp. 48–57.)

✓ *Generic or descriptive names* are least desirable. They are not distinctive in consumers' minds and they can't be protected legally. Interestingly, many online companies with generic names have gone out of business, such as Auctions.com, Business.com, Buy.com, Computer.com, eToys.com, Food.com, Furniture.com, Garden.com, Mall.com, Mortgage.com, Pets.com, or Stamps.com. (Note: Others have subsequently purchased many of these URLs and are trying their luck at them. So much for all those once exorbitantly expensive URLs!)

Generic descriptors are frequently used for subbrands, when you want most of the credit to go to the parent brand. For instance, at Element K our branding structure features generic descriptor subbrands because (a) Element K is a new brand that we need to build quickly, (b) our resources are too limited to build multiple brands and, most importantly, (c) we are touting a blended solution across all of our products and businesses (see Exhibit 7-1).

In summary, *coined names* are used for products and services that are distinctive, that provide sustainable competitive advantages, and that will receive substantial marketing support over time. *Associative descriptive names* are used for important products or services, but primarily those that need to have their meaning built quickly or that will not receive the sustained level of marketing support required of coined names. *Generic or descriptive names* are reserved for non–mission-critical subbrands.

Strong names allude to the benefit, such as Amazon.com, Passion perfume, Ford Explorer, or Roadrunner Internet access service. Ideally, any name you choose should be short, easy to spell, and easy to pronounce. Say the name out loud and see how easily it rolls off of the tongue and how pleasing it is to the ear. Pay attention to cadence, rhythm, and balance. Alliteration and repetition of sounds can add to the strength of the name. Consider Roadrunner, Kodak, and Coca-Cola. I prefer a two-syllable word starting with a strong consonant and possessing rich vowel sounds.

Here are two points to consider when naming your brand:

- ✔ Names formed from acronyms or initials are up to 40 percent less memorable than any type of pronounceable word, real or coined.[2]

- ✔ Perhaps the worst names of all are those built from generic word parts such as "com" and "sys" and "compu" (WorldCom, UniSys). These

EXHIBIT 7-1. ELEMENT K BRAND ARCHITECTURE.

Entity	Name (brand/subbrand)
Company	Element K
E-learning division	Element K Online
Courseware division	Element K Courseware
Journals division	Element K Journals
Rochester, N.Y., learning center	Element K Learning Center

names seem to be confused with every other brand name created from similar word parts and they are very difficult to recall.

Naming Decision Trees

Organizations with more than one brand should develop decision trees to aid people in naming new products and services. The decision tree (see Exhibit 7-2) should outline when an existing brand should be used and when a new brand is necessary. It should also identify the type of brand to be created (subbrand, endorsed brand, etc.) and the naming convention for that brand (coined, associative/descriptive, etc.). This should be based upon the following factors:

- ✓ Importance of the new product or service to the market and to the organization
- ✓ Projected life span of the new product or service
- ✓ Unique differentiating benefits delivered by the new product or service
- ✓ Intent and capacity to communicate the new brand in a significant way over time

In general, new brands should be created only when a new product or service delivers on a brand promise different from one of the organization's existing brands. To do otherwise would be costly and confusing to consumers.

Brand Logos

It is at least as important for a logo to be recognizable as it is for it to be readable. Often, people are only able to get a quick glance at the logo, and then only at a distance. In those instances, recognition, not readability, is all that counts. That is why it is so important to integrate recognizable icons, shapes, type fonts, and colors into a logo's design.

Some logos were created during the era of big department stores and were designed as signatures to fit on the side of buildings. As a result, these logos tend to be more square in orientation than they are horizontal. Many of these logos now seem outdated (if they haven't been updated). Hallmark's logo belongs to this class (see Figure 7-1). Others were designed as corporate logos to reinforce leadership and stability (AT&T, IBM). Many of these now seem cold and sterile. Some logos are more fun—communicating more of a personality (Apple, MTV, eBay).

Today, logos must be designed with the foresight that they will be used in multimedia environments (from TV to the Internet). That means colors, animation, and sound sequences (like NBC, Intel, AOL, Harley-Davidson [engine sound], and Maxwell House) should be considered.

EXHIBIT 7-2. BRAND NAMING DECISION TREE.

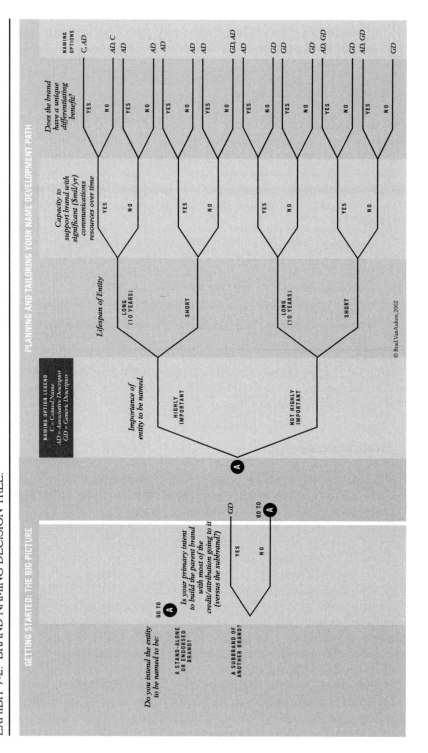

GETTING STARTED: THE BIG PICTURE

Do you intend the entity to be named to be:

A STAND-ALONE OR ENDORSED BRAND?
GO TO Ⓐ

A SUBBRAND OF ANOTHER BRAND?

Is your primary intent to build the parent brand with most of the credit/attribution going to it (versus the subbrand?)

YES — GD

NO — GO TO Ⓐ

NAMING OPTION LEGEND
C = Coined Name
AD = Associative Descriptor
GD = Generic Descriptor

PLANNING AND TAILORING YOUR NAME DEVELOPMENT PATH

Importance of entity to be named.

Ⓐ

HIGHLY IMPORTANT

Lifespan of Entity

LONG (10 YEARS)

Capacity to support brand with significant ($mil/yr) communications resources over time

YES

Does the brand have a unique differentiating benefit?

YES — C, AD
NO — AD, C

NO
YES — AD
NO — AD

SHORT
YES — AD
NO — AD

NOT HIGHLY IMPORTANT

LONG (10 YEARS)
YES
YES — GD, AD
NO — AD

NO
YES — GD
NO — GD

SHORT
YES
YES — GD
NO — AD, GD

NO
YES — GD
NO — AD, GD

YES — GD
NO — GD

NAMING OPTIONS

© Brad VanAuken, 2002

FIGURE 7-1. HALLMARK LOGO.

◼ The Importance of Color

Color is an important consideration in your brand identity system. Colors have a significant impact on people's emotional state. They also have been shown to impact people's ability to concentrate and learn. They have a wide variety of specific mental associations. In fact, the effects are physiological, psychological, and sociological. For instance:[3]

- ✔ Nonprimary colors are more calming than primary colors.
- ✔ Blue is the most calming of the primary colors, followed closely by a lighter red.
- ✔ Test takers score higher and weight lifters lift more in blue rooms.
- ✔ Blue text increases reading retention.
- ✔ Yellow evokes cheerfulness. Houses with yellow trim or flower gardens sell faster.
- ✔ Reds and oranges encourage diners to eat quickly and leave. Red also makes food more appealing and influences people to eat more. (It is no coincidence that fast food restaurants almost always use these colors.)
- ✔ Pink enhances appetites and has been shown to calm prison inmates.
- ✔ Blue and black suppress appetites.
- ✔ Children prefer primary colors. (Notice that children's toys and books often use these colors.)
- ✔ Forest green and burgundy appeal to the wealthiest 3 percent of Americans and often raise the perceived price of an item.
- ✔ Orange is often used to make an expensive item seem less expensive.
- ✔ Red clothing can convey power.
- ✔ Red trim is used in bars and casinos because it can cause people to lose track of time.
- ✔ White is typically associated with cool, clean, and fresh.
- ✔ Red is often associated with Christmas, and orange with Halloween and Thanksgiving.

- ✓ Red and black are often associated with sexy and seductive and are favored by porn sites.
- ✓ Black clothes make people look thinner (as most people know).
- ✓ Black is also associated with elegance and sophistication. It also seems mysterious.
- ✓ Black is the favorite color of Goths.

Favorite Colors of American Consumers

1. Blue
2. Red
3. Green
4. White
5. Pink
6. Purple
7. Orange
8. Yellow

(*Source*: Carlton Wagner, founder of the Wagner Institute for Color Research in Santa Barbara, Calif.)

Colors also have a functional impact on readability, eye-strain, ability to attract attention, ability to be seen at night, etc. This is important in choosing colors for signing, Web site pages, prints ads, and other marketing media.

- ✓ The most visible color is yellow.
- ✓ The most legible of all color combinations are black on yellow and green on white followed by red on white. (It is no surprise that most traffic signs use these color combinations.)
- ✓ Black on white is the easiest to read, both on paper and on computer screens.
- ✓ "Hard" colors (red, orange and yellow) are more visible and tend to make objects look larger and closer. They are easier to focus upon. They create excitement and cause people to overestimate available time.
- ✓ "Soft" colors (violet, blue and green) are less visible and tend to make objects look smaller and further away. They aren't as easy to focus upon. They have a calming effect, increase concentration, and cause people to underestimate remaining time.

Usually, it is advantageous for a brand to consistently "own" certain colors, which provide an additional recognition cue. The George Eastman House International Museum of Photography and Film in Rochester, New York has taken a different, but equally effective approach. They intended to communicate that they are a fun and vibrant organization that features much more than artistic black and white photography. So, the "e" icon in their logo appears in a rainbow of colors. Each business card features the logo with a different color. The name itself always only appears in black and white.

Obviously, colors are an important part of any brand identity system. Testing the effect of a new brand identity system's colors is well advised. It is important to consider that color associations will vary by individual, and especially by culture, due to the cultural context and a person's previous experiences with the colors. All of the impacts of colors are equally true of music, scents, and sounds. For instance, studies have identified that music has an impact on supermarket sales, mental concentration, achievement on standardized tests, factory productivity, clerical performance, and staff turnover, among other things.

Tools to Maintain Brand Identity Consistency

To ensure that external audiences are hearing consistent messages about the brand, companies often "script" their sales and their service organizations. At Element K, the marketing department worked with company management and the ad agency that developed our "E-learning with the Human Touch" campaign to craft a detailed script (together with a PowerPoint slide presentation and other presentation aids). This script was designed to reinforce our brand positioning, "E-learning with the Human Touch," and we required our sales and service organizations to memorize those scripts.

In addition to scripts, organizations use the following tools to ensure brand identity consistency across the enterprise (and by business partners):

✔ Published brand identity standards and systems (historically, these were printed hard copy manuals and CDs, but more recently they're featured on intranet sites, which offer the substantial advantages of providing instant, low-cost universal updates and digital access.) These published standards usually include brand architecture, brand style guides, naming conventions, and a naming decision tree.

✔ Brand photo libraries.

✔ Brand message guidelines. These are often divided into dos and don'ts columns, such as: Do say "Make a Xerox branded photocopy," but don't say "Make a Xerox."

✔ Brand management intranet sites usually include the following items:

   ✔ Brand essence, promise and personality statements

   ✔ Brand pricing guidelines

   ✔ Brand distribution guidelines

   ✔ Brand research summaries

   ✔ Brand management contact information

   ✔ Examples of recent brand ads

✔ Brand management intranet sites sometimes include the following items:

   ✔ Video clip of corporate officers talking about the importance of living the brand

   ✔ Video clip of customers talking about the brand

   ✔ Recognition of people and activities throughout the organization that have delivered upon the brand promise

   ✔ Brand history, myths, and legends

   ✔ Quizzes and other fun exercises designed to teach employees about the brand and its promise

✔ Digital brand asset management systems. More and more organizations are using these to maintain consistency and control throughout their enterprise. These systems are typically fully hosted on the Internet by third parties (ASP model). They provide the ultimate control over decentralized sales and marketing organizations (or retail networks) that develop localized advertising, promotions and other marketing programs. Two firms that specialize in digital brand asset management include Imation (www.imation.com) and Saepio (www.saepio.com).

✔ Naming a brand identity manager or specialist. This is also extremely helpful. This person reviews and approves all new executions of the brand and its subbrands and all new interpretations of its identity. He or she should be well respected throughout the organization, possess strong interpersonal skills, and should be assertive and persuasive.

✔ Creating a cross-divisional brand identity council. Such a council, composed of key design (and editorial) managers from departments and divisions throughout the organization, is also very helpful. The council raises awareness of brand identity issues, builds a consensus around their resolution, becomes a "brain trust" for the brand's identity, and provides peer pressure for interpreting the brand accurately and consistently.

    Use the checklist in Exhibit 7-3 to assess the efficacy of your brand management practices in the area covered by this chapter. The more questions to which you can answer "yes," the better you are doing. The checklist also provides a brief summary of the material covered in the chapter.

EXHIBIT 7-3. BRAND MANAGEMENT CHECKLIST.

BRAND IDENTITY STANDARDS AND SYSTEMS

	YES	NO
As St. James Associates says, some brands are "all symbols but no soul." First and foremost, does your brand have a soul?	___	___
Is your brand's name proprietary? Does it differentiate the brand instead of just describing its products and services?	___	___
Is your brand's name suggestive of a key differentiating benefit, but not too narrow so as to decrease the brand's ability to claim new benefits in the future?	___	___
Do consumers like your brand's name? Is it memorable?	___	___
Do you avoid generic subbrand names?	___	___
Do you have comprehensive brand identity standards and systems that address all uses of your brand's identity elements?	___	___
Are those standards and systems actively in use?	___	___
Are they available in manuals, on CDs, or through your intranet?	___	___
Are all business units and subbrands subject to those standards, with none outside the jurisdiction of the standards?	___	___
At a minimum, does the system include standards for the visual identifier, color, typography, backgrounds, contrast, staging area, relative size, positioning, key applications, and unacceptable uses?	___	___
Is your logotype horizontally shaped? That orientation delivers the greatest visual impact and is a functional necessity when the logotype is used in retail environments.	___	___
Will your system work globally? The meanings of specific words, colors, and symbols in different countries are especially important to understand.	___	___
Does your system include distinctive shapes, colors, typestyles, and voices?	___	___

(continues)

EXHIBIT 7-3. (CONTINUED).

Does your brand own a color that is different from that of your major competitors? _____ _____

Does your system include a slogan or jingle? _____ _____

Does it include sounds and other mnemonic devices? _____ _____

Is your system effective in multimedia environments? _____ _____

Does it address cobranding, comarketing, brand licensing, strategic alliance, and sponsorship situations? _____ _____

Are there simple and consistent ways in which subbrands relate to corporate or parent brands? _____ _____

Are there simple rules for when a brand is endorsed by a corporate or parent brand and when it is not? _____ _____

Does everyone agree upon what names, symbols, colors, visual styles, voices, etc. are used across all applications, subbrands, and product lines on behalf of the parent brand and its identity? _____ _____

In each point of contact with the consumer (advertising, retail environment, product packaging, etc.), have you decided how much emphasis will be placed on the parent brand versus the subbrand? Have you decided which elements will be associated with the parent brand and which will be associated with the subbrand? _____ _____

Does the system deliver strong brand recall and recognition in all contexts? _____ _____

Is the system functional for all intended uses? _____ _____

Is the system flexible enough to address even the most complicated situations? _____ _____

Does your system address internal applications (memos, employee newsletters and other internal publications, computer screen savers, etc.)? _____ _____

Does the system reinforce intended brand associations? _____ _____

Have you built at least nine random, nonfunctional design elements into your brand's trade dress to make it easier for you to legally protect your brand? _____ _____

Do you confer with intellectual property lawyers when designing new products and brands to ensure what you've created has maximum protection under the law? _____ _____

Do you have an ongoing process set up to proactively protect your brand's identity against dilution or confusion, including regular reviews of possible competitive infringements? _____ _____

Do you have a corporate brand identity council (or another process) to manage the brand identity on an ongoing basis? _____ _____

Do you conduct periodic communications audits to monitor adherence to corporate brand identity standards? _____ _____

Is your brand identity system as simple as possible? _____ _____

Ultimately, is it immediately clear which brand is the source for all points of contact you have with the consumer? _____ _____

Notes

1. *The Wall Street Journal,* as quoted in *emarketing* magazine's April 2001 issue, p. 52.
2. "Naming Strategies: 33 Tips & Tactics for Generating Names," *The Naming Newsletter* (Ravkin & Associates), June 26, 2001. p.5.http://www.namingnewsletter.com/33Tips.htm.
3. The primary source for this discussion is "Color Psychology: Meanings and Effects of Colors," May 17, 2001. wysiwyg://33/http://psychology.about.com.

PART THREE

BUILDING THE BRAND

CHAPTER 8

Driving the Consumer from Brand Awareness to Brand Insistence

MY COMPANY BELIEVES that the ultimate goal of brand equity building is to move the consumer from brand awareness to brand insistence. Our brand insistence model incorporates five elements that drive a consumer to insist upon a particular brand to meet his or her needs—brand awareness, accessibility, value, relevant differentiation, and emotional connection (see Figure 8-1). We believe that these five areas of emphasis and activity are the primary drivers of consumer brand insistence.

FIGURE 8-1. BRANDFORWARD'S BRAND INSISTENCE MODEL.

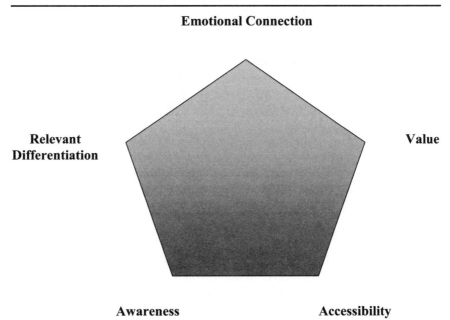

Emotional Connection

Relevant Differentiation

Value

Awareness

Accessibility

Brand Awareness

Brand building begins with awareness. Consumers first must be aware that there are different brands in the product categories in which your brand operates. Next, they must be aware of *your* brand. Ideally, your brand should be the first one that comes to their minds within specific product categories and also be the first one they associate with key consumer benefits. Consumers should:

- ✓ Be able to identify which products and services your brand offers
- ✓ Be able to identify which benefits are associated with the brand
- ✓ Have some idea of where your brand is sold

Accessibility

Your brand must be available where consumers shop. It's much easier for consumers to insist upon your brand if it is widely available, and slight brand

---

McDonald's: The Power of the Arches

During the 1996 Summer Olympics, a study was done of the most recognized symbols across several nations. What was right up there in the top five behind the Olympic rings but ahead of the Christian cross? The McDonald's golden arches, of course. How did this icon get to be so well recognized? To answer this, you only have to go to a McDonald's restaurant. From the time you turn into the restaurant parking lot and enter the restaurant until the time you are finished eating and leave, count the number of times you are exposed to the arches. Also make note of the most unusual places in which you discover the arches. You will have witnessed the power of an effective brand identity system and icon repetition.

---

preference goes a long way toward insistence when the brand is widely available. The importance of convenience cannot be overestimated in today's world. (Brands whose market place positionings have "exclusivity" as a key component are an exception to this. In those cases, scarcity, and limited distribution, can stimulate demand.)

The Coca-Cola Company: The Power of Brand Accessibility

Brand Asset Value

In 1997, *Financial World* valued the Coca-Cola brand at $48 billion. (More recently, it was valued at $72.5 billion. For the sake of comparison—Microsoft's brand was valued at $70.2 billion, IBM at $53.2 billion, and Intel at $39.0 billion.)

What does that really mean? If all of Coke's plants were burned to the ground, if every one of its employees were to quit, if all of its retail distribution was lost to competitors, if every single remaining tangible asset was sold, the person who owned rights to the Coke name and trademark could go to any bank in the world and, based on the value of that trademark, borrow money to completely rebuild the company. In other words, the Coke name alone is worth some $72.5 billion dollars—more than the value of all the company's other assets combined. After all, it's Coke that consumers insist upon, not any of the other stuff.

From the Three A's to the Three P's

Coca-Cola used to focus its strategy on the three A's: availability, acceptability, and affordability. While these provided for tremendous growth, they also led to lowered entry barriers. Today, Coca-Cola's mantra is the three P's: preference, pervasive penetration, and price-related value.

The Power of Brand Accessibility

If you were another soft drink company, you might define your competitive frame of reference as the cola market or the soft drink market or even the beverage market. But Coke thinks of its business and its market share in terms of "share of human liquid consumption." This makes water a competitor. In fact, a Coke executive has said that he won't be satisfied until "there is a Coca-Cola faucet in every home." Coca-Cola's mantra is "within an arm's reach of desire."

Another indication of Coke's drive for accessibility, beyond the vending machines that seem to be everywhere, is illustrated in a recent trip I took to Peru. We had spent several days traveling down Rio Madre de

Dios on a riverboat, moving deeper and deeper into the Amazon river basin, jungle, and Manu World Biosphere Reserve. When we finally encountered a riverside village of indigenous people and thatched huts, what was waiting for us? A Coke sign and fresh Coke.

Coca-Cola Is Serious About Brand Building
    Each month, Coca-Cola tests 20 brand attributes with 4,000 consumers to measure movement. The company also compensates (bonus and other compensation components) a large portion of its senior managers based on brand preference.

One Final Coca-Cola Fact
    Coca-Cola's 1995 annual report reported that the second most recognized expression in the world after "okay" is "Coca-Cola."

Value

Does your brand deliver a good value for the price? Do consumers believe it is worth the price? Regardless of whether it is expensive or inexpensive, high end or low end, it must deliver at least a good value.

Important Things to Know About Pricing[1]

Reference Prices

People often compare a product's price to a "reference price" that they maintain in their minds for the product or product category in question. A "reference price" is the price that people expect or deem to be reasonable for a certain type of product. Several factors affect reference prices:

✓ Memory of past prices.
✓ Frame of reference (compared to competitive prices, pre-sale prices, manufacturer's suggested prices, channel-specific prices, marked prices before discounts, substitute product prices, etc.). Creating the most advantageous (and believable) competitive frame of reference is essential to achieving a price premium.
✓ Prices of other products on the same shelf, in the same catalog, or in the same product line. The addition of a more premium-priced product typi-

cally increases sales of other lower-priced products in the same product line

✓ The way the price is presented. For instance:

  ✓ Absolute number versus per quart, per pound, per hour of use, per application, or for the result achieved

  ✓ Four separate payments of $69.95 versus $279.80

  ✓ Total purchase price versus monthly loan payment versus monthly lease payment (e.g., for automobiles)

✓ The order in which people see a range of prices—such as a realtor using the trick of showing the poorest value house first.

Price Sensitivity

It is extremely important to be able to estimate the impact of price changes on sales and profits. That is, it is important to know how a price change will impact consumer response, competitive response, and unit volume. Many business people erroneously believe that a price increase is *the* most cost-effective revenue-generating marketing tactic. I have heard generally intelligent business people share their excitement about how a price increase will drop to the "bottom line" dollar-for-dollar. Most of the time, this is simply not true.

People display different price sensitivities to different products in different situations. Often people are relatively price insensitive, but only within a relevant price range. Once a price exceeds that range, people become very sensitive. Raising the price across that threshold is akin to walking off of a cliff.

The following factors decrease price sensitivity:

✓ Relevant brand/product differentiation

✓ Marketing and selling on factors other than price

✓ Convincing consumers that quality differs significantly among products and brands in the category

✓ Self-expressive or "image" products or brands. (For example, if I wear sports apparel featuring Nike's swoosh, it implies that I have the "Just do it" attitude of Nike's "authentic athletic performance" essence; if I carry a Gucci hand bag or wear a Rolex watch or drive a Mercedes Benz, it says that "I have arrived," that I have social status; if I wear a Harvard ball cap, it says I am extremely smart and successful; and if I wear a Harley-Davidson tattoo, it says that I know the freedom of the road, that I am a free spirit.)

✓ Brand advertising

✓ Situations in which price is a signal to quality—usually for relatively new or unknown products or brands

- ✓ When it is difficult to ascertain a "reference price" within the category
- ✓ When there are significant switching costs—in dollars, time, effort, risk, or emotional impact
- ✓ Product categories for which the risk of failure is an important issue
- ✓ When the price is insignificant relative to the total budget or discretionary income
- ✓ For businesses, when the item does not significantly contribute to the cost of the products and services that they sell
- ✓ When the price falls within the expected price range for products in the category
- ✓ When offering "value-added services" versus "price discounts" to motivate purchases
- ✓ New markets

The following factors increase price sensitivity:

- ✓ Price promotions, especially when people are able to stock up on the price-discounted items
- ✓ Mature and declining markets

Price Segmentation

Price segmentation (offering different prices to different market segments) increases overall revenues and profits, and it is particularly beneficial to industries that have high fixed cost structures. Obviously, price segmentation works better when there are real customer need segments and when you can effectively isolate those segments.

As an example, imagine that your business only offers one product priced at $5. But you know that some consumers would be willing to pay up to $8. You are leaving $3 on the table for each of them. Other consumers are more price-sensitive and only willing to pay $3. You do not get any of their business. Exhibit 8-1 illustrates how much more revenue you can generate by offering three prices—$3, $5 and $8—instead of just one—$5. Although this is a simplified example, it illustrates the financial advantages of price segmentation.

Prices can be segmented in the following ways:

- ✓ By time (e.g., higher hotel room rates for holidays and other peak tourist seasons)
- ✓ By location (e.g., higher prices in locations with less competition or where less price-sensitive shoppers shop; orchestra versus balcony seats in a theater)

EXHIBIT 8-1. PRICE SEGMENTATION.

Segment	Number of people in segment	Maximum price people in that segment are willing to pay	Maximum possible revenues from that segment if you only offer one item at $5	Maximum possible revenues from that segment if you offer three items—one at $3, one at $5, and one at $8
A	10	$3	0	$30
B	10	$5	$50	$50
C	10	$8	$50	$80
TOTAL	30		$100	$160

✓ By volume (volume discounts for large orders)

✓ By product attribute (first class versus coach section on airplanes; solid brass versus plastic faucets)

✓ By product bundling—for example:
Selling software in product suites versus by the program
Selling e-learning by library versus the individual course
Fixed price versus à la carte menus
"Fully-loaded" models versus "basic" models with additional options available
Single admission ticket at theme parks versus charging per ride

✓ By customer segment (brand-loyal versus price-sensitive versus convenience-oriented; or image-conscious versus economy-oriented)

Other price/value considerations are:

✓ In your pricing strategy you should consider these factors:

1. *Perceived* customer value

2. Competitive response

3. Channels of distribution

4. Cost parameters

5. Congruence with the brand position

✓ Constantly explore new ways to uniquely add customer value to your products and services.

✓ In creating greater customer value, always ask, "How can we make it quicker, easier, less risky, or more pleasant to do business with us?" Ask, "What could we do that would favorably surprise and delight our customers?"

✓ Communicate the value of services that you provide for free.

✓ Remember that providing value-added products and services at "no charge" is superior to price discounting as a short-term purchase incentive because it preserves the value of the brand

✔ Be careful to price your products and services to reward brand-loyal (versus brand-switching) behavior

Pricing is becoming an increasingly sophisticated discipline. The three topics we just discussed (reference prices, price sensitivity, and price segmentation) are just a few of the important considerations when developing pricing strategies and tactics. (Introductory pricing [skimming versus penetration, trial pricing], product mix pricing, fixed and variable price components, price adjustments [reason, amount, and frequency], pricing to meet buying system requirements, loss-leader pricing, prestige pricing and even-odd pricing are other pricing approaches/considerations of note.) I would highly recommend reading *The Strategy and Tactics of Pricing* by Thomas T. Nagle and Reed K. Holden to better understand how to develop effective pricing strategies and tactics.[2] Online pricing resources include www.pricing-advisor.com and www.profitablepricing.com.

Relevant Differentiation

Relevant differentiation is the most important thing a brand can deliver. Relevant differentiation today is a leading-edge indicator of profitability and market share tomorrow. Does your brand own consumer-relevant, consumer-compelling benefits that are unique and believable? Today, services and the "total brand experience" often become the differentiators.

Emotional Connection

As we've discussed, the consumer must first *know* your brand, then *like* your brand, and finally *trust* your brand and feel an emotional connection to it (Figure 8-2).

People become emotionally connected to a brand for a number of reasons:

✔ The brand stands for something important to them.
✔ The brand is intense and vibrant. It connects with people on multiple levels across several senses.
✔ The brand is unique.
✔ The brand is admirable.
✔ The brand consistently interacts with them. It never disappoints them.
✔ The brand makes them feel good.

There are many innovative ways to achieve this emotional connection—from advertising and the quality of front-line consumer contact to consumer membership organizations and company-sponsored consumer events.

The Power of Breaking Consumer Compromise

"Breaking consumer compromises" is one of the most powerful concepts in business today. Introduced by George Stalk, Jr., David K. Pecaut, and Benjamin Burnett ("Breaking Compromises, Breakaway Growth," *Harvard Business Review*, September–October 1996, pp. 131–139), it states that the best way to create breakaway business growth is to identify all the ways in which a business has made compromises with the consumer and then break them all so that that consumer gets exactly what he needs and wants.

For example, consider CarMax and the used car industry. An industry outsider (Circuit City) carefully analyzed the very large and profitable used car industry to identify all the consumer compromises—limited variety at any one place, no maintenance records, limited knowledge about the car's history, high pressure sales tactics, perceived lack of honesty, etc. By breaking all of these compromises, Circuit City gained a substantial market share very quickly with its CarMax business.

The trick is to constantly reinvent your business even if you think you have something to lose by doing so. That is why it is often the most difficult for an industry insider to transform their industry by breaking compromises. Consider Kodak. It must have been difficult for Kodak to enter the digital imaging world with a passion when most of their current business is based on chemical photography. And, it was very difficult for Hallmark, in the late 1990's, to introduce a very large selection of 99-cent cards (Out of the Blue, Children's Seasonal, and Hallmark Warm Wishes greeting cards) with the very-real concern of possible trade down. But, to their credit, Hallmark did it, and broke the consumer compromise.

It is especially important to ensure that all of your employees with front-line customer contact are like Boy Scouts—that is, that they are trustworthy, helpful, friendly, courteous, kind, and cheerful. Add to that list empathetic, good listeners, and reassuring. Accomplish this by establishing the appropriate hiring criteria, training, and organization culture. Remember, good service is all about creating positive feelings, treating people well, and solving people's problems.

FIGURE 8-2. HIERARCHY OF EFFECTS.

Ultimately, emotional connection will come from positive shared experiences with the brand over time. While this trust is built over time, offering an unconditional guarantee is a quick way to reduce the risk of a new unknown brand and to generate some minimum level of trust immediately.

Other loyalty-inducing approaches:

✓ The brand encourages frequent, habit-forming interaction (as long as the interaction is pleasant or beneficial and not against people's wills).

✓ The brand finds ways to build cumulative value for customers over time, especially if the value is not transferable to the use of competitive products and services.

Did You Know?

✔ It costs seven times more to get a new consumer for the brand than it does to get a current consumer to make an incremental purchase.

✔ In some sectors, an increase in the consumer base by just 1 percent is otherwise equivalent to a 10 percent cost reduction. (*Source*: Robert Passikoff, Ph.D., president of Brand Keys, Inc.)

✔ Depending on the category, a 5 percent increase in customer loyalty will lift the lifetime profits per customer by up to 95 percent. (*Source*: Robert Passikoff. Also, according to Larry Light, on average, a 5 percent increase in loyalty results in a 25 percent increase in profitability.)

✔ Increasingly, brands are shifting their focus from penetration to usage. Greater success comes from getting a larger portion of a smaller segment's business (versus getting more consumers to buy your brand). This can be accomplished in many ways, including offering more and different products and services that deliver against your brand's promise.

In his book, *The Dream Society,* Rolf Jensen makes the case for a shift from an information society to a dream society in which imagination and storytelling become the primary drivers of value.[3] He identifies six emerging emotion-based markets:

1. Adventure
2. Community (togetherness, friendship, and love)
3. Providing and receiving care
4. Self-expression ("Who-Am-I?")
5. Peace of mind
6. Standing for something (convictions)

Any brand that seeks to create emotional connection should find ways to tap into these and other underlying human motives. See Exhibit 8-2 for illustrations of strong emotional connections.

EXHIBIT 8-2. BRAND EMOTIONAL CONNECTION.
_____

You know you have a vital, relevant, compelling brand when customers think or say the following things about your brand. (These statements are taken from real customer feedback on brands with strong emotional connection.)

It affects people at a visceral level.
It "gets in your blood."
It evokes strong emotions.
It speaks from the heart.
It speaks to the heart.
It opens up people's sense of what is possible.
It creates a sense of possibility.
It opens people up a whole new world.
It is inspiring.
It is empowering.
It is invigorating.
It helps people see that they can make a difference.
It makes people believe that they can change the world.
It helps people articulate what they have been trying to say.
It is the first time that people feel as if they really have been heard.
It is unique.
It is fresh.
It is original.
It is one-of-a-kind.
It breaks all of the rules.
It breaks down all the boundaries.
It is "a breath of fresh air."
It defines the category.
It is quintessential.
It sets the standard.
It stands apart from all the rest
It can't be categorized.
It is in a class all of its own.
No one else is doing anything like that.
It has new ideas.
It is very influential.
It is seminal.
Everything else is derivative.
It reinvents the category.
It is genuine.
It is sincere.
It is real.
It is pure.
It is trustworthy.

It is approachable.
It is endearing.
It stands for something.
It believes in something.
It is passionate.
It has a distinctive attitude.
People in that organization love what they do.
It is powerful.
It possesses great energy.
It is entertaining.
It is elegant, beautiful, and/or haunting.
It is admirable.
It is visionary.
It possesses a timeless quality.
It possesses a universal quality.
It has successfully stood the test of time.
It is still relevant years later.
It is as it is meant to be.
It is "bigger than life."
It has a presence that you can't ignore.
It demands to be heard.
It is legendary.
It is enshrouded in mystery.
There is a certain mystique about it.
It is profound.
It is captivating.
It is otherworldly.
It is mesmerizing.
It is indescribable.
The only way that people can fully understand the brand is by
    experiencing it for themselves.
It is unstoppable.
It is extraordinary.
It is flawless.
It is genius.
It is a "crowning jewel."
It is riveting.
It is "mind blowing."
It doesn't get any better than that.

A Quiz: What Brand?

What brand has built enormous equity without huge advertising budgets?

What brand has defined its business not narrowly as a product, but broadly as an experience and a state of mind, despite the fact that the vast majority of its revenues result from one single product category?

What brand has created tremendous brand loyalty by creating a social organization for owners of its products?

What brand sponsors frequent events for owners of its products, which the company's management attends in order to understand the consumer, his/her experience, and his/her needs first hand?

What brand proactively leverages publicity as a key component of its marketing plan?

What brand tried to legally protect the sound its product makes as a key element of its brand identity system?

What brand, having been on the brink of bankruptcy twice since the 1960s, has achieved a stunning transformation into a world-class brand?

What brand evokes so much loyalty in its consumers that many of them tattoo its logo on their bodies?

Harley-Davidson, of course.

CASE STUDY

Brand Equity Case Study:
Hallmark

While serving as director of brand management and marketing at Hallmark, I spent the better part of three years developing and refining a brand equity framework and scorecard for Hallmark. As awareness of the Hallmark brand was very high and its image was very positive, we were less interested in measuring and managing these aspects of the brand's equity than we were in identifying the attributes that drove customers to insist upon the brand. This ultimately led to what is now my organization's brand insistence brand equity model (as addressed earlier in this chapter) with key drivers: awareness, accessibility, value, relevant differentiation, and emotional connection. Hallmark scored extraordinarily high on awareness, accessibility, and emotional connection. While relevant differentiation was constantly a focus (as it should be for all established brands), we primarily focused on improving value. Although Hallmark's greeting cards were actually less expensive than competitive cards, they were universally thought to be more expensive. People perceived Hallmark cards to be priced between $2.75 and $2.95 (one dollar higher than the actual average price paid), while they perceived mass channel brands' cards to be priced at $2 (very near the actual average price paid after in-store discounts). So, people connected the following in their minds: "Hallmark = The Best = Expensive" (or "When you care enough to send the very best"). This perception was reinforced in several ways:

✔ People were especially price conscious in card shops (Hallmark's primary channel at the time) as they assumed products would be more expensive there. Card shops seldom, if ever, offer price discounts. If one shops in Wal-Mart, with its promise of "Always the Low Price—Always," its prominent "X percent off" displays, and, in the case of greeting cards, its generic brands, one is less likely to be on the lookout for high prices.

✔ In a card shop's typical market basket of four greeting cards, card prices were obvious (a total bill of $12 easily translates to $3 a card). This compares to a typical mass channel market basket, which may be comprised of a wide variety of items and cost many times that amount.

Our brand equity measurement system identified this as an issue in two ways: Hallmark received a mediocre score on "value," and the system identified "expensive" as Hallmark's only negative brand association.

Altering price perceptions for a leading premium brand is a tricky exercise. It's kind of like diffusing a bomb. The trick is to snip the right wire—the "The Best = Expensive" wire, not the "Hallmark = The Best" wire.

Changing Hallmark price perceptions was also critical to the success of our strategy of launching "Expressions from Hallmark" to the mass channel (see the Hallmark case study, Leveraging the Brand, on page 208).

After our brand scorecard identified "value" as an issue, we got management's buy-in to develop and test aggressive measures to alter the "expensive" price perception. Here is what we did:

✔ We developed two lines of 99-cent cards as proof points— children's (occasion and nonoccasion) cards and "Out of the Blue," a new line of "anyday" friendship cards. We devoted 248 skus and 8 linear feet of product to this new line, which provided a proof point of (and statement about) our commitment to the new line.

✓ Because we knew our competitors could not match this, we created pocket identifiers (signs above each card on the display) that highlighted that the cards that were priced under $2 (65 percent of Hallmark's cards, only 11 percent of our competitors' cards).

✓ We prominently featured "99-cent" signs at appropriate places throughout the card department.

✓ We advertised the fact that Hallmark now had 99-cent cards.

✓ Introducing "Expressions from Hallmark" cards to Wal-Mart and other mass channel stores reinforced the point that Hallmark must not be that expensive (borrowing upon Wal-Mart's "low price" brand perceptions).

✓ We did all of this as a part of a test market in Las Vegas.

✓ We tested the impact of this action on many brand equity components in that test market, not just "value." For instance, we tested brand preference, quality perceptions, and brand insistence itself to validate that increased "value" led to increased brand equity and insistence.

Here is what we found from the Las Vegas test market:

✓ Greeting card category price perceptions improved significantly

✓ All Hallmark brand equity measures increased significantly

✓ People gave Hallmark credit for listening to their concerns about price

✓ Hallmark sales and market share increased significantly

Based upon the success of this test market, we launched this program nationally, and we achieved the same results nationally. This is a simple example of how a brand equity measurement system led to actions that significantly improved brand perceptions, sales, and market share.

Use the checklist in Exhibit 8-3 to assess the efficacy of your brand management practices in the area covered by this chapter. The more questions to which you can answer "yes," the better you are doing. The checklist also provides a brief summary of the material covered in the chapter.

EXHIBIT 8-3. BRAND MANAGEMENT CHECKLIST.

DRIVING THE CONSUMER FROM BRAND AWARENESS TO BRAND INSISTENCE.

	YES	NO
Was your brand first to market?	____	____
Was it the first to communicate with consumers in significant ways?	____	____
Is your brand the top-of-mind brand in its product/ service category?	____	____
Is it the only brand that comes to mind for its primary differentiating benefit?	____	____
Do consumers perceive your brand to be easily accessible and convenient?	____	____
Have you carefully crafted brand pricing strategies and tactics based upon a solid understanding of contribution margins, consumer price sensitivities, reference prices, likely competitive responses, and basic pricing principles?	____	____
Does your brand deliver a good value for the price? Do consumers think your brand is worth the price?	____	____
Is your brand differentiated in at least one highly relevant and compelling way?	____	____
Does your brand reflect the attitudes and values of its target customers?	____	____
Does your brand touch people at some deep emotional level? Does it stand for something important to them?	____	____
Does your brand achieve any of the following?		
✔ Does it make people feel more in control?	____	____
✔ Is it nostalgic of something from their childhood?	____	____
✔ Does it make them feel warm and safe?	____	____
✔ Does it offer a sensual experience?	____	____
✔ Does it make them feel smart or frugal or important when they use it?	____	____
✔ Does it make them feel like "masters of the universe"?	____	____
✔ Does it help them play out unfulfilled fantasies?	____	____

(continues)

EXHIBIT 8-3. (CONTINUED).

    ✔ Does it make them feel as though they have become the people that they had always wanted to be?   _____ _____

    ✔ Does it make them feel more connected to the group they most admire?   _____ _____

    ✔ Does it make them feel superior to others?   _____ _____

Does your brand invite people into its world? Is it inviting and engaging?   _____ _____

Is your brand the most preferred brand in its category?   _____ _____

Do your customers perceive your brand to be vital, popular, or leading-edge?   _____ _____

Do people like your brand?   _____ _____

Do people trust your brand?   _____ _____

Is your brand on most potential customers' short lists? Is it typically the only brand that they consider?   _____ _____

Are your customers attitudinally loyal to your brand?   _____ _____

Do people enthusiastically recommend your brand to others?   _____ _____

Notes

1. Much of this section (especially the list of factors that decrease and increase price sensitivity) is informed by Thomas T. Nagle and Reed K. Holden's book, *The Strategy and Tactics of Pricing: A Guide to Profitable Decision Making* (Upper Saddle River, N.J.: Prentice Hall, 1995). It also largely draws upon my experience crafting pricing strategy for Hallmark.

2. Nagle and Holden, *The Strategy and Tactics of Pricing.*

3. Rolf Jensen, *The Dream Society: How the Coming Shift from Information to Imagination Will Transform Your Business* (New York: McGraw-Hill, 1999).

CHAPTER 9

Brand Advertising

ADVERTISING IS ONE of the most frequently used and powerful communications mediums for brand building. How then does one maximize the effectiveness and efficiency of this medium?

Selecting an Ad Agency*

First, if you don't have an advertising agency, select one. Begin by thoughtfully defining what is most important to you in an agency, and clarify where you need the most help. This will be an important touchstone throughout the remainder of the process.

Cut out your favorite magazine ads and tape your favorite television commercials. A good place to find great ads is *www.adcritic.com,* as are *One Show* and *Communication Arts* awards books. Also, most cities have ad clubs that judge and recognize the best ads from local agencies. Check with these clubs as well. Once you have selected several ads that you like, find out which agencies created them. Of those agencies, find out which are already working for your competitors. Rule them out. Talk with marketing peers at other companies about their perceptions of the agencies that are left. Ask about the agencies' capabilities in each of the following areas: product, company and market place knowledge, creative, strategic insight, media planning, and production. (I have found that the two most important aspects of an effective agency are strategic insight and translating that insight to creative communication.) Contact the top three to four agencies of those that are left.

When you meet, ask to see their best ads. Have the agencies demonstrate how they would address your most pressing strategic issues. You might also ask each agency to create three campaigns to move your brand forward. (Be sure to pay each of the agencies for their work. This protects you if you use

---

* Much of this section is adapted from an approach David Ogilvy outlines in his book, *Ogilvy on Advertising* (New York: Vintage Books, 1985), pp. 66–69, combined with my personal experience.

an agency's ideas but do not end up hiring that agency.) Look for the agency that you can best work with based upon personal chemistry.

Some other tips:

- ✓ Don't assume that going with the biggest well-known agency is best. Unless you have an enormous advertising budget, you are likely to be assigned to their "C team" and may not be happy with the "C team's" work.
- ✓ There are significant advantages to choosing an agency that has strengths in multiple areas: strategy, creative, media planning and buying, direct marketing, online marketing, Web site design, trade shows, etc. It will make it easier to manage your overall marketing budget and, more importantly, all of your communication is more likely to be consistent and "on brand."

  Unfortunately, very few agencies are tops in more than a few aspects of marketing. I prefer to work with a small number of "best in class" agencies. This requires a strong coordination effort, including frequent (quarterly) "brand champion summits" (to which all agency partners are invited to remain informed and aligned with the strategy and key messages), well-thought-out and accessible brand identity standards, and an accessible brand image library. It is particularly important to coordinate the efforts of advertising strategy and creative with that of media planning and buying if performed by separate agencies. The two agencies should meet often and learn to work well together.

- ✓ Some agencies are best at (and enjoy most) the development of new breakthrough campaigns. They are critical to your brand's success but also tend to be more expensive. Other agencies don't have a "strategic bone in their bodies" but provide on-spec collateral pieces at a fraction of the cost. I use both types of agencies. Some agencies try to address both needs at different hourly rates, using different individuals and processes. Sometimes that works. Sometimes it doesn't.

  See Exhibit 9-1 for tips on how to get the most out of your advertising agency.

Importance of a Well-Designed Brand to Brand Advertising

As you begin to work with an agency (even during an agency review), you will make greater strides if you have already designed and positioned the brand. Remember, your brand's promise should leverage all three of the following: (a) a compelling point of difference in the consumer's mind, (b) your organization's unique strengths, and (c) your competitors' vulnerabilities. This implies that you have identified the brand's target consumer, essence, promise and personality. The brand promise, in turn, implies that you understand your brand's competitive frame of reference and the consumer's benefit struc-

EXHIBIT 9-1. THE CARE AND FEEDING OF ADVERTISING AGENCIES, OR, HOW TO GET THE MOST OUT OF YOUR ADVERTISING AGENCY.

Give them clear assignments with clear deliverables (see "agency brief").
Tell them that you expect their best work.
Treat them with respect.
Expose them to your customers and all of your customer research.
Get out of their way. Don't micromanage them.
Run internal "interference" for them. Don't let internal review and
   approval processes adulterate their product.
Pay them fairly for their work.
Praise them when they do good work.

ture within that frame of reference. The brand design and positioning will drive brand advertising and every other brand marketing activity. Make sure your ad agency thoroughly understands and embraces your brand's design. (Although you should take the lead in crafting your brand's design, ideally your advertising agency should be actively involved in the process, including immersing themselves in the underlying consumer research.)

Specifying the Marketing Objective for Advertising

The next step in advertising development is specifying the marketing objective for the advertising. That is, what do you want the advertising to achieve? Do you want it to increase brand awareness, attract new customers, increase brand loyalty, encourage add-on purchases, motivate people to switch from competitive brands to your brand, increase frequency of use, reinforce ongoing use, etc.? Make sure the objective is quantifiable and measurable.

As an example, the marketing objective for Hallmark's brand insistence advertising campaign in the mid-1990s was very simple and tactical: to get consumers to flip the card over and look for the brand name on the back cover.

During your brand positioning work, you should have developed the brand promise including identification of the brand's relevant differentiating benefit. Next you augment the brand promise with proof points (reasons to believe). Proof points may include the following:

✓ Product features and attributes (including the design itself or its formula or ingredients)

✓ Performance features, statistics and research results

✓ Performance guarantees

✓ Service claims

   ✔ Side-by-side comparisons

   ✔ Third-party endorsements

Writing the Agency Brief

The marketing objective and the brand promise with its proof points are key elements of the agency brief, a document that communicates the strategic direction of a new advertising campaign. Once you have completed the agency brief, your ad agency will use the brief to develop campaign ideas/concepts (storyboards, print ads, etc.). They will likely show you several different campaign ideas.

Exhibit 9-2 lists the elements of the agency brief.

EXHIBIT 9-2. AGENCY BRIEF.

Background/Overview: (provide history, context, and a general overview of the competitive environment and the problem)

Marketing Objective: (desired tangible result, usually in target customer's attitude or behavior–intended effect with quantifiable success criteria)
- ✔ **Current State:** (what the customer thinks today)
- ✔ **Desired State:** (what we want them to think *and* what we want them to do)

Assignment: (deliverable, timing, and budget)

Product or Service: (if product/service-specific)

Target Customer: (be as specific as possible)

Brand Essence: (the "heart and soul" of the brand expressed as "adjective, adjective, noun")

Brand Promise: (Only [brand] delivers [relevant differentiated benefit])

Proof Points: (reasons to believe)

Brand Personality, Voice and Visual Style: (from the positioning statement—list of adjectives that describe the brand, for instance: *voice*: down-to-earth, assertive, confident, warm, sarcastic, witty, reassuring, eloquent, simple, etc.; *visual style*: bold, bright, energetic, soft, textured, ornate, understated, nostalgic, futuristic, etc.)

Mandatories: (Those items that are givens. It is best to provide as few constraints as possible. I usually specify the brand identity standards and system as the only mandatory. There may be legal or regulatory mandatories as well.)

Evaluating Advertising Effectiveness

When evaluating the potential effectiveness of different campaign ideas, I use the following questions:

1. *All Advertising*

- ✔ Does the ad clearly identify your brand? Does it do so immediately and throughout the ad?
- ✔ Does the ad clearly and forcefully communicate your brand's unique promise?
- ✔ Does the ad feature a tag line that reinforces the brand's promise?
- ✔ Are the ad's tone, voice, and style true to your brand's essence and personality?
- ✔ Does the ad reinforce your brand's identity?
- ✔ Does the ad connect with the reader on an emotional level? Does it win the reader's heart or capture his or her imagination?
- ✔ Is there something about the ad that makes the reader admire the brand?
- ✔ Is your ad significantly different from that of your competitors? Does it look and feel different from anything else featured in the same media?
- ✔ Does the ad reinforce the positive value and values of your brand?
- ✔ Does the ad seem truly inspired?
- ✔ Is your ad so powerful that it has the potential to keep your competitors awake at night worrying about your brand?
- ✔ Is the ad persuasive?
- ✔ Could another competitor make the same claim? If you inserted a competitor's logo in the ad, would it make no sense or be unbelievable?
- ✔ Does the ad lead the reader/viewer to believe that he or she will be better off in some way for having interacted with your brand? Does it create a more favorably perceived end-state for him or her? Does it leave a vivid picture in his or her mind?

2. *Print Advertising*

(The benefits of print advertising are: good reach and frequency, can handle complicated propositions, reaches consumers in a receptive context, can be very targeted.)

- ✔ Does the headline immediately "grab" the reader? (In his book *Ogilvy on Advertising*, advertising guru David Ogilvy's states that five times as

Did You Know?

Psychologist Erich Dichter found that consumers are more apt to relax and accept advertiser recommendations when the tone is that of a friend or an unbiased authority. (Source: Emanuel Rosen, *The Anatomy of Buzz: How to Create Word of Mouth Marketing,* New York, Doubleday, 2000, p. 210.)

many people read headlines as read body copy.) Ideally, the headline is nine words or less.

✓ Does the headline promise an important benefit? (Ogilvy also states that ads with headlines that promise benefits are read by four times more people than those that don't.)

✓ Is the body copy long enough to provide the reader with useful information and ample proof points for your brand's promise? Long copy is more effective than short copy. This is particularly true for business-to-business advertising. (Alternatively, Roper Starch Worldwide, which maintains a database of more than 2 million print ads, has found that excessive copy reduces the effectiveness of ads and recommends keeping ad copy to fifty words or less. With whole generations having now grown up on "sound bytes" of information, some cohort groups will respond better to shorter copy.)

✓ Increasing white space around the ad or the headline increases the ad's effectiveness. Exhibit 9-3 ranks ad placement and size according to impact.

3. *Television Advertising*

(Television advertising benefits are: broad reach, greatest ability to dramatize the brand.)

✓ Do you try to grab peoples' attention immediately so that they do not become preoccupied with other activities?

✓ Do you have enough time too tell a story with your commercial? (Two-minute commercials are more powerful than thirty-second commercials.)

✓ Have you carefully selected the music for your commercial? (Music can make or break a commercial.)

✓ Have you consistently used a sound or visual mnemonic to reinforce the brand in your commercials?

EXHIBIT 9-3. RANKING ORDER OF MAGAZINE ADVERTISING SIZE IMPACT.

1. Three single-page ads following each other on the right side.
2. Two single-page ads in different sections of the same magazine on the right side.
3. Double-page spread.
4. Single-page ads on right.
5. Single-page ads on left with strip on right.
6. Single-page ads on left.
7. Checkerboard ads on right.
8. Checkerboard ads on left.
9. Half-page ad, upper right.
10. Half-page ad, lower right.
11. Strip on both right and left sides.
12. Half-page ad, upper left.
13. Half-page ad, lower left.
14. Third-page block, lower right.
15. Strip (one column) extreme right.
16. Strip, extreme left.

SOURCE: A study performed by the PreTesting Company and reported by "The MPA Research Newsletter/No. 60" (Magazine Publishers of America), as featured on the Magazines Canada Web site (http://www.magazinescanada.com/research_archives/7_Ad_Postioning_60/1.shtml).

4. *Radio Advertising*

(Radio advertising benefits are: very efficient, a good frequency medium, coverage flexibility.)

✔ Does the first five seconds "grab" the listener?

✔ Have you chosen the right voice?

✔ Does the dialogue sound natural?

5. *Outdoor Advertising*

(Outdoor advertising benefits are: very low CPM, a true local medium, ability to communicate a single "idea" effectively.)

✔ Does the billboard have no more than seven words? Does it have less than five? ("Got Milk?") Remember, motorists often have to "get it" (your message) in a second or less!

✔ Is the ad "big" in every way? Is it outrageous? Does it turn heads? Does it pique the reader's curiosity? Does it shock the reader? Does it make the reader laugh?

▦ Successful Advertising Approaches

Here is a list of effective general ad techniques:

- ✓ Always dramatize your brand's most important benefit
- ✓ Create simple ads—they are usually more powerful
- ✓ Create copy in smaller chunks—sentences, paragraphs, etc.
- ✓ Use natural and "real life" writing or dialog
- ✓ *Subtly* tap into peoples' fears and anxieties

Here are some print advertising techniques that have proven to be effective:

- ✓ Try to evoke the reader's curiosity. Begin by asking a provocative question and/or feature an image that piques the reader's curiosity.
- ✓ Put quotes around your headlines.
- ✓ Romance/dramatize your product or service.
- ✓ Try to trigger multiple senses—use words that help people feel, hear, smell and taste your product.
- ✓ Tell a story.
- ✓ Communicate "news."
- ✓ Provide information that is useful to the reader.
- ✓ Always write in the present tense.
- ✓ Be as specific as possible.
- ✓ Include customer testimonials (they should seem natural, not scripted or polished).
- ✓ Know how readers read ads (from right to left, top to bottom) and place your headlines, illustrations, captions and copy accordingly. (In his book *Secret Formulas of the Wizard of Ads*, Roy H. Williams indicates that savvy photographers and graphic artists have known for some time that there is a spot on a piece of artwork to which the eye is irresistibly drawn, roughly between the middle and upper right corner of the artwork.)
- ✓ Use white space to focus the reader's attention on something important.
- ✓ Use words that sell: *at last, now, new, introducing, announcing, finally, limited, save, free, win, easy, guarantee, breakthrough, wanted*, etc. (Keep in mind that as consumers become more sophisticated and savvy, there may be instances where these words might be clichés or overused and, thus, may not be as effective.)

- ✔ Avoid metaphors, analogies, puns, double entendres, "insider" references, and other non-straightforward language. Alliteration is sometimes effective.
- ✔ Avoid jargon, dialect, acronyms, and model numbers, especially in headlines.

Here are some successful approaches to television advertisements:[1]

- ✔ Company leader as brand spokesperson. (Examples are Richard Branson of Virgin Atlantic, Dave Thomas of Wendy's, Lee Iacocca of Chrysler, and Ben Cohen and Jerry Greenfield of Ben & Jerry's.)
- ✔ Interesting character as brand spokesperson (Mr. Whipple for Charmin).
- ✔ Customer testimonial.
- ✔ Visualization of the brand benefit and/or the "reason why."
- ✔ Product demonstration (demonstrate product usage and show brand benefit).
- ✔ Torture test (Timex: "Takes a lickin'—Keeps on tickin'").
- ✔ Problem-solution.
- ✔ Before-after. To some large degree, advertising sells the hope of an improved future with the use of a particular brand of product or service. Before-after advertising reinforces this hope.
- ✔ Competitive comparison, although it is usually not wise to identify the competitive brand by name. A special case would be the comparison to premium brand(s), although this can lead to greater category price sensitivity.[2]
- ✔ Slice-of-life vignette (tells a story about the benefits of the brand).
- ✔ Presenter/"talking head" (in which a person attempts to persuade the viewer about the benefits of the brand).

In his book, *Cutting Edge Advertising*, Jim Aitchison indicates that every ad must have an idea. He suggests that ideas may come from any of the following: "product name or logo," "packaging," "how the product is made," "where the product is made," "the product's history," "the product's old advertising," "something that is happening around you," "what happens with the product," "what happens without the product," "what happens with and without the product in the same ad," and "where the ad will run."

The following will likely result in bad brand advertising:

- ✔ Design by committee.
- ✔ Opinionated reviewers and approvers who don't understand marketing.

✓ Writing ads that appeal to you rather than the target consumer.

✓ Using flowery language that sounds good but that means nothing. (This is a common ailment of neophyte copywriters. Substance is good. Using an economy of words is good. Simple, persuasive copy is good. Fluff and filler are bad.)

✓ Squeezing as many features and benefits into the ad as possible (unsophisticated advertising clients often request this).

✓ Revising an emotional or metaphorical ad to make it more literal (another common ailment of unsophisticated advertising clients).

✓ Focusing on reach versus frequency. (See discussion on reach versus frequency later in this chapter.)

✓ Assuming that business-to-business advertising is significantly different from consumer advertising (e.g., "it needs to be factual and informative, not emotional"). Don't forget, business decision makers are people too. And people are ruled as much by their hearts as by their heads. Harding's 1996 study of buyers in ten corporations demonstrated that corporate buyers overwhelmingly rely on personal and emotional reasons over rational ones in their purchase choice.

✓ Jingles. Unless they are very, very good (and most are not very, very good), they will distract from the brand message.

✓ Celebrity endorsements tend not to be believable.

✓ Making claims that your brand can't support.

And, although this may not result in bad advertising, for consistency's sake, the following is not a good idea:

✓ A new marketing manager, feeling the need to "make his or her mark" on the brand, hires a new advertising agency and creates a totally new advertising campaign (whether the old campaign was working or not)

When building the brand, the best advertising vehicles to use tend to be radio, television, and with the widespread emergence of broadband, the Internet, due to the auditory elements. These vehicles create a slower build but are more effective in the long run. Trade magazines and shows and direct marketing (mail, e-mail, etc.) are effective for business-to-business marketing because the target audiences typically are geographically dispersed but highly targeted. Newspapers and the radio are often used to promote brand-building events as they can efficiently and effectively deliver a more immediate message. Radio advertising should be scheduled for immediate effect, and radio ads should be scheduled to run just before or during a sale or other event.

The Art of Persuasion

There are certain techniques that advertisers, politicians, salespeople, speech-writers, preachers, and others have long known to be effective in persuading people. Social psychologists have studied many of these in great detail. Anthony Pratkanis and Elliot Aronson, in their book, *Age of Propaganda: The Everyday Use and Abuse of Persuasion*, outline four basic strategies to effectively influence others: (1) defining/structuring how an issue is discussed (setting the agenda, creating the frame of reference), (2) establishing credibility (authority, likeability, and trustworthiness), (3) vividly focusing the audience's attention on the key point the communicator intends to make, and (4) arousing emotions in a way that can only be satisfactorily addressed by taking the communicator's desired course of action.

In his book, *Influence: The Psychology of Persuasion*, Robert B. Cialdini, Ph.D., focuses on six principles of persuasion: (1) reciprocation (people try to repay favors out of a sense of obligation), (2) commitment and consistency (people behave in ways that support an earlier action or decision), (3) social proof (seeing other people doing something makes it more acceptable and appealing), (4) liking (people are more likely to say yes to people and brands that they know, like and trust), (5) authority (people are inclined to yield to authority), and (6) scarcity (people are more motivated by the thought of losing something than by the thought of gaining something).

Cialdini also indicates that many approaches lead to "liking": physical attractiveness (which studies have shown to be a function of body/facial symmetry), similarity (people feel comfortable with you and can relate to you), compliments, familiarity (through contact and cooperation), and direct or indirect association with other likeable entities.

Both books are quite interesting and well worth reading, if only to help you better understand how third parties attempt to persuade you on a daily basis.

Other considerations in creating highly persuasive communication:

- ✔ Always design the message to play off of the audience's preexisting beliefs and values.
- ✔ To be effective, your point of departure must be from a place of agreement.
- ✔ Try to define the issue in a way that your brand can't help but "win." This is why it is so important to choose the optimal "frame of reference" in brand positioning.
- ✔ Sometimes, just asking the right questions can reorient people's thinking about a topic in your favor.
- ✔ Comparisons/contrasts alter perceptions of the items being compared/contrasted. For example, when I moved to Rochester, my realtor first showed me a number of overpriced houses that required much

work. When we got to the houses that she wanted me to buy, they seemed even more appealing than they might have otherwise if she hadn't first shown me the other houses. This concept is also used in establishing reference pricing. Create reference prices that make your price seem more reasonable or even a "bargain."

✓ Be careful when labeling, categorizing, or describing competing brands or approaches in ways that cast them in a negative light. While it is an effective technique (that is, it usually works), in the long run, it may cast a less favorable light on your brand.

✓ Making people feel as though they are a part of a group (assigning brand labels, brand-as-a-badge) helps sell products and brands.

✓ Fear and guilt sell. (Example: "When you care enough to send the very best.")

✓ Paint vivid pictures of desired or dreaded end states with words or images or both.

✓ Let people touch, try, use, and otherwise interact with your product or brand before they buy it. Once they have done so, they are much more likely to want to purchase it. This works for a wide variety of situations: from automobile test-drives and in-home free-trial use to staying overnight on the campus of a college that you are considering attending (assuming the experience is positive).

✓ Neurolinguistic programming (NLP) is a well-studied technique that increases persuasion. Through NLP, you can establish a strong rapport with the audience by mirroring the mannerisms and expressions of the audience. After you have done this, you can more easily lead them in the direction of your choice.

✓ "Largest," "fastest growing," "most popular," "highest rated," and other similar claims provide strong third-party endorsements for a product or brand. (Alternatively, they may be perceived to be puffery by a jaded audience unless you back them up with credible proof points.)

✓ Repetition increases the effectiveness of communication.

Advertising Research

Although advertising is part art and part science, there is more science to it than one might realize. There are many "rules of thumb" that ad agencies and advertisers have developed over time, based on experience or research or both. I have found the following types of research to be important to creating strong brand advertising:

✓ **Qualitative research** (focus group, mini-group, one-on-one, anthropological, etc.) to better understand the target customer's hopes, needs, desires, aspirations, fears, and concerns.

✔ **Brand preference testing** (before and after exposure to the ad). Asking people what they would tell others about your products and services before and after exposure to the ad is also insightful. (David Ogilvy's book, *Ogilvy on Advertising*, states that people whose brand preference increases after having seen an ad are three times more likely to purchase the brand than those whose preference does not change.)

✔ **The split-run technique.** This technique allows you to test two forms of the ad in the marketplace to determine which one is the most effective.

✔ **Understanding customer response.** Occasionally, you may want to understand how existing loyal customers are responding to your ads, especially if your ad's intent is to attract new customers. For instance, are the ads offering new customers something that you are not offering existing customers? Are the ads promising something that current customers have found not to be true? Are your ads helping existing customers to feel better about your brand? Are they reinforcing the wisdom of having purchased your brand?

When measuring the effectiveness of your ads, increased top-of-mind awareness and purchase intent are the two most important measures. Ad likeability, another useful measure, correlates highly with purchase intent.[3] Other measures tend to be: specific changes in customer attitude or behavior based upon the specific marketing objective for the ad.

Keep in mind, too, that because advertising's effect is gradual and cumulative (much like the growth of a child), it is difficult to measure the effect of an individual ad on sales or market share. For that reason (and for diagnostic reasons) it is important to measure the effect of ads on attitudes. Ad recognition and recall and message takeaways also help diagnose an ad (which is particularly important when an ad is not working).

A word of caution regarding advertising research: It is unwise to delegate this task to your advertising agency. It is best to conduct it yourself or to employ a third party to conduct it. Checks and balances are a good thing. And there is no sense in "hiring the fox to guard the chicken coop."

If you are interested in learning more about advertising research, you should consult the Advertising Research Foundation's Web site (http://www.arfsite.org/) and consider subscribing to their *Journal of Advertising Research*. Another source is the American Marketing Association's *Journal of Marketing Research* (www.marketingpower.com).

▨ Advertising Rules of Thumb

✔ Try to budget between 8 percent and 12 percent of revenues on advertising and other marketing activities. This obviously varies significantly by company and industry. An average company spends approximately 6 percent of sales on advertising alone. Advertising expenditures for computer and office equipment are as low as .09 percent versus 16.8 percent for toys, dolls, and games.[4] Industrial companies tend to spend less on advertising (1 percent to 5 percent typically) than consumer products companies.

✓ You should spend more on advertising and marketing if the following conditions exist:[5]

   ✓ You are building a new brand

   ✓ You are launching a new product or service

   ✓ Your product offering is large and complex

   ✓ You charge premium prices

   ✓ You sell products and services in a "low involvement" category (typically low priced items for which there is little risk of failure)

   ✓ You are selling commodity products (advertising will be the primary differentiator)

✓ Spend approximately $1 on proactive publicity for every $10 you spend on advertising. (PR budgets are 1 percent of a company's revenues, on average.[6]) It will multiply the effectiveness of your advertising. (Advertising in trade magazines also gives you a relationship with the publications, alerts you to editorial opportunities, and *sometimes* impacts your brand's presence in articles.)

✓ Production costs are usually 10 percent of the media buy.

✓ Know what your brand's "share of voice" is—or the amount of advertising (or consumer communication) dollars your company spends compared to competitors' spending for a given product category. It is a good rough measure, despite its flaws that include:

   ✓ Its focus is on traditional advertising spending only

   ✓ Competitors are usually in different portfolios of businesses and it is difficult to break the spending out for the same categories across all competitors

   ✓ Advertising effectiveness for the same level of spending varies widely

✓ It is nearly always more productive to focus on frequency versus reach. Many will say that it is more efficient to focus on reach because there are diminishing returns with each new ad exposure. That is, the advertising response curve is usually concave. This is particularly true if your goal is to create an immediate sale of a ubiquitously purchased consumer product. In that situation, reach almost always delivers "more bang for your buck." However, if your funds are limited and your audience is highly targeted, you would do better to focus on a reach schedule of 3+, seeking out media with significant audience overlap.[7] For brand-building purposes, I usually focus on advertising frequency targeted at those who are most likely to influence the remainder of the market: primary target opinion leaders and "hard core" users.

- ✓ Ads produce better results if they highlight or dramatize the brand's unique compelling benefit.
- ✓ The most effective ads combine a subtle emotional appeal with a practical benefit.[8]
- ✓ The more an ad can get people to identify with one of its characters, the more powerful its effect will be.
- ✓ If the ad is designed so that people overhear something rather than being told about it, they will be less rigorous and defensive in their analysis of the message.[9]
- ✓ If a significant portion of your product's sales result from repeat purchases, it may be more important for your advertising to reinforce the purchase than to persuade people to purchase your product for the first time.
- ✓ Carrying a particular brand voice and visual style (and mnemonic device) from one ad campaign to another increases the effectiveness of the new ad campaign.
- ✓ Scents have the greatest ability to evoke memories. Music has the second greatest ability to do so. Both are mnemonic devices.
- ✓ Repeatedly featuring a product's packaging in advertising makes its more noticeable at point-of-purchase (and therefore, more likely to be purchased).[10]
- ✓ Fifteen-second commercials are seldom effective, because it is difficult for them to break through the clutter and they are far too short to tell a story. They are best used as reminder commercials (reinforcing messages from previous longer commercials).
- ✓ The following factors have been shown to increase advertising effectiveness:[11]
  - ✓ Differentiating brand message
  - ✓ Product demonstration (use, result and benefit)
  - ✓ Total time viewed
- ✓ The following factors have been shown to decrease advertising effectiveness:[12]
  - ✓ Detailed component or ingredient information
  - ✓ Multiple propositions
- ✓ For manufacturers, advertising can affect sales in two ways: One, it persuades the end consumer to purchase your brand, and two, it persuades the intermediary (retailer) to carry your brand, increasing the brand's accessibility.

What Comes to Mind When You Hear the Following?

1. You deserve a break today.
2. Be all that you can be.
3. Just do it.
4. It's the real thing.
5. Where's the beef?
6. It takes a tough man to make a tender chicken.
7. We try harder.
8. Oh, what a feeling . . .
9. You've come a long way, baby.
10. Mmm mmm good . . .
11. It's everywhere you want to be.
12. It takes a licking and keeps on ticking.

Answers:
1. McDonald's
2. U.S. Army
3. Nike
4. Coca-Cola
5. Wendy's
6. Perdue
7. Avis
8. Toyota
9. Virginia Slims
10. Campbell's
11. VISA
12. Timex

✔ Persuasive ads diminish in their effectiveness over time. This argues for front-loading GRPs (gross ratings points) to maximize the effect.[13]

✔ There is a strong correlation between how much a company spends on advertising and its share of market.[14]

✔ Brand familiarity and popularity increase with increased advertising.[15]

✔ Advertising affects purchase decisions by affecting the order in which alternatives are evoked (top-of-mind awareness) and the desirability of a particular alternative (positioning). The former is the most important effect. It puts an alternative in people's consideration sets.[16]

✔ Over 70 percent of the impact of advertising on market share results from increasing brand awareness (versus creating or building brand image).[17]

> ## Did You Know?
>
> ✔ There is a direct correlation between advertising spending, brand awareness, and market share (given that the brand's distribution is equal to that of other brands in the category and consumers like the brand's point of difference). In fact, James Gregory and the Corporate Branding Partnership (and others) have linked advertising spending to increases in sales, earnings, market share, and stock price.
>
> ✔ A brand's perceived quality increases with increases in advertising impressions, regardless of message.

✔ As the number of messages in an advertisement increase, two things happen: Demand increases and recall decreases. The ratio of these effects varies by media and for high- and low-involvement categories.[18]

✔ It is extraordinarily difficult to try to change the consumer's mind about your brand. You would do best not to try. If you must, link the change in perception to something that consumers currently believe about your brand.

✔ Themes and slogans that reinforce the current brand image generate awareness faster than those that support a new positioning.[19]

✔ In general, the more unique the message, the more successful its communication.[20]

✔ Highly recalled messages tend to be the result of "well-funded long-standing advertising campaigns."[21]

✔ The more often a brand repeats a claim, the more likely people are to believe that the claim is true, especially if there is no evidence to the contrary.[22]

✔ For low involvement categories (in which the alternatives are often virtually identical), advertising can tip the balance in the favor of the advertised brand. For these categories, it is particularly important that the ads break through the clutter and focus on one simple message.[23]

✔ For high involvement categories, advertising plays less of a role overall. Typically, its role is to put the brand in the consideration set, not to influence the final buying decision.[24]

✔ People actively seek out information in high involvement categories. Print media, more information, and longer copy work well with this audience.

✔ It is acceptable, and even preferable, to include a "call to action" in brand advertising. (An impact on short-term sales results will help you justify the expenditure.)

Advertising Quick Assessment Tool

✔ Does the headline/opening grab people?

✔ Does the ad clearly and forcefully communicate the intended brand benefit?

✔ Is the ad distinctive and "ownable"?

✔ Does the ad feature a strong reason why (proof points)?

✔ Does the ad communicate something admirable about the company?

✔ Will this ad resonate with the target audience?

✔ Does the ad connect with people on an emotional level?

✔ Does the ad reinforce the brand essence, promise, and personality?

✔ Does the ad reinforce the brand identity standards?

Media Planning

It is best to leave media planning to media planning professionals. The following are some of the things that they will consider when they develop a media plan for you:

✔ Reach (percentage of people—or target audience—exposed)

✔ Frequency (number of times, on average, a person is exposed)

✔ Impressions (the number of times the target market comes in contact with a media vehicle)

✔ CPM (cost per thousand exposures)—measures efficiency

✔ CPM™ (cost per thousand target market exposures)—measures effective efficiency

✔ Most appropriate media vehicles (audience fit with target market, environmental fit with advertising message)

   ✔ For instance, Web sites and trade shows provide a high capacity to process information when customer information needs are high, while short TV spots are best used when information processing needs are lower.[25]

✓ Some media are more appropriate when the purchase decision is based primarily on facts, while others are more appropriate when feelings and emotions are the key influencers.

✓ Evaluating vehicle effectiveness (clutter, distractions)

✓ Adjusting potential exposures to actual exposures (for television, it has been found to vary from 50 percent to 70 percent)

✓ Developing a media strategy and schedule that maximizes advertising response (against the advertising objective)

Did You Know?

✓ **Research has shown that the media environment affects advertising claims (see Aaker and Brown's study of vehicle source effects of 1972). For instance, quality claims are more effective in elite or prestigious magazines because people associate the claim with the media environment.**

✓ **Aspirational, upscale and high status brands have the potential to alienate customers who lack confidence. While these customers might admire these brands, they don't feel comfortable using them. Building warmth, humor and less formality into the brands to make them more approachable helps overcome this problem. (*Source*: Max Blackston, "Observations: Building Brand Equity by Managing the Brand's Relationships," *Journal of Advertising Research* 32, May/June 1992, pp. 79–83.)**

When we conducted laddering research at Hallmark, we discovered that most product and brand benefits ultimately supported the underlying need to preserve self-esteem. (*Laddering* is a research technique that probes consumers to better understand underlying basic human values the brand addresses. It investigates benefits that underlie product attributes, consequences that result from the benefits and values that underlie the consequences. The results are often mapped to outline the brand's benefit structure.) Different benefits may have followed different paths to that end, but, ultimately, the need that they fulfilled was the same fundamental one: to preserve self-esteem. Some emotional end benefits—self-affirmations that contribute to different aspects of a person's self-esteem—that we explored are:

✓ I am frugal

✓ I am a good mother

- ✓ I am a good wife
- ✓ I am a good friend
- ✓ I am competent
- ✓ I am successful
- ✓ I am unique
- ✓ I am lovable
- ✓ I am in control of my life
- ✓ I am making a positive difference in the world

I have observed that the most powerful brands and products are those that help people stay healthy physically, mentally, emotionally, and spiritually. In fact, brands and products that can help people with the following (largely spiritual needs) are extraordinarily powerful:

- ✓ A sense of purpose
- ✓ A sense of self-worth
- ✓ Personal empowerment
- ✓ A sense of well-being
- ✓ Healthy, trusting relationships
- ✓ A sense of community
- ✓ Peace
- ✓ Hope
- ✓ Joy

To that list you could also add communication that taps into any of the higher order needs from Maslow's hierarchy of needs: affiliation, esteem, or self-actualization.

Use the checklist in Exhibit 9-4 to assess the efficacy of your brand management practices in the area covered by this chapter. The more questions to which you can answer "yes," the better you are doing. The checklist also provides a brief summary of the material covered in the chapter.

EXHIBIT 9-4. BRAND MANAGEMENT CHECKLIST.

BRAND ADVERTISING

	YES	NO
Have you conducted extensive customer research prior to developing your ads?	_____	_____

Do you have a carefully crafted brand promise? Have you identified the most powerful (believable) proof points for that promise?　　　—— ——

Does your ad agency fully understand and embrace your brand design and plans?　　　—— ——

Do your other external marketing agencies embrace them as well?　　　—— ——

Is there centralized management of the client/agency relationship?　　　—— ——

Do your ads immediately capture peoples' attention?　　　—— ——

Does your advertising clearly communicate your brand's promise? Do your ads clearly and forcefully communicate the intended brand benefit?　　　—— ——

Are your ads distinctive and "ownable"?　　　—— ——

Do your ads feature a strong "reason why" (proof points)?　　　—— ——

Do your ads reinforce your brand's essence, promise and personality?　　　—— ——

Have you kept you ads simple and devoid of meaningless detail?　　　—— ——

Do your ads connect with people on an emotional level?　　　—— ——

Are your ads focused on building brand awareness and differentiation?　　　—— ——

Are your brand's ads unique?　　　—— ——

Are your ads clever enough in and of themselves to create brand buzz?　　　—— ——

Do you have a way to measure the effectiveness of your ads? Is your advertising effectiveness measured by a party other than your ad agency?　　　—— ——

Have you maximized the frequency of your ads?　　　—— ——

Have you been consistent in advertising your brand over time? Have you communicated a consistent brand message over time?　　　—— ——

Do your brand's successive advertising campaigns share the same brand identity and mnemonic device (to provide a bridge)?　　　—— ——

(continues)

EXHIBIT 9-4. (CONTINUED).

Do you know how your advertising-to-sales ratio compares to that of your direct competitors? Is it higher?	_____	_____
Do you know what your brand's share of voice is? Is it higher than or equal to its share of market?	_____	_____
Do you know how effective your advertising is, not only in growing your brand's share of market but also in maintaining or growing the health of its product category? (This is especially important if you are the share leader in the industry.)	_____	_____
Does everyone in your organization understand that brand advertising is an investment leading to increased revenues and market share over time?	_____	_____
Does your organization only reduce your advertising budget as a last resort in down markets? Do you realize that maintaining or increasing advertising in a down market increases brand equity and share of market?	_____	_____

Notes

1. Richard D. Czerniawski and Michael W. Maloney, *Creating Brand Loyalty: The Management of Power Positioning and Really Great Advertising* (New York: AMACOM, 1999), pp.194–215. Also, David Olgilvy, *Ogilvy on Advertising* (New York: Vintage Books, 1985), pp. 103–113.

2. Ajay Kalra and Ronald C. Goodstein, "The Impact of Advertising Positioning Strategies on Consumer Price Sensitivity," *Journal of Marketing Research* 35 (May 1998), pp. 210–224.

3. Carlos Harding and Patrick Le Brigand, "Brand Tracking Is Good, But Is It Enough?" Transcript of Proceedings, Advertising Research Foundation Advertising and Brand Tracking Workshop, November 12–13, 1996, p. 101.

4. Paul A. Scipione, "Too Much or Too Little? Public Perceptions of Advertising Expenditures," *Journal of Advertising Research* 24, 6 (December 1984/January 1985), pp. 23–26.

5. William M. Luther, *The Marketing Plan: How to Prepare and Implement It* (New York: AMACOM, 2001), pp. 134–135.

6. Source: Christian Harper, Managing Director, BSMG Worldwide.

7. Hugh M. Cannon, "Addressing New Media with Conventional Media Planning," *Journal of Interactive Advertising* 1(2) Spring [Online] http://jiad.org/vol1/no2/cannon/8/11/01.

8. David N. Martin, *Be the Brand: How to Find a Powerful Identity and Use It to Drive Sales* (Richmond, Va.: The Oaklea Press, 2000), p. 22.

9. Max Sutherland and Alice K. Sylvester, *Advertising and the Mind of the Consumer: What Works, What Doesn't and Why.* (St. Leonards NSW: Allen & Unwin, 2000), p. 120.

10. Ibid, p. 23.

11. David W. Stewart and David H. Furse "Analysis of the Impact of Executional Factors in Advertising Performance," *Journal of Advertising Research* 27, 6 (December 1987/January 1988), pp. 45–50.

12. Stewart and Furse "Analysis of the Impact of Executional Factors in Advertising Performance" *Journal of Advertising Research* 40, 6 (November/December 2000), pp. 85–88.

13. Margaret Henderson Blair, "An Empirical Investigation of Advertising Wearin and Wearout," *Journal of Advertising Research* 40, 6 (November/December 2000), pp. 95–100.

14. Paul Georgiou and Stephen Miller, "Ten Years of Advertising Tracking in the Rent-A-Car Business," Transcript of Proceedings, Advertising Research Foundation Advertising and Brand Tracking Workshop, November 12–13, 1996, p. 3.

15. Sutherland and Sylvester, *Advertising and the Mind of the Consumer*, p. 54.

16. Ibid, p. 14.

17. Georgiou and Miller, "Ten Years for Advertising Tracking in the Rent-A-Car Business," p. 7.

18. Kevin J Clancy and Robert S. Shulman, *Marketing Myths That are Killing Business: The Cure for Death Wish Marketing* (New York: McGraw-Hill, 1995), pp. 151–153.

19. Georgiou and Miller, "Ten Years for Advertising Tracking in the Rent-A-Car Business," pp. 10–11.

20. Ibid, p. 10.

21. Ibid, p. 10.

22. Sutherland and Sylvester, *Advertising and the Mind of the Consumer*, p. 9.

23. Ibid, pp. 7, 200.

24. Ibid, p. 12.

25. Cannon, "Addressing New Media with Conventional Media Planning." http://jiad.org/vol1/no2/cannon/.

CHAPTER 10

Nontraditional Marketing Approaches That Work

ADVERTISING IS USUALLY the most important element in any brand marketing plan, but many companies are finding that other approaches are also effective. Some have pursued these approaches out of necessity, being unable to support national advertising campaigns, while others are just more innovative than most in developing their marketing repertoires.

Following are some examples of nontraditional marketing techniques:

- ✔ **Membership Organizations** (Harley Owners Group [HOG], Hallmark Keepsake Ornament Collectors Club, Pond's Institute).

- ✔ **Special Events** (HOG Rallies, Saturn Owners Homecoming, Jeep Jamboree).

- ✔ **Museums and Factory Tours.** Examples include the World of Coca-Cola Museum in Atlanta and Las Vegas; CNN Factory Tour in Atlanta, Kellogg's Cereal City USA in Battle Creek, Michigan; the American Girl Place in Chicago; the Crayola Factory tour and store in Easton, Pennsylvania; the Hallmark Visitors' Center in Kansas City, Missouri; the Ben & Jerry's factory tour in Waterbury Center, Vermont; Hershey's Chocolate World in Hershey, Pennsylvania; The Vermont Teddy Bear factory tour and store in Shelburne, Vermont; Dewar's World of Whisky in Aberfeldy, Scotland; MacWorld Expo (85,000 make this pilgrimage!), and the annual Saturn Owners Homecoming in Spring Hill, Tennessee.

- ✔ **Theme Parks** (Disney World, Cadbury's Theme Park, Legoland, Busch Garden, Knottsberry Farm).

- ✔ **Flagship Stores** (Niketown, Warner Brothers Store, and the new Disney store that opened on Times Square in 2002). A more recent phenomenon: new ultra-deluxe flagship megastores from fashion designers DKNY, Donna Karan, Gucci, Hermes, Hugo Boss, Hickey Freeman, Louis Vuitton, Prada, and Tommy Hilfiger.[1]

✓ *Limited distribution for Product Launches.* Create a sense of scarcity. Focus on those outlets known to be frequented by enthusiasts.

✓ *Sponsorships* (Rolex and high-end sports events, such as horse shows and races, yacht races, polo; Continental Arena, Allstate Arena, Capital One Bowl).

✓ *Sponsorship Ambush.* Converse was an official sponsor of the summer Olympics in Los Angles in 1984. Nike upstaged Converse, however by creating huge tributes to Nike-sponsored athletes on downtown L.A. buildings. In 2000, Reebok was an official sponsor of the Olympics. Nike upstaged Reebok by contracting with many athletes to wear Nike-branded athletic wear. In both instances, Nike received a much greater "share of mind" than the official sponsors in its category. (Of course, using this technique says something about the brand that uses it. The technique is not compatible with many brands' intended personalities.)

✓ *Larger-Than-Life Brand Owners.* At the December 1999 Brand Master Conference, Sixtus Oechsle, the manager of corporate communications and advertising for Shell Oil Company, said that 40 percent of a company's reputation is based on the reputation of its CEO. Examples include Richard Branson (of Virgin), Anita Roddick (of The Body Shop), Dave Thomas (of Wendy's), Bill Gates (of Microsoft), Ted Turner (of TNT), Jeff Bezos (of Amazon.com), Steve Jobs (of Apple), Michael Eisner (of Disney), and Lee Iacocca (of Ford and later Chrysler).

✓ *Frequency Programs* (Hallmark Gold Crown Card, Continental Airlines OnePass).

✓ *Businesses with a Social Conscience* (Ben & Jerry's, The Body Shop, Toms of Maine, Paul Newman products).

✓ *Cleverness That Creates Buzz.* Consider Wendy's "Where's the Beef?," The Dairy Council's "Got Milk?," and Absolute Vodka's advertising of its bottle shape.

✓ *Cause-Related Marketing* (McDonald's sponsoring Ronald McDonald House; American Express alleviating world hunger; and Pfizer donating fluconazole, an AIDS drug, to South Africa).

✓ *Special Events* (especially community-based and grass-roots events, such as Adidas holding streetball festivals and track & field clinics).

✓ *Proactive Publicity.* This can be one of the most powerful and cost effective marketing tools. Publicity is free, approximately six times as many people read articles as read ads,[2] and articles are more credible as they are perceived to be third-party endorsements versus self-promotion. And, the average salary of an in-house copywriter is very low compared to the average ad agency fee for creating an ad. Here are some examples of proactive publicity:

   ✓ When Hallmark launched the industry's first personalized, computer-generated cards, they sent cards to talk show hosts.

✓ Easyjet invested a large portion of its marketing dollars in a lawsuit against KLM, claiming unfair competitive practices, positioning itself as the underdog on the side of the public.[3]

✓ Trivial Pursuit marketers sent games samples to celebrities featured in the game and to radio personalities who had an affinity for trivia.[4]

✓ *Outrageous Marketing Breakthroughs.*

    ✓ I recommended the following to a nonprofit organization whose mission was to encourage woman over age 40 to get mammograms annually. They wanted a message that would "break through." I suggested they feature a bare-chested woman with a double mastectomy on outdoor signs along major highways, using shocking copy such as "Over 40? Don't wait until it is too late. Get a mammogram today." Or, "Which pain is worse? Over 40? Get a mammogram today." (Imagine the buzz this would create.)

    ✓ To create buzz about the movie *Frenzy*, Alfred Hitchcock floated a dummy of himself down the Thames River.[5]

✓ *Brand as a Badge* (Nike swoosh, BMW). For this to work, the brand must stand for something the consumer wants to say about himself or herself.

How to Get the News Media to Cover Your Story

Stories have a better chance of being covered if they:

✓ Tie into what people are talking about today

✓ Add to discussions on current "hot" issues or topics

✓ Reference prominent people, places or things

✓ Have visual impact

✓ Are dramatic

✓ Are unexpected, controversial or outrageous

✓ Directly impact a publication's readership

✓ Have "human interest"

✓ Educate or entertain a publication's readers

✓ Have a "local" angle

✓ Tie into a holiday or special occasion

✓ Represent a significant milestone or a major honor

✓ **Cobranding** (Kmart and Martha Stewart; Hallmark Confections and Fannie Mae Celebrated Collection).

✓ **Ingredient Branding** (Dolby, Nutrasweet, Intel, Kevlar, Lycra, Nylon, Gore-Tex and Culligan).

✓ **Comarketing with Complementary Products.** Identify organizations with which your target customer is likely to interact at the same time that he or she might be ready to buy your product or service. Better yet, find a quality branded product that your customer would use in conjunction with your product. Best, find another product that matches the above criteria and that provides complementary distribution opportunities. For example, bundling a free sample of a washing detergent with the purchase of a new washing machine, or accounting firms referring clients to financial service firms and estate planning attorneys, and vice versa.

✓ **Contests** (Crayola: Kids Coloring Contest and new crayon color contest; Mar's "Choose the next M&M color" contest).

✓ **Brand Magazines and Newsletters** (Crayola Kids).

✓ **Network Marketing** (Primerica, MCI's Friends & Family, Amway, Mary Kay, Avon, Tupperware).

✓ **Colossal Ads** (500-foot-high working Swatch watch draped from tallest skyscraper in Frankfurt, Germany).[6]

✓ **Word of Mouth, Folklore, Testimonials, and Referrals** (Saturn's television commercial spreading the news about one of its dealers flying to Alaska on a rented plane to replace a part on a recalled car in the customer's own garage).

  ✓ Focus on hard core users, opinion leaders, and what Emanuel Rosen, in his book *The Anatomy of Buzz,* calls "network hubs": They read, they travel, they attend trade shows and conferences, they serve on committees, they participate in best practices benchmarking studies, they speak, they write books, articles, newsletters, and letters to editors, they teach courses, they consult, they advise others.

  ✓ Expose people to things that make great "cocktail party talk."

  ✓ Give them sneak previews, "inside information," "behind the scene stories," and factory tours. Let them meet the product designers.

  ✓ Give new products to the trendsetters (seeding).

  ✓ Ask your employees to spread the word to everyone they know. Give them free products as a perk. This will attract people who like the product category and brand. It will also familiarize them with your brand's products so that they can make better sales people.

✓ **Shopping Channel.** Many companies have discovered that the channel QVC is a great way to promote new products.

✓ **The Neiman Marcus Catalog.** For example, in the catalog BMW offered a limited edition of its Z3 Roadster with a "Specially Equipped 007" dash

The Power of Word of Mouth

In his book, *Eating the Big Fish: How Challenger Brands Can Compete Against Brand Leaders* (New York: John Wiley, 1999), Adam Morgan indicates that people enthusiastically share information for one of four reasons: (1) bragging rights, (2) product enthusiasm, (3) aspirational identification, or (4) news value.

Stories and anecdotes make a point real to people and imbed it in their memories. Brand stories and anecdotes can become legends. As they are told and retold, they can raise the brand to a mythological level. Stories are often told about consumer experiences that far exceed expectations. This could be the result of extraordinary customer service or some other incredible experience with the brand. Going out of your way as an organization to create these experiences will pay huge dividends—word-of-mouth marketing can not be underestimated. Ideally, you create experiences that reinforce your brand's point of difference.

For instance, a Hallmark card shop owner cared so much for one of her customers that when the customer could not find what she was looking for in the store, the owner drove several miles away to a few other Hallmark stores until she found what the customer was looking for. She hand delivered it to the customer's house that evening, at no charge, reinforcing Hallmark's essence of "caring shared." Now *that* is the stuff of legends. Delivering this type of service, even occasionally, generates significant word-of-mouth brand advocacy.

plaque. After they sold all 100 cars, there were still approximately 6000 people on the waiting list![7]

✓ **Product Placement.** Featuring your brands and products in movies.

✓ **Covert or "Stealth" Marketing.** For example, companies pay (a) doorman to stack packages featuring their logos in building lobbies, (b) people to sing the praises of a specific brand of alcoholic beverage in bars, (c) actors to pose as tourists asking passers-by to take their picture with a new camera/cell-phone product, and (d) models to ride their scooters around town.[8] (When companies are caught doing this, it may have a negative effect on brand equity and cause consumers to become even more jaded, especially if the tactic is more deceptive than it is creative.)

✓ *Airline Radio and Television Shows.*

✓ *Unusual Advertising Media.* Companies have used everything from sidewalks (written in chalk), walls above men's room urinals, and posters on bulletin boards, to the sides of trucks and buses, athlete's clothes, and crop art (images created by plowing fields in certain patterns). In France, PlayStation inserted airsick bags in magazines to communicate the realism of its latest Formula One racing game.[9] A German company is now printing advertising messages on toilet paper. Evian funded the repair of a run-down pool in London in return for featuring its brand's identity in the pool's tile design, which could be seen by people flying into and out of nearby Heathrow airport. Proctor & Gamble placed upscale Porta Potties (air conditioned, hardwood floors, aromatherapy candles) at state fairs in the summer of 2001 to reinforce the luxury of its Charmin toilet paper.[10]

✓ *The Internet* (particularly Amazon.com), which is covered in greater detail later in Chapter 11.

Traditional Marketing Techniques "on Steroids"

Here are some traditional techniques taken to an extraordinary level of success:

✓ *Packaging* (Gateway's cowhide pattern on its boxes, Absolute vodka's consistently advertised distinctive bottle shape, Ty Nant's use of cobalt blue bottles to break into the mineral water category, Voss' use of aesthetically pleasing cylindrical glass bottles to do the same, *New York Times* use of blue bags for home-delivered papers).

✓ *The Product Itself* (Apple's iMac, Chrysler's PT Cruiser). Never underestimate the power of design to differentiate!

✓ *Vehicles, Uniforms, and Signing.* Coca-Cola, FedEx, and UPS use trucks as billboards. UPS uses their delivery peoples' distinctive brown uniforms. Lucent displays large branded signs in front of each of its offices.

✓ *Point-of-Sale Signing and Merchandising.* Mass displays of Coca Cola cases at the ends of aisles (in grocery and other mass channel stores) are designed to bring the brand to the top-of-mind. Signs, posters, and coasters featuring a particular brand of alcohol are intended to accomplish the same in bars and taverns.

✓ *Free Product Trial.* AOL did this very successfully by distributing hundreds of millions of free software disks featuring one month's service free. Element K is doing this with e-learning IDs featuring run-of-site (over 800 courses) for free for three months. This works especially well with low variable cost items for which there is some perceived risk of purchase.

Small Business Marketing Techniques

- ✓ Conduct demonstrations, classes and workshops. A restaurant's chef can teach a cooking class for a continuing education program or for a department or cooking supply store.
- ✓ Speak at conferences and for professional associations. Join your local chapter of the National Speakers Association and register with speakers bureaus. Publicize your speaking engagements.
- ✓ Hold contests.
- ✓ Write articles for newspapers, periodicals and professional journals.
- ✓ List yourself as an expert (*Radio-TV Interview Report*, *Yearbook of Experts, Authorities and Spokespersons*, Broadcast Interview Source, Inc., ProfNet, etc.).
- ✓ Be a guest on or host a local radio or television show on your area of expertise.
- ✓ Network online and offline (in professional associations, conferences, trade shows, benchmarking groups, chambers of commerce, usenet groups, chats, online forums, etc.).
- ✓ Publish newsletters (online or offline).
- ✓ Write a book.
- ✓ Hire a publicist.
- ✓ Maintain relationships with the press.
- ✓ Get involved in civic organizations.
- ✓ Donate money to local charities, especially complementary causes.
- ✓ Volunteer to judge competitions.
- ✓ Wear branded shirts and other clothing.
- ✓ Cross-promote with complementary or nearby businesses.
- ✓ Give away insignia merchandise (featuring your business's name, logo, tag line, and contact information).
- ✓ Write letters to new residents introducing them to your business (perhaps offering them a free or reduced-price trial).
- ✓ Script your customer service and tech support people to cross-sell and up-sell products and services as appropriate. (Be careful not to over-incent people to do this. They should only do this in the most helpful way as appropriate.)

Business-to-Business Techniques

- ✓ Create and actively interact with customer advisory boards. Invite the most influential opinion leaders to participate.

✓ Create and actively interact with strategic partner boards.

✓ Create external "expert councils" for all major new products. Invite the most knowledgeable and influential outside experts to participate, involve them in the product design itself.

✓ Hold conferences and seminars, inviting current satisfied customers, prospective customers, and internal and external industry experts. Present case studies, discuss the latest innovations, let the experts speak, and allow time for networking.

✓ For software companies, "beta test" your software with major influential customers and those that would provide compelling case studies and testimonials.

✓ Hold product launch parties for important customers.

✓ Record testimonials from your most supportive customers and subtly interweave these with the background music that plays when people calling your company are put on hold. (This could become annoying to some people who are waiting to speak to a customer service or technical support rep regarding a major problem. Hopefully, they aren't on hold for long!)

✓ Develop and disseminate a portfolio of customer case studies to reinforce specific brand benefits to specific target customers.

✓ Publish and widely disseminate white papers to position your organization and brand as experts in your field.

✓ Develop a speakers' bureau and actively orchestrate speaking engagements at key industry events—conferences, trade shows, industry association meetings, etc. At our company, we started a local chapter of Toastmasters and assigned the speakers bureau responsibility to a specific individual.

✓ Actively seek industry association committee assignments and board positions.

✓ Constantly keep the following people and organizations aware of your brand and its latest accomplishments:

   ✓ Industry analysts

   ✓ Financial analysts

   ✓ Resellers and other strategic partners

   ✓ Your organization's professional partners (lawyers, accountants, management consultants, advertising agencies, etc.)

   ✓ Trade magazine editors and writers

   ✓ People who write about your industry for the general business press

   ✓ People who write books about your industry

   ✓ Other opinion leaders

Distribution of Business Marketing Budget

- ✔ Trade Magazines 23%
- ✔ Trade Shows 18%
- ✔ Direct Mail 10%
- ✔ Promotion/Market Support 9%
- ✔ Dealer/Distributor Materials 5%
- ✔ General Magazine Advertising 6%
- ✔ Internet/Electronic Media 9%
- ✔ Directories 5%
- ✔ Telemarketing/Telecommunications 3%
- ✔ Publicity/Public Relations 7%
- ✔ Market Research 4%
- ✔ Other 1%

Total 100%

(Source: Cahners Advertising Research Reports.)

Direct Marketing

Direct marketing is a very specific subdiscipline with its own rules within marketing. It offers several advantages to the marketer:[11]

- ✔ It allows you to target specific people.
- ✔ It enables you to tailor your message for each person.
- ✔ It is action oriented.
- ✔ It is confidential.
- ✔ It is economical.
- ✔ You can track and measure the response rate and the return on investment.
- ✔ You will be able to significantly and continuously improve its effectiveness over time.

The three most important elements of direct mail response are the list, the offer, and the creative. Of the three, the list is by far the most important.

The List

- ✔ You will have the most success with your current customer list (typically, it provides two to ten times the response rate of a rented list). Beyond that, always seek out frequently updated lists.
- ✔ Use a list broker that you trust.
- ✔ Profile your current (or prospective) customer base (behavioral and demographic characteristics) and compare that to the profiles of the various lists that you are considering.
- ✔ Test each of the lists that you are considering (ask for free names or rent the minimum number of names possible).

The Offer

- ✔ Provide an incentive for the recipient to act immediately ("free" . . . , free product trial, percent off, premiums, sweepstakes; for B2B: kits, white papers, research reports).
- ✔ Maximize the perceived value of the offer.
- ✔ Provide an easy way to respond (1-800 number, postage-paid response card, coupons, or Web site address).
- ✔ Code the response devices to be able to track the effectiveness of the offer.
- ✔ Make the offer time sensitive in some way.
- ✔ Specify a response deadline (not too short, not too long).
- ✔ Provide a guarantee if appropriate.
- ✔ Avoid offers that are vague, generic, offered by most of your competitors, or that seem too good to be true.
- ✔ Test responses to various offers.

The Creative

- ✔ Use the Johnson Box area (top right corner of the letter) to plainly state your offer.
- ✔ Start the letter with a powerful, attention-grabbing, benefit-driven statement.
- ✔ Talk to the recipient in his or her own language—be conversational.
- ✔ Use the word "you" as much as possible.
- ✔ Always use the "active voice."
- ✔ Write long copy, but use short words, sentences, and paragraphs.
- ✔ Maximize subheads to call out important offers, benefits, and points of differentiation

✓ Sell benefits, not features.

✓ Appeal to the "head" and to the "heart."

✓ Personalize the letter to the extent possible.

✓ Make your copy sympathetic to the recipient's problems.

✓ Use words to "paint a picture"—help the recipient to envision a desired or undesired end state.

✓ Know that the "fear of loss" is more powerful that the "hope of gain."

✓ Include testimonials and case studies.

✓ Include a strong, clear call to action.

✓ Use the problem-solution construct that almost always works—think about the five P's: picture, problem, promise, proof, and push.

✓ Always use a P.S. (restate your proposition here). After the Johnson Box, this is the most read portion of the letter.

✓ Test various versions of the copy.

Other Considerations

✓ Personalize the envelope.

✓ Design the envelope/packaging to maximize its possibility of being opened.

✓ Use dimensional packaging—it has a much higher chance of being opened.

✓ Test envelope solutions.

✓ Time the mailing for maximum response.

✓ Carefully time follow-up contacts to substantially increase response rates.

✓ Always take the opportunity to thank your current customers—again and again.

Customer Relationship Management

Customer relationship management (CRM) is huge. Most companies use it to increase customer loyalty and retention, and it will continue to grow with the emerging accessibility of the Internet and e-mail worldwide.

Although CRM potentially results in significant benefits to an organization, a recent Conference Board report on the subject[12] indicates that only a quarter of all firms report that their CRM projects had been "very successful."

Ideation and Creative Problem Solving

The mostly highly admired brands are usually unique, original, fresh, and leading edge. In fact, many have invented or reinvented entire categories. To be that kind of a brand, an organization must be highly innovative. Element K CEO Bruce Barnes likes to talk about the "Virtuous Circle of Investment/ Innovation." It is very simple:

✓ Investing in customer-relevant product/service innovation leads to increased revenues

✓ Increased revenues enable continued product/service innovation

Innovative brands with innovative products, services, and marketing approaches typically make extensive use of creative problem solving and ideation (idea generation) techniques.

Creative problem solving usually requires two distinct phases: divergent thinking (ideation) and convergent thinking (idea analysis and evaluation). The purpose of ideation is to generate as many ideas as possible in as condensed a timeframe as possible.

Did You Know?

✓ In general, it is much more important for a brand to focus on gaining the zealous support of its primary customers than it is to try to gain the business of a much broader audience. If the primary customers are "brand fans," others will follow.

✓ Risk taking, innovation, breaking industry rules, products that overperform and services that exceed customer expectations strongly contribute to brand vitality. "Adequate," "suffice," and "good enough" are not a part of a vital brand's vocabulary.

✓ The products and services that achieve the most "buzz" and that benefit the most from "buzz" are innovative, leading-edge, and of superior quality—often creating a new standard for customer experience.

Brainstorming

The most popular ideation technique is brainstorming. It requires the following components to be successful:

- A well-defined problem.
- Two or more people together in a room. Ideally, you have a mix of people from different disciplines, including someone who knows nothing about the subject (to offer perspective) and a subject matter expert. Also, participants should be screened for divergent thinkers with diverse experiences, who are willing to actively share their thoughts and ideas.
- Relaxation training, autogenics, psychodrama, sociodrama, and other techniques can help prepare people to ideate effectively. The intent is to break down mental blocks and preconceived notions and to get people to relax and to feel confident and safe from criticism. A warm-up exercise also helps to get people to think about things in new ways, to encourage "boundary-less" thinking.
- Providing participants with crayons and paper, Play-Dough, clay, Tinker Toys, and other activities often helps people open up in their thinking.
- The exchange of ideas to generate more ideas.
- Session ground rules: no criticism or judgments allowed.
- The facilitator ensures that each person's ideas are drawn out.
- No ideas are filtered out by the session facilitator—all are captured as presented, typically on a flip chart.
- The facilitator keeps the session moving so that people don't have time to make premature judgments.
- The facilitator interjects questions to stimulate additional ideas when ideas are waning. Facilitators should have prepared a set of conceptual block-busting questions before the session. What if it were bigger? What if it were the opposite of what it is? What if we morphed it? What if it were only one-dimensional? What could we do to solve the problem if we had no money to do so? What could we do if we had unlimited financial resources? What if it were round? What if it were red? What is the high-tech solution? What is the low-tech solution? How would environmentalists solve the problem? How would farmers solve the problem? How would Albert Einstein solve the problem? How would a five-year-old girl solve the problem? How would the Chinese government solve the problem? How would your cat solve the problem? How does nature address this? What if you were the problem? What would you do? What if you were the solution? How would you feel? Etc.

Other ideation techniques include the following:[13]

- Visualization, guided imagery, fantasizing, and envisioning the future
- Attribute listing, discovering connections between those attributes
- Mind mapping, diagramming relationships
- Questioning the problem and its assumptions, broadening the problem, looking at the problem at a meta-level

✓ Applying ideas from one context to another (metaphorical thinking)

✓ Creating connections for two previously unconnected items (bisociation)

✓ Free associations (What is the first word that comes to your mind when I say . . . ?)

✓ Forced relationships (or forcing an association between the problem or solution and random words)

✓ Conceiving of two unrelated entities occupying the same space (homospatial thinking)

✓ Stopping to further consider associations that initially make us laugh (laughter results from the unexpected connection between two things)

✓ Sketching and doodling

✓ Stream-of-consciousness writing

✓ Experiencing the problem emotionally, intellectually, spiritually, and physically

✓ Incubation (walking away from the problem after intensely thinking about it)

✓ Living a life of diverse experience

Who drives the pace of change in your industry, you or one of your competitors? Go to www.brandforward.com for a list of online ideation and creative thinking resources.

Use the checklist in Exhibit 10-1 to assess the efficacy of your brand management practices in the area covered by this chapter. The more questions to which you can answer "yes," the better you are doing. The checklist also provides a brief summary of the material covered in the chapter.

EXHIBIT 10-1. BRAND MANAGEMENT CHECKLIST.

NONTRADITIONAL MARKETING APPROACHES THAT WORK

	YES	NO
Is marketing perceived to be an investment (versus a cost) at your company?	___	___
Are there clear objectives and performance targets for each marketing program you initiate?	___	___
Do you know the payback or return on investment (or better yet, the marginal return on investment) for each of the following marketing strategies: increasing household penetration, increasing capture, increasing		

(continues)

EXHIBIT 10-1. (CONTINUED).

conversion, incenting trial, encouraging repeat purchase, increasing share of requirements (or share of wallet or share of dollar—the concept is to identify the percentage of every unit or dollar sale within a category that goes to the brand in question), increasing price premium, reinforcing purchase (post purchase), increasing brand loyalty, and increasing brand advocacy? *(Note: Don Schultz, Angora, Inc., and Targetbase can help you measure marketing ROI.)* _____ _____

Have you made a conscious decision regarding how much you should spend on marketing activities in total? _____ _____

Is your marketing focused on consumer "pull" (versus trade "push")? _____ _____

Is there agreement that the majority of your marketing resources will be spent on brand building versus product sales promotion? _____ _____

Are you spending more on brand building than you are on trade deals? Do you know the answer to this question (without having to research it first)? If you are not happy with the spending balance, do you have specific, realistic plans to change the balance? _____ _____

Do you know your consumers as well as you know your products? _____ _____

Do you know what consumers value most about your brand? _____ _____

Do you know who your best customers are? Do you know why they are your best customers? Have you designed programs to retain those customers? Are you actively trying to increase share in your high profit, heavy user market segment? _____ _____

Do you have a database of your best customers? _____ _____

Have you established a robust customer relationship management (CRM) system? _____ _____

Do you use an innovative mix of marketing elements tailored to achieve your brand's key objectives, instead of relying primarily on advertising?
Do you stick with marketing programs that are working well (versus changing them whenever someone new arrives on the job)? _____ _____

Are your consumer and trade marketing efforts integrated across all marketing elements? _____ _____

Are your marketing programs and consumer communications seldom if ever diluted, compromised, or killed by multiple layers of review and approval? _____ _____

Do your marketing plans and programs include the following elements: products, packaging, pricing, sales, advertising, promotion, publicity, distribution, signing, merchandising, point-of-purchase materials, product placement, marketing events, and sponsorships? _____ _____

Have you carefully designed your promotions to reinforce the brand promise (versus primarily delivering price incentives)? _____ _____

Does your packaging reinforce the brand promise and other key brand messages? _____ _____

Are customer service departments and customer contacts always included in your marketing programs? _____ _____

Do you know all of the points of contact your brand has with consumers? Are you measuring the quality of contact at all of those points? Are you actively managing what you are communicating at each of those points of contact? _____ _____

Do you have brand training for all people who come in contact with your consumers on behalf of your brands (whether they are your employees or not)? _____ _____

Do you create brand and product scripts for your salespeople, customer and technical service representatives, and other front-line employees? _____ _____

Do you leverage point-of-purchase as a major consumer communication platform? _____ _____

Is your brand available wherever and whenever your consumers want it (versus being channel-constrained due to internal or trade issues)? _____ _____

Do you use your Web site to transact business and to communicate key brand values and to create an emotional connection with the consumer? _____ _____

(continues)

EXHIBIT 10-1. (CONTINUED).
_____

Does your Web site provide an engaging interactive experience for your consumers? ____ ____

Do you use database marketing? ____ ____

Do you use proactive publicity to build the brand? ____ ____

Do you use event marketing? ____ ____

Do you use cause-related marketing? ____ ____

Do you use word-of-mouth marketing? ____ ____

Have you identified the industry opinion leaders and "network hubs"? Do you communicate with them on a regular basis? ____ ____

Have you created flagship stores to showcase your brand and its promise? ____ ____

Have you created factory tours, a visitor's center, or a company museum to communicate your brands' promises to the public? ____ ____

Have you considered creating consumer membership organizations to increase emotional connection and loyalty to the brand? ____ ____

Have you created other ways (online and offline) for your customers and potential customers to interact with one another on a regular basis? ____ ____

Have you considered establishing your brand as a consumer badge? Do you offer insignia merchandise to increase the brand's badge value? ____ ____

Are there media to which your brand has privileged access, such as magazines, television programming, radio stations, television networks, billboards, theme parks, retail stores, Web sites, etc.? Are you fully exploiting them? ____ ____

Do you leverage secondary brand associations to build brand equity (cobranding, endorsements, sponsorships, licensing, etc.)? ____ ____

Do your marketing programs build brand awareness? ____ ____

Do your marketing programs communicate brand essence, promise, personality, and other intended associations? ____ ____

Do they create an emotional connection with the
consumer?   _____ _____

Do they communicate good value?   _____ _____

Are they memorable and engaging?   _____ _____

Do they clearly communicate differentiating benefits
that are relevant and compelling to the consumer?   _____ _____

If you are marketing your brand globally, have you
considered how the brand's geographic origin affects
consumers' perception of the brand? (Often, countries
and regions have their own "brand images" which
may influence the perceptions of brands from those
places.)   _____ _____

Do you know which of your marketing programs
provide the highest return on investment? Do you
know which ones provide the lowest? Based on this,
are you constantly adjusting your program mix?
*(Note: Media Market Assessment at www.mma.com
can help you measure your program efficiency.)*   _____ _____

Does your organization frequently use creative
problem solving and ideation techniques to promote
innovation? Does the organization encourage "out-of-
the-box" thinking?   _____ _____

Do you measure business innovation? Do you have a
constant stream of consumer relevant innovations?   _____ _____

Do at least 20 percent of your annual revenues result
from new products and services?   _____ _____

Notes

1. "Designer Stores, in Extra Large" *Wall Street Journal*, June 6, 2001, pp. B1, B12.
2. David Olgilvy, *Ogilvy on Advertising* (New York: Vintage Books, 1985), p. 90.
3. Adam Morgan, *Eating the Big Fish: How Challenger Brands Compete Against Brand Leaders* (New York: John Wiley, 1999), pp. 168–169.
4. Emanuel Rosen, *The Anatomy of Buzz: How to Create Word of Mouth Marketing* (New York: Doubleday, 2000), p. 119.
5. Ibid, pp. 182–183.
6. Morgan, *Eating the Big Fish*, pp. 117–118.
7. Rosen, *The Anatomy of Buzz*, p. 177.
8. Daniel Eisenberg, "It's an Ad, Ad, Ad World" TIME.com 60, 10. September 2, 2002.

9. Morgan, *Eating the Big Fish*, p. 180.

10. Eisenberg, "It's an Ad, Ad, Ad World."

11. Ray Jutkins, "13 Platinum Advantages Direct Response Marketing Offers the 21st-Century Marketer," November 17, 2001. http://www.directmailquotes .com/expertadvice/.

12. "Customer Relationship Management: New Ways of Keeping the Customer Satisfied," August 2001, R-1299-01 RR. www.conference-board.org.

13. Diane Montgomery, Kay Sather Bull, and Sara Leigh Kimball, "Stimulating Creativity in Computer Mediated Learning: Individual and Collaborative Approaches," August 4, 2001. http://home.okstste,edu/homepages.nsf/toc/ EPSY5720cm119.

C H A P T E R **11**

Brand Building on the Internet

REGARDLESS OF WHAT you may have read or heard about the "dot-bomb," the Internet is alive and well. In fact, the Internet continues to expand the possibilities—and the requirements—for brand building.[1] The organization that ignores the Internet as a brand-building medium does so at its own risk.

Web sites are effective at building brand relevance, differentiation, and loyalty, but they should not be relied on to build awareness and recognition. Why? Because consumers must seek out your site—your site is not broadcast (like television). Kristin Zhivago likened consumer behavior on the World Wide Web to providing a pond of water and inviting consumers to "come for a swim." She continues, "Prospects can visit your pond anytime they like, stay as long as they want, and dive in as deeply as they want."[2]

Brand Building in Cyberspace vs. Brand Building in the Brick & Mortar World

The following are other ways in which brand building in cyberspace is different than brand building in the brick & mortar world:

- ✔ Web sites offer two-way (versus one-way) communication with your customers. In addition, some Web sites offer "many to many" conversations which can make or break your brand.

- ✔ Ability to customize content depending on the individual user, target audience, time of day, point of entry, or virtually any other criteria.

- ✔ A wide variety of brand-building elements come together to create a total brand experience in one medium.

This chapter is a revised and updated version of "Branding.com: Building and Leveraging Brands Online," *The Advertiser*, October/November 2000, pp. 70–76 (copyright Association of National Advertisers), and of "Branding.com: Brand Building on the Internet," *Admap*, Issue 421, October 2001, pp. 21–25 (copyright World Advertising Research Center).

- ✔ The consumer is in control of the brand experience—he selects what to see and for how long.
- ✔ It is easier to gather far more (and far more specific) information on the consumer than in the brick & mortar world.
- ✔ Results are easier to measure.

The Internet Levels the Playing Field for Small Companies

In some ways, the Internet favors smaller companies:

- ✔ In the brick & mortar world, product accessibility is primarily driven by number of retail locations—and large companies have many such locations. In cyberspace, only one (Web)site is needed—which doesn't necessarily require the resources of a large company.
- ✔ Smaller companies are usually too small to have functional silos and therefore can deliver a more coherent brand message, environment, and experience on the Internet.
- ✔ Small companies provide the personalized attention that fulfills the promise of the Internet. (In fact, Internet culture tends to favor the underdog, allowing smaller companies to prosper in spite of tough competition from national brands.)
- ✔ Smaller companies are often much quicker and more agile to adopt new ideas and technology (a very important attribute on the Internet).
- ✔ Web sites of smaller companies are usually more critical and important components of their businesses in comparison to larger companies. Simply put, the Web site receives more attention at a smaller organization . . . and thus, so do Web customers.

Conversely, some aspects of the Internet definitely favor larger enterprises, including the rising cost of keeping site content fresh, maintaining a high site search engine ranking, and placing online ads.

The Internet Increases Consumer Power

The Internet also increases consumer power in the following ways:

- ✔ Consumers choose where they go and what they see.
- ✔ The Internet makes price comparisons easy—especially with the emergence of intelligent agents such as mysimon.com and froogle.com (intelligent agents search the Web for specified items and notify the user where the items can be found and at which prices).

✓ Every day on the Internet, thousands of users communicate for the sole purpose of buying your product more cheaply. In fact, Web sites have emerged that provide nothing more than information on where to get the best deal on products.

✓ The Internet makes it much easier for people to make their complaints public.

✓ In the case of digital media (e.g., music, movies, and software) the amount of piracy and peer-to-peer sharing on the Internet provides a serious challenge to increasing legitimate sales.

✓ New tools are emerging constantly: buying clubs, reverse auctions, and more. With the advent of cell-phone-based Internet, it's not uncommon to find customers in a brick & mortar world store using their cell phones to compare prices with online retailers.

Internet User Segments

Ketchum Interactive, the global public relations agency, has identified four different Internet user segments (see Exhibit 11-1) based on their approach to finding information on the Web. These segments should clearly impact an organization's site design and Internet strategy.[3]

Web Site Objectives

Organizational Web site objectives vary, but typically the objectives include one or more of the following:

✓ Make it easier for consumers to do business with us (accessibility).

✓ Reduce our costs of doing business (customer value and business profitability).

✓ Enhance our relationship with our customer (creating emotional connection).

✓ Build our brand.

Regardless of the objective, effective Web sites should accomplish the following:

✓ Be findable by users conducting a search.

✓ Drive desired actions from users.

✓ Provide a true brand experience.

✓ Create an engaging, interactive, informative, and helpful consumer experience.

EXHIBIT 11-1. INTERNET USER SEGMENTS.

	Adventurer	Expert	Investigator	Wanderer
Is the user brand knowledge-able?	Yes	Yes	No	No
Does the users know what he is looking for?	No	Yes	Yes	No
Segment summary	"There was nothing there to draw me in because I wasn't looking for a product, I was just look-ing for stimula-tion."	"If I'm looking for information, I just want to get it without unnecessary detours. What's frus-trating about the Web is that you go places you weren't ex-pecting and it wastes your time."	"Don't insult me when I come to your site by adver-tising to me. You've already got me in the store, so give me some help. Ask smart questions that could help di-agnose what I really need."	"The Web is a place to go to make sure I'm not missing out on some-thing."
Ways to appeal to segment	Entertainment, special promo-tional offers and participa-tion in virtual community activities	Fast downloads, easy naviga-tion, intuitive site maps and search ca-pabilities	Consultative navigation, search tools that link needs with the appro-priate informa-tion, products or services	Create a "buzz" about the site, pro-vide opportu-nities for community members to in-teract over time

- ✓ Create an opportunity to expand the customer relationship—provide a reason to bookmark the site, to return to the site, to sign up for a news-letter . . . anything that strengthens the relationship between the cus-tomer and the Web site.
- ✓ Unobtrusively capture consumer information to build a database.
- ✓ Integrate and blend content and commerce in a way that pleases the Internet user segments mentioned above.
- ✓ Provide detailed information about your products and services—more than typically available offline.
- ✓ Generate incremental sales (online and in the brick & mortar world).

Building a Strong Web Site

Successful Web development begins with the brand experience and then backs into visual design. Questions such as "what experiences can we provide users that will bring them closer to our brand?" and "what brand promises have we made in the offline world that we can fulfill online?" must be raised early on. The site should be thought of as a two-way communication mechanism—an opportunity to exchange—rather than as a static receptacle for information.

How to build that brand experience online? With a clear understanding of your brand, here are some steps to consider before beginning the design and development of a site:

- ✓ Which audiences will we be reaching online, and who won't we reach (customers, potential customers, industry analysts, financial analysts, reporters and editors, resellers, prospective employees)?
- ✓ What aspects of our brand would be most effective in cyberspace?
- ✓ How will we measure the performance of the site? What behavior would we want to see from users to indicate that we are gaining brand equity?
- ✓ What online experiences can we provide that would reinforce those most important parts of the brand AND would drive the performance measures we've envisioned?

For example, Wegmans Food Markets builds its brand online by providing unique, brand-specific tools and information. Wegmans differentiation is around "making great meals easy" and has built online services that deliver "easiness" in a number of ways. For example, an extensive recipe database—searchable by course, keyword, or dietary specifics—allows the user to easily find many ideas for dinner. Recipes are ranked by users (who can also submit comments). Wegmans also provides one-click selection of vegetarian, lactose free, gluten free, or other types of special diet recipes.

Wegmans allows users to say at which store they're planning to shop, and sorts their shopping list according to the aisles of the selected store. The site is also supplemented with extensive information on cooking techniques. That's delivering the brand promise online. Better still, the Web site drives traffic to Wegmans brick & mortar stores—it complements the brand rather than competing with it.

- ✓ A well-designed Web site should provide brand experiences that attract, inform, and compel transactions (inquiries, subscriptions, and orders) among all of the user audiences.
- ✓ It's important that you think about how all communication, experiences, and information on the site eventually maps to a database that eventually will provide many answers to online branding questions. And you need to do all this before designing a single screen or writing a single line of code.

The following are also important considerations when building a strong Web site:

✔ The site must download quickly. The average person waits only ten seconds or less for a page to download. Keep in mind that your target customer may not be using a high-speed connection.

✔ The home page must capture users' attention and invite them deeper into the site. "Splash" or "Intro" pages are a big mistake.

✔ Use your homepage to communicate your purpose, personality, and point of difference.

✔ Provide navigation that allows users to make quick and easy choices about where to click next.

✔ Provide powerful content that is detailed, well organized, and up-to-date.

✔ Keep users active while navigating (they want to click and scroll, not read). Once they have found what they're looking for, provide lots of detail; remember, they are trying to accomplish something!

✔ In general, allow users to reach any page in three clicks or less. Note: if you give users seven or so options on each page, then three clicks (7 options × 7 options × 7 options) should allow them to access 343 pages!

✔ Make copy more accessible by breaking it up into chunks, with sub-headings, bullets, and boxes providing a visual hierarchy to the content.

✔ Keep detailed content concise and factual—once users have found what they're looking for it's time for them to read the page . . . this is not a good place to embed "fluff."

✔ Provide a simple site search engine and a clear, easily accessible site map.

✔ Architect intuitive site navigation—avoid jargon and legalese.

✔ Ideally, every page should have home, search/site map, and contact us buttons.

✔ Provide FAQs (frequently asked questions) throughout the content of the site—don't separate them into a special section.

✔ Provide activities to unobtrusively build a database. These activities should provide a real benefit to the user, such as games, contests, online services, surveys, e-mail, or newsletters.

✔ If your site is one that users would visit every day—or many times a day—then consider personalizing the site to the user's preferences: wallpaper, first page viewed, customized content. (Note: it's a rare site that a user visits every day.)

✓ Make sure that new content and features are easy to identify and access.

✓ Create a feedback loop through e-mail (be sure to staff the e-mail for timely response). An immediate autoresponder message followed up by a personalized response is ideal.

✓ Offer customer services such as a store locator service, checklists, and consultative or diagnostic tools. These are ideal places to gather information about your customers for your database.

✓ If you have lots of detailed information on a certain topic (recipes, product details, etc.) , consider putting that information in a database that is searchable against multiple criteria. For a great example of this type of feature, see http://www.wegmans.com/greatMeals/recipes/advancedsearch.asp

Lastly, keep in mind that a successful Web site must work for a wide variety of technical platforms: operating systems, browsers, plug-ins, monitor sizes and resolutions, e-mail programs, etc. Your Web site should be developed by professional Web site developers to insure that it is platform-independent.

Creating a Brand-Building Site

To create a brand-building site, the following considerations are also necessary:

✓ The domain name (URL) should be the brand name (to provide intuitive site access). People increasingly are trying to type the name as the URL. If that doesn't work, they use a search engine.

✓ Own the URLs for all variations of the brand name, including acronyms, abbreviations, misspellings, etc. Also consider owning the .com, .org, .net, .biz, etc. URLs. Redirect people who use those URLs to your site.

✓ Protect your domain name through ongoing surveillance and enforcement. (www.Cyveillance.com and www.Cobion.com provide this online service.)

✓ Weave a story about the brand's history, heritage, and character. A wonderful example of this at work is at the Polo Web Site: http://entertainment.polo.com

✓ Use these elements of your brand to provide unique brand experiences to the user. For example, Google uses its name as a playful part of the brand experience: Ten pages of search results can be accessed by clicking on any of the "O"s in "Goooooooooogle" displayed at the bottom of the page. And Google's new price comparison site is called "Froogle."

✓ The site must be true to your brand's identity and attitude. Your brand should not take on a new persona in cyberspace just to be "hip."

✓ Brand-building sites should avail themselves to the full spectrum of brand identity elements; not just name and logo, but also typography, colors, design and graphic elements, brand voice and visual style, theme lines, animation, sound, etc.

✓ A well-branded site will have a consistent look and feel across all of its pages. Ideally, the brand name and logo appear in the upper left corner on each page.

✓ Brand-building sites should establish a sense of community and create an emotional connection with the brand.

Creating Community Online

The following are effective community building techniques:

✓ Directories (with hypertext links to specific pages on other sites).

✓ Bulletin boards and chat rooms. Bulletin boards usually provide a searchable archive of all discussions; in contrast, you need to be actively participating in a chat room to understand the discussion. A great example of a thriving bulletin board is http://discussion .brighthand.com/ where several thousand Palm and Pocket PC users converge to discuss their gadgets.

✓ Surveys/reviews. People love to express their opinions, just look at the comments on Amazon.com . . . or browse through epinions.com—this entire site is dedicated to customer reviews!

✓ Daily tips, quotes, tricks, or rules of thumb.

✓ Personal user lists kept on your site. Amazon's "listmania" feature is a great example.

✓ Guest books or "cave drawings" (these are features that allow people to leave their own mark on your site).

✓ Custom-published Web magazines. www.salon.com and www.theoni on.com are two of the most popular.

✓ Extranet sections (password-protected areas for clients/members with value-added services).

✓ Online events. ABCnews.com makes extensive use of online events.

✓ Featuring regularly updated news headlines on topics related to the site's purpose

✔ Searchable library of articles by subject matter experts (About.com)

✔ Track where consumers are going. Ask them what they like. Change the experience based on their responses (www.siteintelligence.co.uk provides a detailed analysis of how people use your Web site).

✔ Provide ample opportunities for community members to interact with each other over time. You will be amazed at the close bonds users will form if you provide them the place and tools.

✔ Several companies specialize in helping Web sites create online communities, including RealCommunities and PeopleLink.

Online Newsletters: Perhaps the Most Powerful Online Marketing Technique

Online newsletters are one of the most effective tools for keeping your brand in people's minds and creating an emotional connection with your brand. They provide global reach twenty-four hours a day for free. Because of that, you can afford to use them to advertise to nonrespondents indefinitely. The more people receive e-mail ads, the more they revisit Web sites. According to CyberAtlas, as many as 70 percent of Internet users say visiting a Web site regularly would influence their decision to place orders.

Here are some more tips for creating successful newsletters:

✔ They should be free.

✔ Let people opt-in (don't spam). That is, give them a simple way to subscribe, and let their subscription be their decision.

✔ Communicate your privacy policy when people subscribe to your newsletters.

✔ Provide useful, fresh content each issue.

✔ Provide hypertext links to useful sites and to deeper areas in your site.

✔ Include a small ad in each newsletter. Specific offers with hypertext links are the most effective.

✔ Explicitly inform people how to unsubscribe to the mailing list. Better yet, provide a simple way to do so in each newsletter. Make sure to provide both e-mail and Web-based methods of managing subscriptions.

✔ Don't send more than one newsletter a week.

✔ Add your newsletter to other sites' online periodical listings (with a hypertext link to your subscription form).

✔ Encourage readers to pass the newsletter on to anyone else who might be interested in the topic. (Testing this approach with BrandForward's newsletter indicates that the power of suggestion is real.)

✓ Always include brand access information (URL, address, e-mail address, telephone number, etc.) in the newsletter.

✓ Copyright all newsletter content.

✓ Feature the "enroll" button in the upper right hand corner of each Web page—this will substantially increase subscription rates.

One caution: Since the late 1990s, newsletters have burgeoned in their popularity as a marketing tool. Increasingly, people will weed out newsletters to which they had previously subscribed based upon the immediate value added. This will make it increasingly important for publishers to focus on delivering useful content in a quick and interesting way if they wish to stay on people's "reading short lists."

E-Mail Blasts[4]

There is a fine line between a "bona fide" e-mail blast and an annoying spam. Tread lightly when experimenting with e-mail blasts.

Direct e-mails are like direct snail mail without the cost of stamps and printing. Cross/up/retention e-mail blasts can be extremely lucrative. However, successful e-mail letters are not identical to their snail mail counterparts. Responses generally occur within forty-eight hours, and copywriting is different.

To create copy that generates results, start with a clear offer and convey it in the subject line. The subject line, not the copy, is the most critical component of a successful response rate because it determines whether the e-mail will be opened or immediately discarded. Test many subject lines in all campaigns and keep a list of top performers.

Next, make the first line of copy succinct and interesting. Like the subject line, it also determines whether the rest of the e-mail will be read or discarded. Tell people what you are offering, what it will do for them, and why they should read further. Next, keep the copy short and use bullet points to convey information rather than long sentences. Keep all information on bullet points on a single line.

Finally, deliver a powerful, time-sensitive call to action with a link to an order page or Web response form. Track gross and net response rates (e-mails opened versus target response) so you know where improvements can be made in the sales cycle. Here are some important details when doing e-mail blasts:

✓ Some recipients will think you're spamming them. Respond politely to their (sometimes very nasty) e-mail and inform them you'll remove them from your list.

✔ Follow all the guidelines for e-mail mechanics that were mentioned in the newsletter section above.

✔ Use e-mail blasts sparingly—with greater frequency they become less effective.

Web Site Promotion

Once you have a strong brand-building site, you will want to promote it online and offline. The first thing you will want to do is submit your site to search engines and online directories. (In January of 2001, the NPD Group, a leading marketing information provider, conducted a study to compare the effectiveness of search listings versus banner ads and titles. "Search listings outperformed banner ads and titles" 2 to 1 or more on awareness, likelihood to read and click, and favorable opinions.)[5] Of the three approaches to this (doing it yourself with the help of online site promotion resources, hiring a company that specializes in search engine and directory placement, or doing both), I recommend doing both.

Web site ranking on search engines is a function of many variables, and each search engine uses a different set of criteria. A few years ago, it was fairly easy to get a high search engine ranking by adding the appropriate keywords to your site's meta-tags. With more and more sites added to the Internet each day, search engines have gotten much more sophisticated in how they rank sites. So, achieving a high ranking has become much more difficult.

Specialists use a variety of techniques including "gateway" or "jump" pages. These pages, which provide hypertext links to your site, are optimized to appeal to specific search engines. Considering this increased sophistication, I recommend hiring specialists to improve your Web site's ranking.

Having said that, there are a few things you should know about how to improve your Web site's chances for a high ranking. Do all of these *before* you submit to search engines.

✔ Including the location and frequency of keywords in your site's title and meta-tags will typically improve your Web site's ranking.

✔ Link popularity, or the number of links to your site, is also very important in increasing your site's ranking. That is why it is important to negotiate reciprocal links with other sites.

✔ Well-thought-through and persuasive Web page titles and descriptions will also help.

✔ Consider using <ALT> text to describe all graphic elements on your site. Many search engines index these. Also, using <ALT> texts makes your Web site more accessible to blind people (as the <ALT> text can be read and converted to the spoken word).

✓ Most search engines have gotten wise to "spamming" and will penalize sites that use invisible or tiny text among other approaches.

The following companies specialize in maximizing Web site search engine rankings:

✓ www.OneUpWeb.com
✓ www.eiCommunications.com
✓ www.top-10.com
✓ www.1stplaceranking.com

Whether you outsource site placement or not, it will behoove you to do the following on a regular basis:

✓ Monitor your listings frequently. Check your ranking placement. Resubmit your site often.
✓ Using WebTrends, Urchin, or other similar software, study your log files to see which search engines send you the most traffic.
✓ Check your competitors' sites to see how they rank using your key words.
✓ Analyze the pages with the highest rankings using your keywords. (Work with your Webmaster to view the pages' code, or right click "view source" on the Web page to view its underlying code.)

Once you are listed with search engines and directories, you will want to promote your Web site in other ways as well. Following are *effective* online site promotion techniques:

✓ Banner ads.
✓ Keyword advertising, or ads that appear only when people enter specific keywords into a search engine (often called "Pay Per Click").
✓ Directory advertising, or advertising on pages with specific directory topics.
✓ Signature line (brand name/logo, tag line, address, telephone number, URL, etc.) included in all e-mail.
✓ "Virtual storefronts in Web malls and virtual shelf spaces within stores on other sites"[6]
✓ Set up an affiliate program (perfected by Amazon.com).
✓ Be a part of portal sites.
✓ Apply for awards (start here: *http://Web siteawards.xe.net/*).
✓ Submit your Web site to "What's New" Web sites (such as *www.whats nu.com*).

✓ E-zine ads. Advertise in your own and other people's newsletters/e-zines.

✓ Lead forum discussions.[7]

✓ Online media relations (www.prWeb.com).

✓ By-lined articles for e-zines and other Web sites.

✓ Microsites—or small sites created to promote a particular product or service. (Movie studios do this for each new film they release. Conference companies often do this for each conference they produce.)

✓ Place notices in chat rooms and on bulletin boards,[8] participate in Usenet newsgroup discussions, or post ads in targeted discussion groups. (Be careful here: Most bulletin boards have special rules and specific locations for such notices.)

✓ Join online mailing lists (www.list-universe.com, www.topica.com, etc.).

✓ Invite site users to return to your site with a follow-up e-mail message.

✓ On your site, suggest that users bookmark your site.

✓ Make it easy for people to suggest your Web site to a friend (simple pre-written e-mail messages or "send to friend" functions).

✓ Design a page on your site to serve as a useful or interesting home page. Then make it easy for people to specify it as their home page.

✓ If your product is created on or distributed by the Web, make it "sticky." That is, include an ingredient brand label (such as "I used Photoshop") and/or a hypertext link back to your Web site on the product itself. (A year and a half after its launch, Hotmail had signed up 18 million subscribers with little to no advertising. A simple line at the bottom of every e-mail message helped them achieve this—"Get your free e-mail at Hotmail.com.")

✓ To create a powerful viral program, invent a product that meets a need or exceeds expectations of quality. Make it unique, offer it for free, and make it easy for people to give away. (Hotmail, again, is a great example.) Once you build a database of users, create a conversion strategy to migrate as many as possible into paying customers. This could include offering something free for a thirty-day trial period, and then sending follow-up conversion e-mails with a first-time user discount.

✓ If possible, build something into your online product or experience that makes it more valuable to the user if they share it as broadly as possible. (For instance, the more friends and family members that I can get to join ICQ, the more valuable the service becomes to me.)

✓ Use creative and entertaining multimedia games and greetings designed to spread like wildfire throughout the Internet (examples: dancing baby, elf bowling, and dancing hamsters).

✓ Submit free content to other sites in exchange for a link to your site.

✓ Obtain reciprocal links by:[9]

　　✓ Creating strategies that bring qualified sites to you, rather than going to them. Advertise a cross-linking program on your site, e-zines, and other media.

✓ Approaching sites with an effective e-mail. Do not blast the same e-mail to multiple site contacts. The response will be abysmal. Hand-pick sites you like and sign up for their e-zines and special offers. Write them a personal letter and congratulate them on the quality of their site and content. Thank them for the commitment to a quality user experience. Tell others about their site and pass along their e-zines and other content to others. Let them know that you are promoting their site already. Then, tell them a little about your site and the experience and value you offer. Let them know how many visitors you have. Translate this into value to them: more traffic and qualified leads, leading to more profitability with no cash outlay, which can be achieved simply by providing cross links to your respective Web properties, and some mutual promotional activities. (For added ROI on your efforts, test directing some links to lead forms, offer pages, or specific site pages, rather than the home page.)

✓ Last but not least: Print your URL on EVERYTHING. All business cards, stationery, company vehicles, billboards, product packaging . . . everything.

Banner Ads

Banner ads are the most prevalent form of online promotion. Banner ads should be evaluated using the following metrics:

✓ Increased brand awareness
✓ Brand attributes communicated
✓ Increased purchase intent

"Click throughs" have decreased in importance as a measure, because much of the brand building benefit is derived from people just seeing the ad and absorbing its message. I use banner ads to increase advertising frequency against a highly targeted audience (by placing them only on highly targeted pages on highly targeted sites).

The following are some tips for maximizing the effectiveness of those ads:[10]

✓ Animated banners with a question or a call to action are the most compelling. Rich media banner advertising (mostly Flash based) will probably be the standard by the time this book is published.

✓ Keep the message simple with as few words as possible.

✓ Use bold colors (assuming they are compatible with your brand's identity).

✔ Always anchor your brand mark at one end of the banner—preferably the left side.

✔ Include your URL in the banner.

✔ Always have a "click here" tag line at the end of the banner.

✔ Incorporate the word "free"—it increases response.

✔ Mentally engage the viewer.

✔ Seek out contexts within which there is minimal clutter surrounding your banner ad.

✔ As with any advertising, increase the frequency of your banner ad.

✔ Learn what works best by constantly testing and modifying the ads: Measure results, modify the ads, and measure the results again.

✔ Changing your banner ads every few weeks maintains click throughs—otherwise they decay with time.

✔ Set up special "target" pages on your Web site. Pointing each of your banner placements to a different target page dramatically improves your ability to measure the effectiveness of different media choices.

A final word on online advertising: When online, consumers are in control. They don't have to put up with invasive advertising, the worst of which are interstitial or "pop up" ads. (Do you wait for those ads to fully load before you close them? I don't. My automatic response is to close them as soon as they come up, especially when they interrupt writing an e-mail message or filling out a form.) For that reason, I strongly believe that online advertising will evolve to less intrusive forms, integrating persuasive messages and appropriate hypertext links with useful content sought by people. (Some studies have found that click-through rates for text-based links are four to ten times higher than for banner ad links.) I also believe that online advertising will increasingly integrate interactive and entertaining elements. In fact, the future of advertising online may be the seamless blending of information, entertainment, and persuasive commercial messages in places where people are engrossed in the medium and particularly receptive to the messages. (While this is likely to be particularly effective, it will raise potential ethical issues, especially regarding advertising directed toward children.)

Do not forget to promote your Web site offline as well. Offline promotion should focus on all of the things it normally would for a brick & mortar world brand *plus* it should drive traffic to the Web site. Given that, your offline marketing plan should include advertising, promotion, publicity, and other standard marketing elements. Most importantly, include your Web site's URL in ALL external communication, and your e-mail addresses where appropriate. List your site with reference publications. Finally, tell everyone about your Web site. Word-of-mouth marketing works.

▓ BrandForward Cyberbranding 2000 Study™

BrandForward conducted its seminal Cyberbranding 2000 Study™ in March of 2000. We designed the study to address the questions marketing executives most often ask about brands and the Internet.

- ✓ How does brand building on the Internet differ from brand building in the brick & mortar world?
- ✓ What opportunities and vulnerabilities exist for pure Internet brands and for brick & mortar brands conducting commerce in cyberspace?
- ✓ How do people shop online and what is the role of brand in that process?
- ✓ How can companies best build and leverage brands online?

The study, which surveyed 1548 Internet users in the United States, answered these and many other questions. The study explored three top e-commerce categories (books, toys & games, and clothes/apparel) and identified patterns that are applicable to all product categories. It compared brick & mortar brands in cyberspace to pure Internet brands on twelve different dimensions of brand equity including awareness, accessibility, quality, value, emotional connection, relevant differentiation, personality, vitality, and loyalty. It identified how people shop online and the role of brand in that process. It also ranked the importance of twenty-three factors to the success of e-commerce sites. Following are some of the findings:

- ✓ The brand name is the single most important way people arrive at Web sites at which purchases are made. As shown in Exhibit 11-2 and Figure 11-1, roughly half of all consumers arrive at a Web site by directly typing in the site's URL (domain name). (If one considers bookmarks to be a sign of brand loyalty and counting searching on product or store name,

EXHIBIT 11-2. HOW CONSUMERS ARRIVED AT WEB SITE WHERE PURCHASE WAS MADE.

	Books	Toys & Games	Clothing
Directly to site via URL	46%	45%	54%
Directly to site via bookmark	28%	11%	16%
Link from another site or newsletter or e-mail	13%	19%	14%
Search engine on product name	5%	9%	NA
Search engine on category name	2%	9%	6%
Search engine on store name	2%	4%	4%
Search engine directory of hypertext links	1%	0%	1%

FIGURE 11-1. HOW CUSTOMERS ARRIVED AT A TOYS AND GAMES E-COMMERCE SITE.

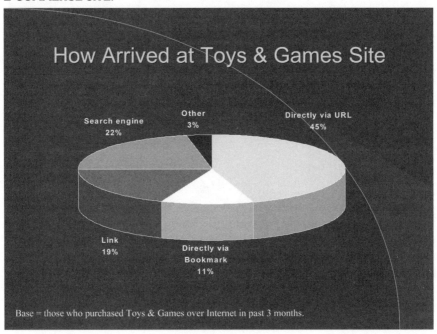

approximately three quarters of all people arrive at Web sites where purchases are made by using the brand's name.)

✓ Top-of-mind awareness of brick & mortar brands far exceeds that of pure Internet brands (see Figure 11-2). (As discussed earlier, awareness is the cornerstone of brand equity. Without it, a brand is unable to differentiate itself or create an emotional connection with people.)

✓ Approximately 15 percent of all consumers arrive at Web sites at which purchases are made through links from other sites and online publications.

✓ The same factors drive brand equity in cyberspace and the brick & mortar world: awareness, accessibility, value, relevant differentiation, and emotional connection, but again—they manifest themselves differently in cyberspace.

✓ The same factors are important in shopping online and in brick & mortar retail: product quality and selection, convenience, and price/value—and again, they manifest themselves differently in cyberspace. For example, the Internet has more convenient hours (24 hours a day, 365 days a year) and, in some instances, a faster way to find a particular product (witness Amazon.com's sophisticated search and browse techniques). But brick & mortar stores offer the convenience of instant gratification—being able to

FIGURE 11-2. BRAND AWARENESS.

When asked to think about brands that sell toys & games, roughly a third mentioned Toys 'R Us first while only 2% mentioned eToys, the top pure Internet brand in the category. Excepting Amazon.com, we found that top-of-mind awareness of brick & mortar brands far exceeded that of pure Internet brands in the same product category. (This study predicted that eToys would go out of business, which it later did.)

- take the product home immediately after purchase, or returning it without the hassle of shipping it.
- ✔ When consumers are made aware of a brick & mortar brand's cyberspace presence, many dimensions of that brand's equity are significantly enhanced. This is particularly true for brick & mortar brands in whose product categories there are no dominant Internet brands.
- ✔ Brick & mortar brands with e-commerce capability are perceived to be more accessible than cyberbrands. The ability to return goods purchased on the Internet to a brick & mortar store provides a substantial advantage.
- ✔ Cyberbrands are perceived to be more "innovative/leading edge" and less "old-fashioned/traditional," and "boring." They are also perceived to be less "friendly," "dependable," and "trustworthy" (largely due to lower brand awareness).
- ✔ Some characteristics of an Internet site that are important to consumers when deciding to make a purchase include clearly marked prices, secure payment methods, inexpensive shipping, no-hassle return policies, detailed item descriptions, and pictures of items.

✔ E-commerce sites will eventually win on information, interactivity, and price (and on some dimensions of convenience). Brick & mortar brands must significantly enhance the store experience (especially its tactile and olfactory elements) to remain viable.

✔ Amazon.com is one of the few pure Internet brands that has achieved a level of brand equity that puts it on par with brick & mortar brands.

Implications

Implications of the Cyberbranding 2000 Study™ findings are as follows:

✔ It is essential that brick & mortar brands have a cyberspace presence.

✔ A brick & mortar brand that is new to the Internet still has the potential to dominate a product or service category online if it has a strong brand name, acts quickly, and can adapt itself to a successful cyberspace business model.

✔ Pure Internet brands are extremely vulnerable to brick & mortar brands due to their very low awareness. They must forcefully and relentlessly build brand awareness through every method possible, including offline. Amazon.com's relentless publicity and affiliate programs and AOL's market saturation approach to software distribution should be considered seriously as models. (In the early- to mid-1990s, AOL had only 300,000 subscribers to CompuServe's 1 million subscribers and Prodigy's 500,000 subscribers. In 1994, AOL began saturating the market with free software disks offering one month's service free. In so doing, AOL surpassed its competitors in far less than a year, reaching 23 million subscribers just a few years later.)

✔ Your brand's URL must be the brand name. You should own URLs for all variations of your brand's name and direct people from those URLs to your brand's primary URL.

✔ Create as many links to your site as possible.

✔ Brick & mortar brands should work toward integrating their cyberspace and brick & mortar processes and systems, especially those that affect customers. (This study found that offering brick & mortar returns for online purchases offers a company substantial advantages. For example, Barnes & Noble has gotten better at integrating this service across its "bricks and clicks" components of its business.)

✔ Shopping on e-commerce sites must offer an advantage over doing the same in the brick & mortar world. Identify the added value and make sure you build it into your site.

✔ Pure Internet brands are much more successful when they can claim leadership in a specific product or service category. Two approaches to this include:

✔ Become dominant in a new category made possible by the Internet (for which there is no good brick & mortar world counterpart). Example: Backup.com.

✔ If there is already a dominant brand in the online category in which you intend to operate, narrow the definition of the category you intend to own. Example: VarsityBooks.com.

A Caution to Web Brands

As more and more Web brands advertise in traditional media, some of them have created ads featuring outrageous stunts. These ads seem to be designed to break through the clutter and create high recall quickly. People behind these brands should understand that brand building is more than creating awareness and recall. *Relevant* differentiation, trust, and emotional connection are also important drivers of brand equity. Shooting gerbils out of cannons is not likely to build brand equity.

Companies often focus their Web sites on brand building or commerce, but not both. I strongly recommend integrating the two. To that end, here is a brief section on online stores.

Online Stores

According to IntelliQuest, a marketing research organization for the technology, Internet, and wireless industries, following are the top five reasons people do not buy online:

1. Worried about fly-by-night retailers (81 percent)
2. Don't want to deal with the hassle of returning something (72 percent)
3. Worried about using their credit card online (69 percent)
4. Think they are going to get a bunch of junk mail (63 percent)
5. Want to see/touch what they buy (62 percent)

The following are key success factors for online stores:[11]

✔ "Don't keep shoppers waiting."
✔ Provide various methods for quick product search: by price point, product category, and brand name.

✔ "Build trust."

  ✔ Feature name brand products.

  ✔ Provide for easy telephone contact (1-800 number).

  ✔ Feature customer testimonials.

  ✔ Prominently display your privacy policy.

  ✔ Offer a no-hassle return policy.

  ✔ Provide an unconditional guarantee (or at least a performance guarantee).

  ✔ Feature pictures of your merchandise.

  ✔ Communicate product sizes and dimensions.

  ✔ Use a secure server and encryption technology—make the consumer aware of this.

  ✔ Cover the fifty-dollar credit-card liability in case of credit card fraud.

  ✔ "Don't hide the price."

✔ Create a foolproof shopping cart and checkout process.

✔ Retain customer information for return visits.

✔ Follow-up with e-mail (autoresponders and human generated).

✔ Provide online customer service chat rooms (like www.1800Flowers.com).

▦ Learn from Strong Brand-Building Web Sites

As you surf the Internet, think about your favorite Web sites. What makes them your favorite sites? What keeps you coming back to those sites? Visit those sites. Identify the features that appeal to you. Notice the site navigation. Notice how the brand identity elements are used throughout the site. After that, if you are still looking for examples of brand-building sites, following are a few others to visit:

✔ *amazon.com:* This Web site has gotten more publicity than any other—and no wonder: *Advertising Age*, in its December 13, 1999 issue, named Amazon.com founder Jeff Bezos "Marketer of the Year." And, while the brand is still in the red, it is doing many, many things right from a marketing perspective. While Amazon.com sells much more than books today, just using its original books section as an example, the online retailer has addressed every key driver of brand insistence (per BrandForward's brand equity model).

  ✔ *Awareness:* At 60.1 percent of all U.S. adults, Amazon.com has the highest awareness of any Internet business. It is no coincidence that it is also the # 1 Internet advertiser—not counting all of the publicity it generates.

- ✓ *Accessibility:* Amazon.com is available 24 hours a day, 7 days a week, 365 days a year—with quick shipping and delivery. It's myriad of browse-and-search approaches makes it much quicker and easier to find what you are looking for on its Web site than at most retail stores. They even keep multiple shipping addresses and credit cards on file to simplify the shopping process. Their extensive Amazon Associates program has extended their online reach even further, often tapping into sites with highly targeted interests and traffic.

- ✓ *Value:* On the price side of the ratio, all hardcover books are 30 percent off and all paperback books are 20 percent off. They also they have a bargain book section in which you can save up to 80 percent and a "10 for under $10" section. On the other side of the value ratio, you can listen to music samples and they offer "complimentary shipping upgrades, free Post-it notes, magnets and bookmarks (with their logo), free gift wrapping"[12] (except for Christmas), book reviews, special orders, many ways to browse or search products, etc.

- ✓ *Relevant Differentiation:* Amazon.com revolutionized the way we buy books (and other products). It owns that spot in our minds. Plus they have many unique features—personal wish lists, customized recommendations, purchase circles and even your own customized store.

- ✓ *Emotional Connection:* Amazon.com personalized suggested book lists (by subject). They maintain your complete order history, which you can access at any time. They let *you* write online reviews of their books, CDs, and other products. Clearly, they are using every brand insistence driver to their advantage.

Perhaps the two most important innovations Amazon.com introduced were (1) a leading-edge CRM approach to online commerce, and (2) a superior way to find a book (vis-à-vis brick & mortar approaches) via its robust search-and-browse techniques.

- ✓ ***patagonia.com:*** Through visuals and words, this site exudes the essence of the Patagonia brand. The "About Patagonia" section prominently features a statement of its brand's essence ("Committed to the Core") along with paths to sub-sections on "our culture," "sports we do," "design philosophy," and "enviro action." The "our culture" section features "our roots" (company heritage and vision), "field reports" (adventure essays) and "Patagoniacs" (profiles and pictures of their employees living the brand) subsections. Given these features and the site's consistently distinctive brand voice and visual style, it's nearly impossible for you not to comprehend Patagonia's essence after having visited their site.

✓ **nextmonet.com:** This site sells fine art for the home and office. It allows you to search their collection by any combination of the following criteria: style, medium, subject, color, artist, price, size, and artwork title or key-word. It allows you to select your favorite art and organize it by your own customized "rooms" for later reference. Its complex set of search criteria helps you search their collection based upon a variety of needs or problems to be solved. Its SmartArt section gives an overview of art appreciation including collecting basics (such as collecting strategies, authenticity, value, and conservation).

✓ **winespectator.com:** This site is chock-full of useful features for the wine enthusiast. It provides wine search, wine ratings, vintage charts, wineries search, wine chat, contests, a weekly poll, personal wine list, restaurant search, food and wine matching, menus, bulletin boards on twenty topics, daily wine news, and other features. It is the easiest way to maintain your personal wine list and it includes reviews, ratings, and "drink before" dates for each bottle of wine.

✓ **morningstar.com:** This investment site allows you to track multiple self-defined portfolios in one of several modes, including a completely custo-mized mode (with frequently updated net worth). Its x-ray feature allows you to view your portfolios in various other ways (diagnostics, stock over-lap, asset class, stock style, stock sector, stock type, stock stats, fees & expenses, world regions, bond style, and overview). The Web site also features news, updates & alerts (based on your portfolio), forums (topic, stock, or fund specific), and Morningstar University.

✓ **travelocity.com:** This full service travel site offers the following features: find/book a flight, find/book a rental car, find/reserve a hotel, vacations & cruises, special deals, and a destination guide. You can search for a flight in one of three ways: best fare, best itinerary (date/fare combination), or schedule. The site maintains a personal profile for you, including frequent flyer numbers and meal and seat preferences. It provides the following travel tools: review your reservations, check your ticket delivery status, edit your personal profile, fare watcher e-mail, weather, and maps.

✓ **ebay.com:** This site redefined commerce. Now anyone can auction off anything to anyone else throughout the world twenty-four hours a day, seven days a week. In 2002, eBay members transacted nearly $15 billion in annualized gross merchandise sales. The site offers a personal shopper service, alerting you to when new items that match your search criteria arrive. It also features an easy search function, seller feedback/rankings, seller's other auctions, message boards, and a library (with a section dedi-cated to collectibles).

✓ **smarterkids.com:** This site allows you to shop by the child's age range, theme, brand, subject, format, and character. It highlights teacher's favor-ites, parent's favorites, best sellers, picks under twenty dollars, and great gift ideas. It even has three specialty centers: special needs center, gifted & talented center, and grandparents center. It has a gift registry and you can create a customized "My Kid's Store." It even features a family resource center with advice, news, activities, and resources, including a learning styles survey and early development checklists. Their products are reviewed and rated by professional educators. Clearly, this site is not just another online toy store. It was carefully designed with the customer's needs in mind—to help children learn, discover, and grow.

✔ **crayola.com:** This site looks and feels like Crayola with a strong and consistent brand identity, including lots of *color* (a key part of its essence). It features separate sections for parents, educators, and kids. It also provides a wide variety of searchable creative ideas for Crayola product use. When your browser contacts the site, a colored Crayola crayon appears in front of the URL above your browser window.

✔ **hallmark.com:** Hallmark's first generation site focused on creating an emotional connection between Hallmark and its consumers. It featured a storytelling bulletin board, joke of the day, weekly comic strip, ornament collectors bulletin board, personal Hallmark Gold Crown card point totals, address book, occasion reminder service, artist profiles, store locator service, Keepsake ornament screensavers, and many other endearing features. The second-generation site is much more focused on commerce, but still offers many of the original features. You can talk Keepsake ornament collecting or join the Maxine club online.

There are many common elements that make these Web sites "strong brand-building Web sites." These common elements include:

✔ Strong and consistent brand identity, voice, and visual style
✔ Robust and intuitive search-and-browse techniques
✔ Features specifically designed to appeal to the target customer, including customer problem-solving features
✔ Creative ways for customers to put a piece of themselves on the site (investment portfolio, personal wine cellar, product wish list, etc.)

A Final Caution

Poorly thought-out and executed Web sites can hurt brand equity. Apply the same thoughtfulness and quality standards to your organization's Web site as you do to its products, services, and other marketing programs. Some companies will permit spelling, typographical, or grammatical errors on their Web sites that they would not tolerate in other media. Some companies also seemingly ignore broken links and leave amateurish "work in progress" pages up for indefinite periods of time. It is amazing how many companies outsource development and maintenance of their Web sites with little direct input or oversight.

Your organization's Web site is its most visible face to the public. Make sure it is building your brand's equity, not depleting it. (For a fee, www .atwatch.com will watch your Web site and alert you to problems in the following areas: average and peak response times, missing content, site down, broken links, hackers, and public postings about your site.)

The Impact of the Internet on Brands: A Summary

- ✔ An Internet presence has become an essential requirement for brand building.
- ✔ A Web site can create an integrated brand experience that consistently reinforces the brand positioning.
- ✔ The Internet will drive brands without a compelling point of difference (or a strong value proposition) out of business.
- ✔ Brands more than ever will help people break through the over-communication clutter.
- ✔ The Web site itself is just one element of brand building on the Internet.
- ✔ You can and should integrate commerce and brand building online.
- ✔ A well-known brand name is the most important factor in directing people to your e-commerce site (top-of-mind awareness is the desired end).
- ✔ To be successful, e-commerce sites must deliver value superior to their brick & mortar competitors. There are four primary ways in which the Internet can add value: information, entertainment, convenience, and cost savings.
- ✔ Brands that integrate a brick & mortar presence with a "cyberspace" presence will be formidable competitors.

Use the checklist in Exhibit 11-3 to assess the efficacy of your brand management practices in the area covered by this chapter. The more questions to which you can answer "yes," the better you are doing. The checklist also provides a brief summary of the material covered in the chapter.

EXHIBIT 11-3. BRAND MANAGEMENT CHECKLIST.

BRAND BUILDING ON THE INTERNET

	YES	NO
Is your domain name (URL) your brand name?		
Do you own URLs for all variations of your brand name? Do you redirect people who enter those URLs to your site?		
Do you contract with someone to protect your brand name and trademark online? (Namesake.com and Cyveillance.com provide this service.)		
Does your website reinforce your brand's essence, promise and personality?		
Is your brand's identity consistently presented throughout the site?		
Does your site weave a story about your brand's history, heritage, character or attitude?		
Does your Web site create an engaging, interactive, interesting, informative and helpful consumer experience?		
Do you use animation (such as Macromedia's Flash and Shockwave) throughout your site to make it interesting?		
Do you use audio on your site?		
Do you feature streaming video on your site (using programs such as QuickTime or Real Audio)?		
Does your site download quickly?		
Do you keep your site visitors active (they want to click and scroll, not read)?		
Can users get to almost any page on your site in three clicks or less?		
Is your site's copy concise, factual and bulletized?		
Do you have a site map that is easy to find and use?		
Do you have a site search engine?		
Is your site's navigation intuitive and consistent?		
Does every page on your site have "Home," "Search," and "Site Map" buttons?		

Does your site work with a wide variety of technical platforms (operating systems, browsers, plug-ins, monitor sizes and resolutions, e-mail programs, etc)?   _____ _____

Does your site create a sense of community? Does it provide ample opportunities for community members to interact with each other over time?   _____ _____

Do you personalize your site to your site visitors' preferences (wallpaper, first page viewed, customized content, etc.)?   _____ _____

Do you give consumers reasons to return to your site on a regular basis?   _____ _____

Do you offer customer services (such as store locator service, checklists and consultative or diagnostic tools)?   _____ _____

Does your site have directories with hypertext links to specific pages on other sites?   _____ _____

Does your site have a searchable library of articles by subject matter experts?   _____ _____

Does your site have bulletin boards?   _____ _____

Does your site have chat rooms?   _____ _____

Do you feature simple surveys and reviews on your site?   _____ _____

Do you keep personal user lists on your site?   _____ _____

Does your site match people with interests (through search and browse techniques)?   _____ _____

Does your site feature user opinion postings?   _____ _____

Do you sponsor online events on your site? Do you lead forum discussions on your site?   _____ _____

Does your site have an extranet section (password-protected area for clients/members with value added services)?   _____ _____

Do you publish a free online newsletter?   _____ _____

Do you provide activities to unobtrusively build a database (games, contests, sweepstakes, surveys and newsletters)?   _____ _____

(continues)

EXHIBIT 11-3. (CONTINUED).

Do you know which word combinations people most often use in search engines to find Web sites like yours? Do you know how your site places in search engine rankings for those key phrases? Do you monitor your listings and check your search engine rankings frequently? _____ _____

Does you site's ranking place it on the first page or two of a search engine's results? If not, are you actively pursuing ways to increase your site's search engine ranking? _____ _____

Have you listed your site in search engine directories? _____ _____

Do you check your competitors' sites to see how they rank using your key words? _____ _____

Do you analyze the pages with the highest search engine rankings using your key words? _____ _____

Is your site featured in portal sites? Is your site a portal site? _____ _____

Do you actively seek reciprocal links with other sites? _____ _____

Do you submit your site for awards? _____ _____

Do you advertise online? _____ _____

Do you use banner ads, keyword advertising, or interstitial advertising? _____ _____

Are your banner ads compelling? _____ _____

Do you post ads in discussion groups? Do you place notices in chat rooms and on bulletin boards? _____ _____

Do you write bylined articles for other Web sites? _____ _____

Do you place e-zine ads? _____ _____

Do you maintain good online media relations? Are you (or is someone from your company) listed as a subject matter expert in online expert lists? _____ _____

Do you create micro-sites to feature specific products, services or events? _____ _____

Do you have virtual storefronts in Web malls and virtual shelf spaces within stores on other sites? _____ _____

Do you include a signature line (brand name/logo, tag line, address, telephone number, URL, etc.) in all of your outgoing e-mail as a standard business practice? _____ _____

Do you include your Web site's URL in ALL external communication (advertising, business cards, letterhead, etc.) as a standard business practice? _____ _____

Do you promote your brand's Web site offline (through advertising, publicity, published articles, word-of-mouth, etc.)? _____ _____

Are you a student of the World Wide Web, constantly noting effective techniques that other sites use? _____ _____

Do you visit your competitors' sites often to better understand how they are interacting with their customers? _____ _____

Do you carefully track who is on your site, where they came from, what they look at and how they found your site (through programs that analyze your log files)? _____ _____

Do you ask your consumers what they like and what they don't like? Do you change the site experience based on their responses? _____ _____

Do you use cookies to capture additional information on site visitors and to provide them with customized content when they return to your site? _____ _____

Do you use a combination of cookies and surveys to compare site/page/ad exposure to brand awareness and perception? _____ _____

Notes

1. Kelly Anthony-Rodriques, "Brand Management: From Print to Broadcast on the Web," Seybold San Francisco/Publishing '98 Web Publishing Conference, September 1, 1998. p. 12 http://www.seyboldseminars.com/Events/sf98/transcripts/ETAPE_14.html. 10/22/99.

2. Peter M. Stevens, "Branding On-Line," p. 6. http://aorangi.vuw.ac.nz/Websearch/BrandPaper/BrandingPaper.html. 10/22/99.

3. Source: Steven M. Cristol and Bob Johnson, "Building Brand Equity on the World Wide Web," Summary of a Presentation to the Business Week Corporate Branding Symposium, Chicago, June 17, 1997, www.haas.berkeley.edu/~wba268/brandWeb.htm. 3/27/99.

4. Courtesy of Jeff Kuzmich, Element K Internet marketing manager.

5. "Search Listings Outperform Banner Ads and Tiles!", www.goto.com/d/about/advertisers/slab/jhtml.

6. Cristol and Johnson, "Building Brand Equity on the World Wide Web."

7. Joseph Jobst, "Branding on the Net," http://linz1.net/freep19.html.

8. Cristol and Johnson, "Building Brand Equity on the World Wide Web."

9. Courtesy of Jeff Kuzmich, Element K Internet marketing manager.

10. Primary sources: www.aibn.com/brandbuild.html, and Rex Briggs, digital marketing and measurement pioneer (at the Second Annual Online Marketing International Summit, April 23-26, 2001).

11. Source: "Brand Interaction: the Oft-Neglected Element of Online Branding" by Rob McEwen, principal of This Quarter, a direct-marketing consultancy, and formerly founder and CEO of M2K, an integrated marketing agency, October 23, 1999.

12. Source: Rob McEwen, "The Little Things That Make a Difference," http//www.searchz.com/Articles/1210983.shtml. 10/23/99.

CHAPTER 12

Developing a Brand-Building Organization

ONE OF THE most difficult tasks in brand management is transforming the organization from one that does not understand the scope or importance of brand management to one that embraces and actively builds the brand as a critically important source of sustainable competitive advantage. Key to this transformation is the organization's *brand promise*.

The following comment is typical of what I hear from marketing executives at more and more companies these days: "We conducted exhaustive consumer research. We carefully positioned our brand. We developed and instituted comprehensive brand identity standards and systems. We are running our new advertising campaign. Now what do we do? How do we get the rest of the organization to understand and care about the brand and its promise? How do we get the organization to deliver on the promise? How do we make the brand promise real?"

Brand management guru David Aaker posed the following very important question when he visited Hallmark a few years ago:

> **Until everyone from** your CEO to your receptionist can accurately and consistently articulate your brand's promise, how do you expect your customers to?

Certainly, the brand promise drives your marketing communication and your brand identity standards and systems. But it must do much more than that. Your products and services, every point of contact your brand makes with consumers, and the total consumer experience your brand creates must reinforce your brand's promise (see Figure 12-1). This has tremendous organizational implications. How can an organization deliver against its promise

This chapter is a revised version of "Developing the Brand Building Organization," *Journal of Brand Management* 7, 4 (2001): 281–90 (copyright Henry Stewart Publications).

FIGURE 12-1. REINFORCING YOUR BRAND'S PROMISE.

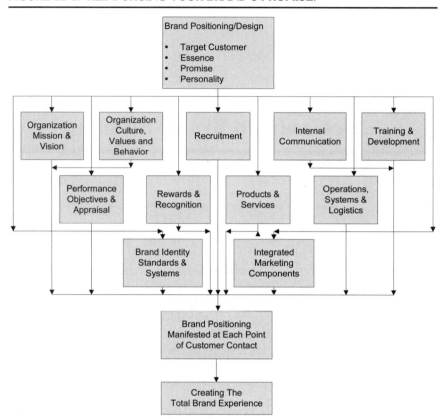

if its front line employees don't know (or care about) what its brand stands for?

At Hallmark, we did a number of things to incorporate the brand at every level of the organization:

- ✔ We worked with our public affairs and communications department to include key brand concepts and messages in all internal and external publications and executive speeches.

- ✔ We worked with the training department to build brand strategy modules into all internal training programs, especially new employee orientations.

- ✔ We gave Franklin Planner page finders featuring the brand essence and promise to all employees.

- ✔ We created a brand management and marketing intranet site so all employees could easily access brand plans, brand research, brand identity standards, and other brand information.

Negative Example: United Airlines Rising

A way to illustrate the importance of developing a brand-building organization is through an example of when it is not working. A good example is the United Airlines "United Airlines Rising" advertising campaign in 1997. This campaign was meant to communicate to the public that United was aware of its problems and was making an effort to raise its service to meet consumers' expectations. But the campaign backfired when they first launched it. Why? Because, just as United was making promises about its new customer satisfaction philosophy, its flight attendents were threatening a labor action called CHAOS™, or "Creating Havoc Around Our System™". The Association of Flight Attendants stated, "No raises, no rising." To add insult to injury, United's customer relations department was also so unresponsive to complaints that a disgruntled customer created the Web site www.untied.com, a site featuring complaints from other United Airlines passengers.

Critical Support Factors

In 1998, The Conference Board conducted a study on "Managing the Corporate Brand." In that study, they discovered four organizational support factors were critical to brand strategy success. They are:

- CEO leadership and support
- A distinctive corporate culture that serves as a platform for the brand promise
- The ability to obtain support from a broad spectrum of employees
- The alignment of brand messages across functions

At the Institute for International Research's December 1999 Brand Masters Conference in Palm Beach, Florida, Sixtus Oechsle, manager of corporate communications and advertising for Shell Oil Company, indicated that in a study of sources of brand favorability, Shell Oil found that interaction with company employees had the greatest impact (much greater than brand ads or news) on brand favorability.

Common Organizational Barriers to Brand Building

Here are some of the most common problems that organizations encounter when trying to implement new brand management programs:

- Senior management is not focused on the brand.
- Senior management has a short attention span and fails to provide the support and resources necessary for the branding to occur.

✔ Some senior leaders do not believe in the brand management concept.

✔ The organization is highly fragmented and resistant to change.

✔ The organization is internally focused.

✔ Difficulties in shifting people's focus from their functional "silos" to cross-functional ownership of the brand.

✔ The organization's culture does not reinforce the brand.

✔ The organization's operations and systems do not support the brand.

✔ The brand message is just one of many among a myriad of corporate messages.

Overcoming Obstacles

In my "Creating a Brand-Building Organization" workshops, the following approaches have been found to be effective in overcoming the obstacles encountered in creating brand-building organizations:

✔ *Issue:* How do you get corporate officers to support brand management initiatives when they don't understand the value of brand management or marketing?
   Ideas:

✔ Influence the leaders with books and speakers.

✔ Enlist the help of credible outside brand experts to spend some time with the corporate officer group.

✔ Provide case studies of how brand management has worked in comparable companies and industries.

✔ Symbolically "clean house" in the marketing department. Hire some new high-profile marketers with a history of success.

✔ Invite senior executives to help you solve brand management problems. Appeal to their egos and their propensity to mentor.

✔ *Issue:* How do you get corporate officers to act as brand champions when they are accountable for other corporate priorities?
   Ideas:

✔ Tie brand performance objectives to their compensation system.

✔ Give them bonuses based on achievement of brand goals.

✔ Educate them. Sell them.

✔ Include "brand passion" as an executive hiring criterion.

✔ Figure out how the brand helps them.

✔ Provide them with a quarterly update on progress against key brand objectives.

✓ **Issue:** Once you have most of the brand pieces in place (brand promise and positioning, brand identity, etc.), how do you translate all of that to a brand-building culture?

Ideas:

✓ "Walk the talk." Challenge others to do so as well.

✓ Throw it back out to the organization to figure out. You don't have to know all the answers up front.

✓ Review the brand tenets with various groups. Ask them where your plans are lacking in helping you achieve brand goals.

✓ Develop a six-month plan including objectives, obstacles, messages, and vehicles.

✓ **Issue:** Identify out-of-the-box tactics to ensure continued employee involvement in and support of brand initiatives.

Ideas:

✓ Hold poster contest. ("Communicate what the three brand tenets mean to you.")

✓ Feature twelve of the posters on a twelve-month calendar.

✓ Hold open houses. (Different areas showcase what they have done to promote brand initiatives.)

✓ Promote (through internal publications or other means) "the person on the street" who has helped build the brand.

✓ Name and recognize a "brand champion of the month."

✓ Create brand "certificates of appreciation." Award them to people who have furthered brand causes.

✓ **Issue:** If we believe front-line employees are 80 percent of the way there in their understanding of the brand, what else should we ask them to know, say or do?

Ideas:

✓ Validate your beliefs with research. Measure their understanding.

✓ Create an employee "focus group." Run it by the people in the focus group (for ideas on what to do next).

✓ Ask them how they are going to "live the brand."

✓ Ask them what actions they are going to take to deliver against the brand promise.

✓ Instead of focusing on dissemination of information, focus on recognition for the appropriate behavior.

✓ **Issue:** How do we convince geographically and functionally diverse groups to embrace the brand promise when we have little authority and can only use influencing skills?

Ideas:

✓ Identify each stakeholder's burning issues and discover ways your brand initiatives can address them. Relate your brand programs back to their issues.

✓ Sell your initiatives to top executives in other divisions and departments.

✓ Set up measures to highlight gaps.

✓ Manage by embarrassment. Publicly expose those who undermined the brand.

✓ Identify influencers. Create a grass roots support for your initiatives.

Brand Building Requires More than Advertising and Brand Identity Management

To create the change required to build a brand, all of the following questions must be addressed:

✓ *Corporate mission and vision.* Are they congruent with the brand essence and promise?

✓ *Business planning process.* Is it linked to the brand planning process?

✓ *Corporate culture, values, and behavior.* Do they support the brand essence, promise, and personality?

✓ *Recruitment.* Are you screening people for congruence between their beliefs, values and personality and your brand's essence, promise and personality?

✓ *Internal communication vehicles.* Are you using them to communicate brand positioning, strategies, and priorities?

✓ *Training and development.* Are you using these to increase understanding of brand positioning, strategies, and priorities?

✓ *Performance objectives* (especially common objectives). Do they include brand objectives?

✓ *Performance appraisal.* Do you provide feedback on how well individuals and groups are delivering against the brand promise?

✓ *Rewards and recognition.* Do you reward and recognize people who have furthered important brand goals? Do you compensate people for achievement of brand objectives?

✓ *Products and services.* Do they deliver against the brand promise?

✓ *Operations, systems, and logistics.* Do they support delivery of the brand promise?

Did You Know?

✔ The typical #1 brand is worth 10% more than the #2 brand to consumers (range: 0% to 35%).

✔ Home Depot and Ralph Lauren use the same paint formula, but the Home Depot house brand charges $9.94 while Ralph Lauren charges $26.95. (The only differences between the two are packaging, price charged, and the brand.)

✔ GE receives a 26% to 40% price premium for its light bulbs, depending on the sku. (*Source*: Jim Harmon, "General Electric: Creating a Global Brand Identity," presentation at the Institute for International Research's Brand Masters Conference, December 1997, Atlanta, Ga.)

✔ 42 ounces of Always Save Oatmeal is $1.69, while the same amount of Quaker Oats is $3.35. 32 ounces of Best Choice Ketchup is $1.29 while the same amount of Heinz is $2.05. 16 ounces of Best Choice spaghetti is $.89 while the same amount of Pata La Bella and De Cecco are $1.05 and $1.89 respectively.

Brand marketing won't work (at least to its fullest potential) if it is confined to an advertising agency, public affairs department, or even a brand management function. This is especially true when the brand in question is the corporate brand. The CEO is the ultimate brand manager, and everyone throughout the organization must be a brand champion (which implies they all know the brand essence and promise). Indeed, the company should be organized to deliver optimally the brand promise, and the corporate culture must support the brand's promise. How can consumers know what your brand stands for if people in your organization don't? Does the person answering your 1-800 number know what the brand stands for? How about the in-store sales associate? The copywriter for your brand catalog? The person developing a brand promotion? The people who design the brand's products?

Hiring employees whose personalities and values match those intended for the brand will ensure that the brand experience is consistently delivered as intended. Hiring employees who are category enthusiasts ensures knowledge, passion, credibility, and the ability to communicate more easily with customers and potential customers. It also helps you tap into customer networks more easily. This is important across functions—from product development, sales, and customer service to marketing research, quality control, and senior management. For example, Oakley looks for employees who have a serious interest in sport. Southwest Airlines hires people for their sense of humor and positive attitude.[1] Virgin Atlantic also hires people based on their congruence with company values.

At the Institute for International Research's *The Branding Trilogy* conference in Santa Barbara, California, Kristine Shattuck, Los Angeles area marketing manager for Southwest Airlines, put it well when she said, "Enthusiastic employees spread enthusiasm to customers. Market to your employees as much as your customers. If your employees don't 'get it,' neither will your customers."

You, your executive team, and all your organization's employees should share your passion about your brand each and every day. What story is uniquely your brand's own? Tell that story, and people will pass it on. As you know, "word of mouth" marketing is one of the more powerful forms of marketing. The story could spread to a key decision maker or an important influencer.

Also investigate possible organizational misalignments. At Hallmark, a key brand objective was to differentiate the Hallmark brand of greeting cards from the Ambassador brand of greeting cards, but products for both brands were developed in the same business units. Those business units had profit and loss responsibility, controlled all of the product development resources, and had sku (stock keeping unit) reduction goals that could not be accomplished except by combining skus across brands and removing the brand identity from the affected skus. That was a powerful incentive against brand differentiation.

Or consider the Hallmark licensing department. It had a strong incentive to license the Hallmark name out to any organization that was willing to pay the appropriate royalties (whether or not the product category was right for the Hallmark brand). Why? Because it was not managed as a part of a strategic brand development group but rather as a part of an independent division that was driven by revenue and profit generation goals. In both of these examples, the organizational design made it more difficult to achieve brand goals.

In both instances, education, persuasion, influencing, and constant communication from the brand group were required to ensure brand goals were not completely compromised. Educating division heads and other executives was a critical component of this. If they understand the importance of brand stewardship, it makes the brand manager's job much easier.

Employee morale is a very important element in maintaining a strong brand. It affects everything from quality of front line service and product defects to word-of-mouth negative comments about the company, some of which will eventually make it into the press (trade and general). It is often true that as you treat your employees, so they will treat your customers. Think about that. As you treat your employees, so they will treat your customers.

What are the ramifications of that for brand design and organizational design? Only an organization that authentically cares about its employees can demonstrate genuine concern for its customers.

Creating employee goodwill is very much linked to creating customer goodwill. At Element K, we offered our employees special touches, such as paid health club membership fees, Weight Watchers classes, on-site seated massages, company picnics, and holiday parties, as well as ice cream socials in the warmer months. I have also found that making insignia merchandise available to employees helps them share their pride about the brand and the company. "Learning maps" are increasingly used to roll out new or repositioned brands, especially when concurrent cultural changes are required.

A very recent trend in some companies is to include the human resource function as a part (and in support) of the marketing function. Michael Porter's customer value chain concept is based on the thought that every activity a company performs should add to customer value, or it should be eliminated. If a company has chosen the right promises for its brands, the concept could be adapted to say that all company activities should contribute to the delivery of brand promises or be eliminated—this includes operations, logistics, marketing and sales, human resource management, organization design, technology development, procurement, etc.

Brands typically are a company's most valuable assets, along with its people. In fact, the value of the brand asset often exceeds a company's annual sales. However, in many companies, people view brand management functions and activities as "overhead," implying they are expendable and non-value-added. (In contrast to this view, in the 1950s Peter Drucker stated that "marketing and innovation add value, everything else in the organization adds costs." He assumed marketing was integrated throughout the enterprise.) Accounting systems that categorize brand spending as "nonproduct" or "nondirect" expenses often reinforce the view of brand activities as "overhead." The long-term perspective of brand building also contributes to this view: A brand-building (or brand-diluting) activity typically does not produce visible results in the current quarter. The results are cumulative and are more visible over time.

If the brand is recognized for what it is—a very important asset that must be built, maintained, and leveraged—then people will begin to view brand activities and spending very differently. This must begin with the CEO and the CFO, but it should be a view shared by all employees. The CFO can become one of the biggest brand supporters if he or she is aware of the financial value of the brand asset. This is why measuring the value of the brand asset is so important.

The New Brand Management Paradigm

The most successful brand-building organizations are creating a new brand management paradigm. Increasingly, the brand is becoming the key source of differentiation that guides customer purchase choice. The brand is also the focal point around which an organization defines how it will uniquely deliver value to the customer for a profit. The brand embodies the "heart and soul" of an organization. Its promise is delivered through its products, services, and consumer communication—the total customer relationship and experience. If the brand promise is well conceived and consistently delivered through all business processes and customer contacts, the organization will grow and prosper.

Ultimately, you want to create a company full of brand maniacs, champions, and evangelists. Not until this happens can you be sure that you have developed a brand building organization.

Use the checklist in Exhibit 12-1 to assess the efficacy of your brand management practices in the area covered by this chapter. The more questions to which you can answer "yes," the better you are doing. The checklist also provides a brief summary of the material covered in the chapter.

EXHIBIT 12-1. BRAND MANAGEMENT CHECKLIST.

DEVELOPING A BRAND-BUILDING ORGANIZATION

	YES	NO
Do the CEO and other corporate officers embrace the brand as a key corporate asset that must be built and leveraged?		
Is your CEO's primary perspective that of brand marketing (versus finance, operations or something else)?		
Has your CEO "internalized" your brand's essence? Does your CEO "live" your brand's promise? Does your CEO personally reinforce the brand's intended personality?		
Does your CEO have a long-term vision for the brand?		
Does the CFO understand that the brand is an important corporate asset?		
Have you calculated the value of your brand as a financial asset? Are all corporate officers aware of this value?		
Do people in your organization know the difference between brand management and product management?		

Does a brand management process drive product decisions (rather than a product management process driving brand decisions)? _____ _____

Are there brand evangelists in your organization? Are there brand champions in senior management? Are your employees brand zealots? _____ _____

Have you identified potential allies outside of the brand management function who understand what you are trying to accomplish with the brand? Have you developed a plan to further indoctrinate them and to use them as brand advocates? Have you actively engaged them as brand advocates? _____ _____

Is there a formal process for managing your brands? _____ _____

Is there a person or group responsible for strategic oversight of your brands? Does this include oversight of individual subbrands? _____ _____

Is someone held accountable for managing your brand's personality? _____ _____

Do your senior managers own brand strategy (rather than a specific department or an ad agency owning it)? _____ _____

Do you manage your brands as a portfolio, versus allowing (or even encouraging) autonomy in the management of individual brands and subbrands? _____ _____

Are differentiating features reserved for the brands whose promises they best reinforce? Are you confident that there is no pressure to copy one brand's best competitive features for the organization's other brands and subbrands? _____ _____

In recruiting people for jobs in your organization, do you screen people for congruence between their beliefs, values and personality and your brand's essence, promise and personality? _____ _____

Do you have a comprehensive internal brand education and communication program? _____ _____

Do you have a published glossary of brand terms to ensure everyone in your organization is using the same nomenclature and the same definitions? _____ _____

Can all employees accurately and consistently articulate your brand's essence and promise? _____ _____

(continues)

EXHIBIT 12-1. (CONTINUED).

Do you test employees for their knowledge of the brand essence and promise? Do you regularly ask them what they are doing to deliver against the promise? _____ _____

Are your suppliers and other business partners well versed in your brand's essence and promise? _____ _____

Do you have a method in place to indoctrinate new employees on your brand's essence and promise? _____ _____

Do you tell stories to "drive home" your brand's promise and its importance to your company's future (in your internal communication)? _____ _____

Do your brand's essence and promise serve as rallying cries for your employees? Have you used the brand essence to galvanize and focus the activities of your organization's employees? Are your brand's essence and promise stated simply enough so that they are easy to remember? _____ _____

Do you tell your brand's story to as many people as you can each day (in your external communication)? _____ _____

Do you have a brand plan? _____ _____

Do your senior managers and corporate officers understand that designing your corporate brand (essence, promise, personality, etc.) is inextricably linked with crafting your corporate mission and vision? _____ _____

Is brand planning integrated as a key element of your business planning process? _____ _____

Does the brand promise drive all business decisions within your organization? _____ _____

Is "impact on brand equity" an important criterion in the following decision-making processes: capital investment, budget allocation, business development/ acquisition and cost reduction? _____ _____

Does *every* decision, action and communication produced by your organization reinforce your brand's essence, promise, personality and positioning? If not, can you identify each one that does not reinforce the brand's design and will you do something to correct it? _____ _____

Do your organization's quality standards align with
your customer's definition of quality? _____ _____

Is there a process by which all marketing elements are
integrated to deliver against the brand promise and
key brand priorities? _____ _____

Are there formal processes that enable you to manage
the brand across organizational boundaries? _____ _____

Do you constantly benchmark your brand practices
against other companies to ensure you are
incorporating best practices into your approach to
brand management? _____ _____

Are you personally a student of brand management
practices? Do you try to learn from the successes and
failures of other brands? _____ _____

Do your organization's common measures include
key brand measures? _____ _____

Are your compensation systems and career
advancement policies tied to advancing the brand
promise and achieving key brand goals? _____ _____

Do you offer special recognition for people who
successfully further brand goals? _____ _____

Do you know what functions in your value chain
contribute most to your consumer's experience of the
brand? Do you have a process to focus organizational
resources on those functions (and redirect them from
other nonessential functions)? _____ _____

Are you redesigning your business processes and
systems, networks of relationships, and customer
service functions to better align with and support your
brand's promise of differentiated consumer benefits? _____ _____

Does your organization structure support delivery of
the brand promise? _____ _____

Does the corporate culture reinforce the brand
promise? _____ _____

Is there a spirit of open communication and
cooperation between the brand management function
and the rest of the organization (versus conflicting
agendas, frequent misunderstandings, mistrust, and a
lack of cooperation)? _____ _____

(continues)

EXHIBIT 12-1. (CONTINUED).

Do people in your organization understand that brand building is a long-term exercise with cumulative results? ___ ___

Is your organization *as* focused on long-term brand building as it is on short-term sales promotion (in contrast to short-term performance goals largely superseding long-term brand building efforts)? ___ ___

Do you have a way of measuring return on marketing investment? ___ ___

Do you know if your brand keeps its promise at each point of contact it makes with consumers? ___ ___

Note

1. Adam Morgan, *Eating the Big Fish: How Challenger Brands Can Compete Against Brand Leaders* (New York: John Wiley, 1999), p. 199.

CHAPTER 13

Integrated Brand Marketing

ALTHOUGH BRAND IDENTITY management and advertising are two of the more important and visible components of brand management, I hope that by the time you have finished reading this book you will agree that brand management is much more holistic and interdependent than that.

For instance, a typical marketing budget is divided among the following activities: advertising, promotion, trade shows, lead generation, other sales support (collateral materials), Web site, Internet marketing, direct mail, telemarketing, publicity, brand identity management, and market research. Some companies devote marketing resources to pricing strategy/management, product marketing, channel marketing, and trade relations. If the company is a consumer products company, add packaging to that. If it has a retail component, add merchandising and possibly purchasing. Some organizations put sales under this umbrella as well. Don't forget about communicating with industry and financial analysts, too. Finally, add internal brand-building activities and brand management legal activities (trademarks, copyrights, etc.), and you have a very complicated, interdependent set of activities that require skill-specific subdisciplines and effective integrating mechanisms.

At most companies, not a day goes by that marketers are not trying to integrate one or more of these activities with other ones. Consider just one marketing discipline: trade shows. Trade shows support product marketing plans and help generate sales leads, which go into the marketing database. Trade shows must also reinforce the brand promise and the most recent brand advertising campaign.

Trade show marketing usually entails a carefully crafted integration of numerous marketing activities, such as:

✓ Inviting current and potential customers to your trade show booth and events through direct mailings, e-mail blasts, trade magazine ad inserts, and Web site announcements.

✓ Interacting with the trade press—maintaining relationships, providing company updates and pitching stories—and also using the shows to maintain relationships with industry analysts and business partners.

✔ Researching product innovations, potential partners, and competitors.

✔ Scheduling sales calls and demo products to potential customers.

✔ Timing of new product announcements and press conferences to occur while the show is in session.

✔ Timing of a local cause-related marketing activity to occur during the show to gain publicity in local newspapers.

✔ Paying to sponsor the show in return for many items of value to a brand building campaign, such as mailing lists, e-mail lists, a better booth floor position, workshop speaking slots, or having your logos plastered on trade show brochures, convention center banners, cyber café computers, buses, and a myriad of other things.

✔ Beefing up your advertising and editorial presence in that month's issue of trade magazines.

✔ Placing ads on convention center hotel room key cards or televisions.

Creative marketing may even include buying outdoor advertising along the route between the convention center and the convention center hotels. With all of these activities, remember, however, that each trade show must have a simple and coherent set of messages. Also remember that trade shows are just one marketing tactic in a brand-building campaign!

Effective Integrating Mechanisms

When integrating your brand marketing efforts, here are some mechanisms you may find useful:

✔ Create a well-communicated brand-positioning statement that includes the target customer and the brand essence, promise, and personality.

✔ Conduct a brand-positioning workshop with organization senior managers, if necessary to build consensus.

✔ Place a brand-marketing visionary at the top of at least the marketing organization (marketing VP or chief marketing officer), or better yet (from a marketer's perspective)—at the top of the enterprise.

✔ Provide the chief marketing officer with as broad a span of control as possible (encompassing as many of the disciplines listed above as possible) and with frequent forums for communicating about marketing issues and initiatives with other senior leaders of the organization.

✔ Set specific brand-management and marketing objectives (long term and short term).

✔ Create a brand-marketing plan.

✔ Integrate brand plans with organization strategic plans.

✔ Establish product, program, and segment marketing plans (driven by or at least congruent with brand marketing plans).

✓ Develop marketing budgets allocated by market segment and subdiscipline (with 10 percent to 20 percent of the overall budget held by the chief marketing officer for unforeseen opportunities).

✓ Develop integrated media plans.

✓ Set up an intranet (or extranet) site devoted to the brand identity standards and systems (and any other published brand information of use to broad audiences).

✓ Set up digital brand asset-management systems (to manage organizations with decentralized marketing control).

✓ Create a brand-identity council comprised of brand management personnel, general managers, and creative directors from each of the organization's divisions.

✓ Hold frequent marketing update meetings for heads of each of the marketing subdisciplines (for people to keep informed about what others are doing).

✓ Hold quarterly marketing planning sessions.

✓ Hold brand management forums or summits at least twice a year.

✓ Situate marketing people as close together as possible.

✓ Situate marketing people close to sales people.

✓ Situate marketing people close to product development people.

✓ Situate marketing people close to customer service people.

✓ Provide monthly or quarterly updates on progress against marketing objectives.

✓ Broadly disseminate brand management and marketing monthly reports.

✓ Carefully script the sales force on the brand story.

✓ Send frequent marketing communications to the field sales force.

✓ Use as few advertising and other marketing agencies as possible. Some organizations will find that using a single full-service advertising/marketing agency will help to integrate their marketing effort with a single brand voice and visual style. Others will find that it is best to use multiple agencies with best-in-class services in specific areas—brand advertising, collateral materials, direct mail, public relations, etc. Those that choose to do the latter put a greater burden on internal efforts to integrate brand marketing.

✓ Designate one internal copywriter and one internal graphic designer as keepers of the brand voice and visual style.

✓ Designate one brand management person as the ultimate enforcer of the brand identity standards. That person should be widely respected throughout the organization, possess outstanding interpersonal skills, and be very assertive.

✔ Train every marketer to always ask, "Have I reinforced the brand promise in this decision or activity?"

The smaller the organization (especially those with under 150 employees), the easier it is to integrate marketing activities across the organization. The larger the organization, the more the integration will need to rely on formal processes and procedures.

Use the checklist in Exhibit 13-1 to assess the efficacy of your brand management practices in the area covered by this chapter. The more questions to which you can answer "yes," the better you are doing. The checklist also provides a brief summary of the material covered in the chapter.

EXHIBIT 13-1. BRAND MANAGEMENT CHECKLIST.

INTEGRATED BRAND MARKETING

	YES	NO
Does our brand always speak with one voice to our customers?	_____	_____
Do we routinely integrate multiple marketing disciplines to achieve brand goals?	_____	_____
Does everyone in our organization and do all of our business partners know our brand's essence, promise and personality?	_____	_____
When we develop brand marketing programs, do we start with the brand marketing objectives and brainstorm the most effective ways to achieve them (versus immediately applying a particular technique such as advertising or direct mail)?	_____	_____
Do most of the marketing people in our organization know what most of the other marketing people are working on at any point in time?	_____	_____
Do marketing people from various disciplines and divisions in our organization frequently collaborate and help one another?	_____	_____
Are your sales promotions designed to help build the brand (or at least not to diminish it)?	_____	_____
Is there a lot of cross-functional teamwork in your organization?	_____	_____
Are people in your organization working against common goals?	_____	_____

CHAPTER 14

Creating the Total Brand
Experience

ULTIMATELY, EVERYTHING—products, services, retail environment, corporate culture, front line employees, marketing, etc.—must come together to create the total brand experience.

Starbucks

Starbucks does this well. Not only is their product extraordinarily different from and better than a normal cup of coffee, but everything else they do also adds to the brand experience. Their stores feature the following carefully crafted, aesthetically coordinated components: the smell of fresh brewed coffee, a wide variety of unusual blends, exotic names (Venti Mocha Frappuccino®), fresh pastries, piped-in jazz, comfortable wing chairs, a fireplace (some stores), live music (some stores), functional but stylish lighting, sophisticated sign graphics, stylish merchandising, etc.

Starbucks store designers must first work behind the counter for a while to better understand the in-store experience. And, their employees (called "partners") receive extensive brand and customer service training and stock options to ensure the quality of the customer experience in the store. On their Web site, they devote space to the history and mystique of coffee brewing. Starbucks delivers an affordable indulgent experience. Everything is designed to make you feel sophisticated in a warm and inviting way.[1] (Buy a cup of Starbuck's coffee and you are swept away from the ordinary for a while!)

Saturn

Saturn offers another example of a company where people carefully thought through the total brand experience. They extensively reengineered their operations to radically alter the consumer car purchase experience (A "different

Engineering the Starbucks Experience

✓ Starbucks brand is its product, its people, and its in-store experience.

✓ *Starbuck's promise*: For curious and discerning adults, Starbucks provides the best coffee experience that enriches lives.

✓ Starbucks strives to create an inviting, enriching experience that is stylish and elegant and that provides people with respite, time out and a personal treat. The experience is designed to enhance sensory signals.

✓ Starbucks romances coffee drinking. It encourages its employees to approach coffee with a wine steward mentality.

✓ Involvement and personal interaction is key to the Starbucks experience. Starbucks strives to be authentic and stand for something through passionate and committed employees. It promotes treating people with respect and dignity.

(*Source:* Excerpted from Nancy Barnet's [strategic liaison director, Starbucks Coffee Company] presentation at the 2002 Summit on Internal Communications, October 22, 2002, Chicago, Ill.)

kind of (car) company"). To make the promise of "salespeople as friends" real, Saturn not only established a "no haggle" pricing policy, it also put the following in place to ensure that salespeople would adhere to that policy:[2]

✓ Restructured compensation packages that emphasized salary over sales commission
✓ Selling Saturn dealerships in groups by region to eliminate the incentive to use price discounting to pull business away from the Saturn dealership "down the road"
✓ Extensive salesperson training
✓ Communicating the approach to external audiences

Ten Thousand Waves

Ten Thousand Waves, a spa in Santa Fe, is a case study in creating sensory experience. From its hillside setting, carefully designed layout, architecture, interior design, landscaping, use of water and gardens, fragrant trees, outdoor lanterns, shampoo (scented with real cedar), hand soap (scented with real coconut), in-room fireplaces, hot tubs, massage sessions, etc., it addresses every human sense in a very sensual and spiritual way.

Automobile Manufacturers

Automobile manufacturers have gotten much better at creating the total brand experience, from the product to the purchase experience. Automobile designers now consider such factors as ergonomics; textures; the propensity of fabrics and other surfaces to maintain comfortable temperatures throughout the year; the "feel" of knobs, buttons and other controls; the look of the car itself (consider the PT Cruiser or the new VW Beetle); minimization of road noises; quality of stereo systems and radio reception; road handling; and responsiveness to controls. And automobile manufacturers have adopted lessons from Saturn's purchase experience success.

Musical Groups

Consider another example—musical groups as brands. Have you ever attended a concert that you will never forget? Was the music powerful? Did it speak to you in a way that is difficult to describe? Did the group establish a rapport with the audience that made everything feel completely in sync? Did you find that you could not help but move to the rhythm of their beat? Was their show multisensory? Did they use lights and other special effects? Did their music evoke strong emotions? Did their music make you think about things differently? Did you completely lose track of time? Did you not want the concert to end? What if your brand could accomplish some of these same ends?

Creating the Optimal Brand Experience

How do you create an optimal brand experience? First, ask the following questions:

- ✔ Will the experience impact all of the human senses: sight, sound, scent, taste, and feel?
- ✔ How will it make people feel?
- ✔ Will people want to linger with your brand's products and services?
- ✔ Will people want to use the brand often? Will they want to return frequently (for applicable product/service categories)? Will they look forward to using the brand's products and services again?

✓ Does your brand reinforce something about who your customers are?

✓ Does your brand have a strong "point of view?" Does it stand for something? Is it clear what it cares about?

✓ Is your brand exciting, soothing, exhilarating, fun, comforting, relaxing, stimulating, centering, calming, rejuvenating, etc.?

✓ Will your brand conjure up images in your customers' minds? Will it evoke memories?

✓ Will your brand have the power to take people to "a different place?" Can it put them "in a different state of mind?" Will it have the power to change their mood?

✓ Will your brand make people feel as though they belong to something important or good or newsworthy?

Use Exhibit 14-1 as a guide in designing a total brand experience.

▓ Crisis Management

Although all organizations intend to create the best possible customer experiences, occasionally something real or perceived happens that produces just the opposite effect: a crisis. Every brand will experience a crisis at one time or another. The hallmark of a strong brand is how well it handles those crises.

The crisis could come as a result of something the company does (such as the Exxon Valdez disaster) or something that is foisted upon it (rumors that McDonald's' hamburgers are made of worms). But, when a crisis occurs, it is time to enact a well-rehearsed crisis management plan.

So, think about a crisis management now (hopefully, long before any actual crisis), and begin with the following considerations:

✓ Steadily and consistently build brand goodwill over time.

✓ Identify and address potential problem areas ahead of any actual crises.

✓ Have a well-thought-through crisis (or emergency response) plan, including scenarios, step-by-step instructions on how to best address each scenario, approved spokespeople, contact information, and key communication documents (fact sheets, backgrounders, press releases, bios, etc.).

✓ Work with crisis management experts and your legal staff in developing those plans.

✓ Conduct crisis management drills at least once a year.

✓ Conduct a crisis vulnerability audit.

✓ During the crisis itself, follow these general rules:

  ✓ Follow your crisis plan.

  ✓ Identify your spokespeople.

  ✓ Respond quickly.

  ✓ Be honest. Don't deny or cover things up—ultimately, they will be exposed.

EXHIBIT 14-1. DESIGNING THE TOTAL BRAND EXPERIENCE.

Purchase Cycle Phase	Pre-purchase		Point of Purchase	Post-purchase			
	Creating Awareness	Developing Preference	Stimulating the Purchase	Reinforcing the Purchase Immediately After Purchase	Reinforcing the Purchase During Usage	Other Post-Purchase Reinforcement	Nurturing Ongoing Loyalty
Generic Tactics	Advertising Publicity Direct mail Conferences Trade shows Seminars Articles Reviews Creating "buzz" Heavy user/expert previews	Relevant differentiation supported by strong proof points and "reasons to believe" Distinctive/value-added product/service bundling Designing the brand as a badge	Persuasive salesperson Persuasive signing Persuasive merchandising Persuasive purchase environment Customer touches/feels/tries product In-home trials Price discounts Value added products and services Product customization Customer co-creates product Testimonials Guarantees Product layaways Favorable financing/payment terms	Thank you notes Thank you gifts Follow up phone calls—soliciting satisfaction feedback Coupons for free or reduced price add-ons or upgrades Coupons for free or reduced price servicing	Superior product performance Product sensory experience Product itself thanks the customer for using it Account statements used to reinforce brand equity drivers Superior ongoing customer service and technical support	Newsletters Customer events Advertising Publicity Product/service awards/rankings Product reviews	Membership clubs Customer events Ongoing dialog with customer Put customer on your advisory council Customer co-creates product enhancements Customer helps you envision new products Free or reduced price performance upgrades Invite customer to refer your brand to others

This process is a continuous loop. It is important to generate ideas and develop actions to reinforce the five brand equity drivers—awareness, accessibility, value, relevant differentiation, and emotional connection—in an integrated and cost-efficient fashion throughout the purchase process. This includes helping the brand to become more emotional, experiential, and self-expressive, and finding ways to stimulate as many senses as possible.

✔ Accept responsibility as appropriate.

✔ Share as much information as is possible and prudent.

✔ Let people know what you are doing to manage the situation.

✔ Show concern for those affected.

✔ Let people know what you are doing to help people who are negatively impacted.

✔ Explain what you are doing to cooperate with the authorities.

✔ Let people know if neighbors or others are in danger and what they can do about it.

✔ Provide the media with telephone and Internet access and the other tools that they need to perform their jobs.

✔ Provide frequent updates to keep the communication lines open.

✔ Act with integrity, reinforcing the brand's personality.

If not handled well, a crisis can undo years of brand equity building. According to Bob Roemer—responsible for BP-Amoco's public and government affairs worldwide emergency response capabilities—the key to effective crisis management is to offer maximum information with minimum delay. If you don't have a well-rehearsed plan, you should work with your public affairs department and a PR agency to develop one.

Use the checklist in Exhibit 14-2 to assess the efficacy of your brand management practices in the area covered by this chapter. The more questions to which you can answer "yes," the better you are doing. The checklist also provides a brief summary of the material covered in the chapter.

EXHIBIT 14-2. BRAND MANAGEMENT CHECKLIST.

CREATING THE TOTAL BRAND EXPERIENCE

	YES	NO
Have you designed (and implemented) the "total customer experience" for your brand?	____	____
Do you draw upon all of the human senses in creating your brand's customer experience?	____	____
Does your brand evoke strong positive emotions?	____	____
Does your brand make people feel good?	____	____
Does your brand consistently exceed people's expectations?	____	____
Does your brand create experiences that are memorable in the most positive sense?	____	____

Do people want to linger with your brand's products
and services?   _____ _____

Do people look forward to interacting with your brand
again and again?   _____ _____

Does your brand steadily and consistently build
goodwill over time?   _____ _____

If your brand is delivered through third parties, have
you put the proper training, control and feedback
mechanisms in place to ensure a consistent and
intended brand experience?   _____ _____

Do you have a written emergency response plan?
Does it include a checklist of key operational and
communication steps to be taken? Do you rehearse
the plan at least once a year?   _____ _____

Notes

1. Adam Morgan, *Eating the Big Fish: How Challenger Brands Can Compete against Brand Leaders* (New York: John Wiley, 1999), p. 33.
2. Morgan, *Eating the Big Fish*, p. 140.

PART FOUR

LEVERAGING
THE BRAND

CHAPTER 15

Brand Extension

A BRAND MAY enter new product categories, new product formats within a category (line extension), or new markets or market segments. Examples of the latter include taking a brand currently targeted to women and extending it to the male market, or taking a brand that currently appeals to adults and extending it to the teen market.

Another example of extending a brand into new markets is extending it down from its current position to the value segment or up from its current position to the premium segment. Often, to designate a premium version or offering, special words or phrases are used in association with the brand name—words such as gold, platinum, limited edition, signature collection, premier, elite, marquis, reserve, private, professional, executive class, etc. But, in general, the more subtle the allusion to a brand's premium status, the more effective the approach.

The brand can be extended with or without using another associated brand. If another brand is used, it may be a subbrand or a brand endorsed by the original brand. Another option is cobranding. Hallmark created the "Confections" subbrand to extend into gift candies, but it did so in conjunction with Fannie Mae's Celebrated Collection (premium) subbrand. The product is cobranded with each company's brand and subbrand. Cobranding may be a faster way to enter a new category and gain credibility within it.

Ways to Extend the Brand

Regardless of the branding treatment, extensions can occur in the following ways:

- ✓ You manufacture the product (or supply the service) yourself.
- ✓ You acquire a company that makes the product (or supplies the service).
- ✓ You source the product or service from some other organization, but put your name on it.

✓ You license your name for use by another company that makes the product or supplies the service. Use brand licensing to extend the brand into new categories, expand the meaning of the brand, reinforce key brand associations, build your brand as a badge, or bring your brand to life in new ways. You should avoid licensing your brand where it doesn't make sense just to make a few extra revenue dollars. Where the licensing department resides in your organization structure will have a large impact on how well licensing is used to build (versus bleed) the brand.

✓ You form an alliance or joint venture with another company to supply the product or service.

Obviously, the pros and cons of the various methods include speed to market, fit with core competencies, upside revenue and profit potential, asset risk, amount of control over the brand delivery, and the degree to which you are committed to the category in the long term.

Did You Know?

- ✔ Typically, it costs between $75 and $100 million to launch a new (mass consumer) brand. (*Source*: Brian Wansink, "Making Old Brands New," *American Demographics*, December 1997, p. 53.)

- ✔ The more extended a brand becomes, the more it needs subbrands to aid with its extensions.

Benefits of Brand Extension

Launching new products and services under (or linked to) an existing brand, if done properly, significantly decreases perceived customer risk and increases product/service acceptance, all at a fraction of the cost that it would have taken to launch a new brand. In addition to generating incremental revenue and profit for your brand, brand extensions can be beneficial in the following ways:

✓ Helping to clarify and broaden brand meaning to consumers (for instance, extending Hallmark into candy and flowers may help redefine the brand, expanding it from "greeting cards" to "ways to show you care")

✔ Reinforcing and building upon key brand associations

✔ Extending the brand's reach and relevance to new consumers

✔ Creating brand "news"/"buzz"

✔ Laying the groundwork for future extensions

Risks of brand extension include the following:

✔ Creating confusion regarding brand meaning

✔ Tarnishing the quality image

✔ Conflicting with or counteracting key brand associations

✔ Creating new, undesired brand associations

✔ "Turning off" current key consumer segments

✔ If done in great excess with no focus, completely diluting brand meaning and overexposing the brand in the market place

▊ Dangers of Extending the Brand into a New Price Segment

One of the biggest dangers is a brand extension that repositions the parent brand in a negative light (like Bayer "aspirin-free" products or "Fat Free" Fig Newtons). One of the trickiest extensions is creating a "value" version of the parent brand. Extending your brand up to a premium segment or down to a value segment has the greatest potential for negative impact, as a brand's quality and value perceptions are often central to its positioning. You don't want to create the perception that the original brand was overpriced.

Often the best solution is creating a new brand or subbrand. If the market is moving away from your brand's position, it may be better in the long run, despite the cost, to create a new brand to meet and own the solution to the evolving needs of consumers. This is a more expensive approach with a higher probability of failure *and* is not a brand extension.

▊ Linking Previously Unlinked Brands

If your company has just acquired another company or is considering entering a strategic alliance with another company, research is required to determine how, if at all, the brands should be linked—cobrand, parent brand/subbrand, endorsed brand, one brand replaces the other, create a new brand, etc.

By understanding the impact of each branding approach on the following, it should help you decide the best approach to take.

✔ The essence, promise, personality and positioning of each brand involved

✔ The perceptions of the products and services sold under each brand name

Brand Extensions and Global Branding

If you are in the process of building your brand globally, especially if your brand is in its infancy in some regions or countries, here is something else to watch out for with brand extensions. If a particular extension, especially one less central to the brand's promise, has a strong presence in a market place before you have a chance to establish the brand essence, promise, and core meaning in that market place, it could be much more difficult to position the brand correctly. It would be better to withhold that extension from the market place until the core brand meaning is established there.

Brand Extension Questions

You should answer these questions as you consider each possible brand extension:

✔ **Business Questions**
  ✔ How "big" is the category or segment?
  ✔ Is the category or segment new?
  ✔ Is it growing?
  ✔ Is there "room" in the category or segment for a new brand?
  ✔ Do you have or can you acquire the assets and competencies necessary to compete successfully in the new category or segment?
  ✔ Have you identified a profitable and robust business model for competing in the new category or segment?
  ✔ What type of competitive reaction might you expect as your brand enters the new category or segment?
✔ **Brand Questions**
  ✔ What are your brand's primary benefits?
  ✔ Does the brand uniquely own those benefits?
  ✔ Do those benefits matter in the new category?
  ✔ Do they matter enough vis-à-vis other (competitive) brands' benefits to make your brand preferable, at least among some subsegment of the category?
  ✔ What impact would entry into the new category have on your brand's essence, promise, and equity?

Brand Extension Steps

Brand extension work often starts with a brand asset study to identify the most promising avenues for brand extension (see Chapter 17 on Brand Research). This is often followed by concept development and screening— from simple "trigger" concepts (a simple, several-word concept description, often not even in sentence form) used in focus groups to "ad form" concepts (a concept that is more fully developed to look like a full-page print ad, typically with a couple of paragraphs of copy and a visual) tested quantitatively against a normative database. Next steps often include developing business and marketing plans (including pro-forma financial statements) for the most promising concepts and then more formal funding reviews and approvals leading to prototyping and eventually market testing.

It is important to pursue brand extensions in a very methodical order so that each extension builds upon the previous one. Know where you ultimately want to take the brand, but do it in steps that build upon one another. For instance, corn flakes → cereals → breakfast foods.

Developing Brand Extension Concepts

The concepts must be developed in a standard fashion to allow for comparison. (Do not stack the odds in your favorite concept's favor by reserving score-enhancing adjectives or superlatives only for that concept.) The ideas should be both "close in" and "far out" to determine brand boundaries and associated risks. They can take the form of "trigger" concepts to "ad form" concepts. Visuals often help in communicating the idea. Ideally, the concepts are presented in the context of a competitive set to allow for comparison.

Concept Screening

You should compare the brand extension concepts to current offerings in the category (and to a normative database of other previously successful concepts) on the following dimensions:

- ✔ Purchase intent
- ✔ Benefit importance within the category
- ✔ Need intensity
- ✔ Degree of satisfaction with existing alternatives—category gap
- ✔ Concept uniqueness
- ✔ Likes (open-ended question)
- ✔ Dislikes (open-ended question)

Many companies offer their own versions of this concept-testing methodology (usually with very large normative data bases). We used The Landis

Group's and Home Testing Institute's methodologies at Hallmark, but there are many others.

Other important areas to explore when concept screening is part of a broader brand-extension evaluation:

- ✓ Concept strengths and weaknesses vis-à-vis competitive concepts
- ✓ Benefits/attributes being transferred by the brand to the new category
- ✓ Importance/motivational strength of the benefits being transferred
- ✓ Impact of the extension on the parent brand
- ✓ Ability of the brand extension to draw new consumers to the brand franchise

Successful Brand Extensions

Here are some examples of successful brand extensions:

- ✓ Jell-O (pudding, pudding snacks)
- ✓ Crayola (markers, pens, and paints)
- ✓ Dole (pineapple juice, fruit juice, fruit salad, fruit juice frozen fruit bars)
- ✓ Ivory (soap, dishwashing liquid, gentle care detergent)
- ✓ Woolite (fabric wash, carpet cleaner spray)
- ✓ Arm & Hammer (toothpaste)

Question: For each brand, what was the transferable core-brand association that made a successful extension possible?

Unsuccessful Brand Extensions: Some Examples

- ✓ Bic perfume (Leveraging the "small disposable pocket items" association???)
- ✓ Levi's tailored classic suits: What is Levi's primary association? (casual clothes)
- ✓ Campbell spaghetti sauce: Why didn't "tomato sauce" transfer from Campbell's soups to spaghetti sauce?
- ✓ McDonald's Arch Deluxe (for adults): What is McDonald's primary association? (fast-food for kids)
- ✓ Bayer "Aspirin-free": What is Bayer's primary association? (aspirin)
- ✓ Volvo 850 GLT sports sedan: What is Volvo's primary association? (safety) What is a primary proof point? (boxy armored-car styling)

✓ Or, my all time favorite, New Coke: What is Coke? ("it's the real thing"—with its long-time secret formula)

The Most Common Brand-Extension Problems

Some of the most common problems with brand extension are:

✓ Extending into a category in which the brand adds nothing but its identity (its products or services are not significantly different from current products or services in the category)

✓ Extending through opportunistic brand licensing without regard to its possible impact on the brand

✓ Extending into lower (and, sometimes higher) quality segments

✓ Not fully understanding brand benefit ownership, transfer, or importance

Evaluating Brand-Extension Concepts

Exhibit 15-1 is a rudimentary matrix that I use to focus clients on the most important questions when evaluating brand extension opportunities. The number of benefits included in the matrix and the weighting of each criterion will vary by client.

Generic New Business Strategies

Whether trying to grow your business through brand extension or by launching new brands, the following are generic approaches to creating new businesses:

✓ Identifying gaps in your product/service portfolio (for the category as currently defined)

✓ Identifying current consumers' unsatisfied needs

✓ Addressing emerging consumer needs

✓ Expanding the definition of your brand's category

✓ Exploiting an expanded brand identity

✓ Exploiting channel opportunities (new distribution)

EXHIBIT 15-1. BRAND EXTENSION EVALUATION MATRIX.

Potential Category for Extension	Category A	Category B	Category C	Category D	Category E	Category F	Category G
Category Size (20)							
Category Growth Rate (10)							
Category Profit Potential (20)							
Primary Brand Benefit Matter in Category? (15)							
Uniquely Own Primary Brand Benefit in Category? (10)							
Secondary Brand Benefit Matter in Category? (10)							
Uniquely Own Secondary Brand Benefit in Category? (5)							
Other Brand Associations Matter in Category? (10)							
Uniquely Own Other Brand Associations in Category? (5)							
Extension Reinforce Brand Essence and Promise? (20)							
Extension Provide Flexibility for Future Growth? (20)							
TOTAL (145)							

- ✓ Applying new technologies
- ✓ Targeting new consumer groups

When developing your growth strategies, you should clarify whether the growth will come primarily from existing customers, competitors' customers, or nonusers. The tactics will vary greatly for each.

Use the checklist in Exhibit 15-2 to assess the efficacy of your brand management practices in the area covered by this chapter. The more questions to which you can answer "yes," the better you are doing. The checklist also provides a brief summary of the material covered in the chapter.

EXHIBIT 15-2. BRAND MANAGEMENT CHECKLIST.

BRAND EXTENSION

	YES	NO
Have you identified what your brand owns in the consumer's mind?	____	____
Have you identified all areas in which the consumer gives your brand permission to operate?	____	____
Do you have a clear understanding of whether your brand is over- or underextended?	____	____
Have you identified all the ways your brand and others in its category have made compromises with the consumer? Have you found ways to redefine your business to break those compromises?	____	____
Have you identified new categories for growth? Can you create new categories that meet previously unmet consumer needs?	____	____
Have you targeted new market segments to which you would like your brand to appeal?	____	____
Have you explored ways to make your brand more relevant to the next generation of consumers?	____	____
Do you know what must be done to ensure the parent brand maintains a relationship with the consumer throughout his or her life (cradle-to-grave marketing)?	____	____
Do you have a plan that specifies what categories your brand will enter next, in what order it will enter them and on what time frame?	____	____
Have you considered taking your brand global as an alternative growth strategy to brand extension?	____	____
Do you have a way to screen all new brand extension proposals for their congruence with the brand promise and impact on brand equity?	____	____
Are you sure that the brand's positive associations will not become negative when associated with a new product category?	____	____
Have you thoroughly researched how proposed brand extensions might reposition the original brand in consumers' minds?	____	____

(continues)

EXHIBIT 15-2. (CONTINUED).

Have you considered acquisition as a way to extend the brand?	_____	_____
Do you have a brand licensing department? Does that department have strict guidelines for licensing your brands out in order to ensure brand image is not hurt and brand meaning is not diluted?	_____	_____
Have you developed decision criteria to determine whether an extension (a) uses an existing brand or (b) requires a new brand and, if (b), whether the new brand is (c) a subbrand or (d) an endorsed brand?	_____	_____
Do you have organizational mechanisms to screen, test, and launch brand extensions?	_____	_____
Do you test each new product or service for its impact on your brand's equity (quality, value, reinforcement of brand essence, promise and personality, etc.)?	_____	_____

CHAPTER 16

Global Branding

WHILE MANY CONSUMER goods markets in the West are stagnating, 65 percent of the world's population is living in societies that are experiencing economic growth of 5 percent or more a year. While the baby boom occurred between 1945 and 1960 in the United States, much of the rest of the world is still experiencing a baby boom that began in 1975. The average person has seen his or her standard of living double in the past fifteen years, far surpassing that of the United States or Western Europe. Put very simply, today most of the growth potential in consumer markets exists outside of the United States and Western Europe.

Benefits of Global Branding

In addition to taking advantage of the outstanding growth opportunities, the following benefits drive the increasing interest in taking brands global:

- ✓ Economies of scale (production and distribution)
- ✓ Lower marketing costs
- ✓ Laying the groundwork for future extensions worldwide
- ✓ Maintaining consistent brand imagery
- ✓ Quicker identification and integration of innovations (discovered world-wide)
- ✓ Preempting international competitors from entering domestic markets or locking you out of other geographic markets
- ✓ Increasing international media reach (especially with the explosion of the Internet)
- ✓ Increasing international business and tourism

When to Leverage a Single Brand Globally

A company is more likely to leverage a single brand globally if:

- ✓ It is already operating worldwide (one brand is more efficient)
- ✓ The brand is an extension of the owner and his or her personality
- ✓ The brand's relationship to its country of origin creates positive associations (like a watch brand from Switzerland or a gourmet food brand from France)

Global Brand Constants

At a minimum, when going global, the following elements should remain constant throughout the world:

- ✓ Corporate brand
- ✓ Brand identity system (especially your logo)
- ✓ Brand essence

Global Brand Variables

The following elements *may* differ from country to country:

- ✓ Corporate slogan
- ✓ Products and services
- ✓ Product names
- ✓ Product features
- ✓ Positionings
- ✓ Marketing mixes (including pricing, distribution, media and advertising execution)

These differences will depend upon:

- ✓ Language differences
- ✓ Different styles of communication
- ✓ Other cultural differences
- ✓ Differences in category and brand development
- ✓ Different consumption patterns
- ✓ Different competitive sets and marketplace conditions
- ✓ Different legal and regulatory environments
- ✓ Different national approaches to marketing (media, pricing, distribution, etc.)

Language Translation

A key question in global branding is this: Do you translate the brand name into the local language or keep it in the original language? You should probably keep it in the original language if (a) there is no intrinsic meaning and it is easy to pronounce or (b) global awareness of the brand name is already high. You should consider translating the name into the local language if it is suggestive of a key benefit (that would be lost if the original name were used).

Global Branding Questions

Other key questions when considering global branding are:

- Have you identified the relative attractiveness of each market for your brand (and have you identified consistent criteria for doing so)?
- Have you conducted an attitude and usage study in each country whose market you are considering entering?
- Do you know the category and brand development indices in each country in which you operate?
- Do you have a global branding scorecard that can be applied country by country?
- Do you have agreement on which decisions are made centrally and which ones are made locally?

Here are some other considerations when taking a brand global:

- Because of the extended global baby boom, youth marketing is a huge opportunity. Brand names, designer labels, and other forms of status will play well to the global youth market, in general.
- Global advertising needs to consider the fact that, for much of the world, the economy is booming and the context is unprecedented optimism. The increasing international tensions caused by terrorism and the volatile situations in Iraq and North Korea notwithstanding, the economies of many nations continue this growth.
- The world's consumers are not naïve. Much of the world has access to English-language television programs.
- Start marketing in countries before their spending power is fully realized. Due to media exposure, people are forming their brand opinions now.
- Representing male/female relationships appropriately will vary from society to society, so be sure that you fully understand the local cultures before attempting to do so.

✔ Using distributors is frequently a good way to break into foreign markets. It is critically important to choose the right distributor when trying to enter a new market.

Ultimately, there is much to be gained by extending your brand globally. The saying "think globally, act locally" makes much sense in this context. The key is determining what elements you will tailor for local markets. That depends upon a thorough understanding of the similarities and differences among the local markets you intend to serve.

Did You Know?

✔ **"Purchase intent" tends to be inflated for declining brands and understated for emerging brands.**

✔ **Advertising is often most effective in increasing share of market when brands are so similar that the advertising message is the primary source of differentiation. (*Source*: John Ehrenberg, Neil Barnard, and John Scriven, "Differentiation or Salience," *Journal of Advertising Research,* November–December 1997, p. 12.)**

CASE STUDY

Leveraging the Brand Case Study:
Hallmark

In the early to mid-1990s, an ever-increasing share of greeting card sales occurred in the mass channels. Wal-Mart alone was projected to achieve a 20 percent share of the total greeting card market by the year 2000. Three brands accounted for the vast majority of sales in these channels: American Greetings, Gibson, and Ambassador— Hallmark's flanker brand. (The sale of Hallmark-branded greeting cards accounted for no more than 20 percent of the overall market. Hallmark-branded products were sold primarily in Hallmark card shops and select chain drug stores. Hallmark's corporate share of greeting card sales was 39 percent including all brands, including Ambassador, Shoebox, etc.).

While Ambassador-brand sales were becoming an ever-increasing proportion of Hallmark's overall corporate sales, Ambassador's margins were eroding due to increased retailer leverage over manufacturers and heightened mass channel competition. This trend of a less and less profitable brand becoming a larger and larger share of corporate sales was not acceptable. We knew that more sophisticated contract negotiations and sales term innovations would not be enough to halt or reverse this negative trend. We had to do no less than change the rules of the game itself.

After some thought, we knew our only hope was to unleash the power of the Hallmark brand in the mass channel. But, that was tricky and unpopular as we did not want to undermine the success of the Hallmark card shops and chain drug stores—channels that were our "cash cows" and to which we felt a strong loyalty. We conducted the most extensive research in Hallmark's history to assess the impact of pursuing this strategy on Hallmark card shop and chain drug store sales—which turned out to be minimal. Nevertheless, prior to the launch of this strategy, we fortified the viability of these two channels through extensive store consolidation, marketing, merchandising, systems, and standards improvements, most notably through the development of the Hallmark Gold Crown program. And we expended great efforts to quantify and communicate the equity and power of the Hallmark name to the mass channel retailers. In fact, one mass channel retailer believed in the power of the Hallmark brand so much that it refused to switch to one of our competitor's brands in return for $100 million in sales term. (Greeting card manufacturers negotiate multiple-year contracts with mass channel retailers in which they receive most or all of a retailer's business for a specified minimum floor space and number of stores for a specified period of time. In return for that privilege, they pay substantial sales terms.)

Here is some salient information to help you understand the strategy: Hallmark's primary competitors had significantly reduced their costs by reducing their internal marketing research and creative development capabilities. They leveraged Hallmark's resources in this area (Hallmark employed over 700 artists and writers and 70 marketing researchers at the time) through well-constructed systems of emulation. All mass channel (non-Hallmark) brands had raised prices faster than inflation for a number of years, due to the apparent lack of price sensitivity for greeting cards (until the major price thresholds of $2 and $3 were surpassed) and the pressures applied by retailers for ever increasing year-over-year sales productivity gains. In fact, while over 65 percent of Hallmark-branded cards were priced *under* $2, 89 percent of competitive mass channel brand's cards were priced *over* $2. Competitors used their lower cost structures and higher product prices to fund ever-accelerating sales terms. They placed their bets that rich sales terms would buy distribution with major mass retail chains, which was in fact what was occurring.

Despite the fact that mass channel share was increasingly based upon which brand could write the biggest check, Hallmark was betting on the fact that it could change the rules by introducing the power of brand equity to the mass channel. After all, Hallmark is the only greeting card brand widely recognized by consumers. (It had unaided top-of-mind awareness of nearly 90 percent and Shoebox—a tiny little division of Hallmark—was the only other greeting card brand with significant top-of-mind awareness or preference.) Hallmark's product also was superior (validated by rigorous market research) and Hallmark products were priced lower than any other major competitive brand.

Compare this with what I was fond of saying about Hallmark's primary competitors to rally the internal troops around this strategy, "Would you rather be our competitors with overpriced, no name, inferior products?" If Hallmark could align consumer price perceptions with reality (Hallmark was perceived to be "expensive" by consumers), I knew we could win with this strategy. Our competitors (both public companies, one of which consistently touted quarter over quarter revenue and profit increases) were locked into multiple-year retailer contracts with very high sales terms. They would not be able to reduce prices without severely affecting their revenues, profits and stock prices.

I could devote at least a whole chapter to the nuances of this strategy, but suffice it to say that Hallmark's static 39 percent greeting card market share increased to 42 percent with increased profitability in the first two years after we implemented this strategy. Since then, Hallmark's share has steadily grown to 55 percent in a few short years. Unleashing the power of the Hallmark brand in the mass channel resulted in substantial market share and profitability gains for Hallmark without taking away from the success of the card shop and chain drug store channels. (Hallmark card shops achieved consistent month over month sales increases for at least three years during this period, validating my held belief that the added marketplace exposure to the Hallmark brand would have a positive impact on all channels carrying Hallmark products.)

Use the checklist in Exhibit 16-1 to assess the efficacy of your brand management practices in the area covered by this chapter. The more questions to which you can answer "yes," the better you are doing. The checklist also provides a brief summary of the material covered in the chapter.

EXHIBIT 16-1. BRAND MANAGEMENT CHECKLIST.

GLOBAL BRANDING

	YES	NO
Does your company operate as a global enterprise versus a domestic company that sells its products internationally or that has separate international operations?	____	____
Do you sell your brand in international markets?	____	____
Do you believe global expansion of your brand will be a significant source of revenue growth for your organization for the next few years?	____	____
If you have grown internationally through acquisition, have you either (a) replaced the local brands you purchased with your global brand (if the local brands did not have strong brand awareness or loyalty), or (b) linked your corporate or parent brand name to the local brand name (if the local brands did have high awareness and loyalty)?	____	____
Is your brand's market share as large or larger, on average, in international markets than it is in your domestic market?	____	____
Is your brand's awareness as high, on average, in international markets as it is in your domestic market?	____	____
Does your brand's essence remain the same throughout the world?	____	____
Have you investigated the meaning of your brand's name (and other nomenclature), symbols, colors and other brand identity elements in each country in which your brand is sold?	____	____
Does your brand's identity system work globally? Is it applied consistently throughout the world?	____	____
Do you have agreement on which decisions are made centrally and which ones are made locally? Is there sound logic underlying that agreement?	____	____
Have you identified the relative attractiveness of each market for your brand (and have you identified consistent criteria for doing so)?	____	____

(continues)

EXHIBIT 16-1. (CONTINUED).

Have you conducted an attitude and usage study in each country whose market you are considering entering?

Have you identified how each of the following vary from country to country (or from region to region): language, culture, consumption patterns, competitive set, marketplace conditions, legal environment, approaches to marketing, etc.?

Do you know the category and brand development indices in each country in which you operate?

Have you varied your approach to each of the following based on the above-mentioned national (or regional) differences: brand slogan, products and services, product names, product features, positionings, marketing mixes (pricing, distribution, media, and advertising)?

Have you made a conscious decision to either translate your brand name into the local language or keep it in the original language for each country in which your brand is sold?

Do you have a global branding scorecard that can be applied country by country?

Are you organized so that your brand and its business are managed globally? If not, is there good communication and cooperation between your domestic and international brand management functions?

If you use more than one advertising agency, do you coordinate the agencies' efforts to achieve an adequate level of consistency in communicating the brand's essence globally?

Would you describe your brand as a "global power brand"?

Note

1. Simon Silvester, "World Waves: Global Trends for Global Brands," Silvester Research, Ltd. www.silvester.com.

PART FIVE

BRAND
METRICS

Brand Research

PREVIOUS CHAPTERS TOUCHED upon research that can help with brand positioning and advertising. The next chapter covers brand equity research in depth. In this chapter, I highlight a number of other research techniques that can be helpful to the brand management process, beginning with brand asset research and followed by brand association measurement.

Brand Asset Research

Brand asset research is an important first step in brand extension. Brand asset research identifies and dimensionalizes a brand's meaning to consumers, including its elasticity across product and service categories. It identifies categories within which consumers give the brand permission to operate. (More often than you might expect, consumers will indicate that a brand offers products in a category that it does not. This clearly identifies "low hanging [brand extension] fruit.")

Typically, brand asset studies are conducted qualitatively (focus groups, mini-groups, one-on-one interviews, etc.) using the following techniques: word association, qualitative mapping, ranking various brands between contrasting viewpoints, brand extendibility probes, and (often in a second phase) identifying the appeal of various concepts as they relate to the brand in question. I have found that the best way to communicate the result is by mapping the categories, concepts, and attributes as they relate to the core essence of the brand.

Think of a dart board with the bull's eye being the brand's core essence. The concepts that are closer to the bull's eye are less risky brand extension opportunities. The ones further away risk diluting the brand's essence and have a greater chance of failure (see Figure 17-1).

Brand Association Measurement[1]

It is important to measure associations both *from* (When I say "Lexus," what comes to mind?) and *to* (When I say "luxury cars," what comes to mind?)

FIGURE 17-1. CORE ESSENCE OF A BRAND.

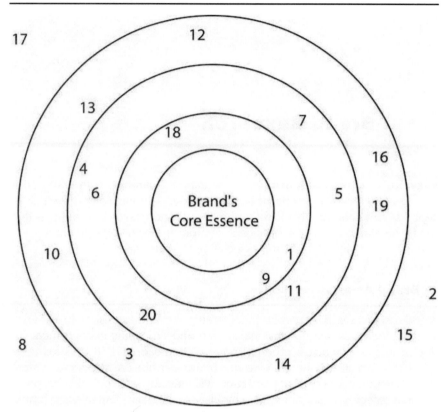

Each number represents a category, concept, feature, or benefit. Item numbers 1, 9, 11 and 18 have the best fit with the brand in question. The proximity of items 1, 9 and 11 to one another indicates that they may form a logical new business grouping.

the brand. Qualitative research is an effective starting point if little is known. Specific qualitative techniques can be used to solicit associations. The Zaltman Metaphor Elicitation Technique (ZMET) and other projective techniques are covered later in this chapter.

Information gathered by qualitative research must be quantified to lay the groundwork for developing successful brand extension concepts. You should consider using both open-ended and scaled responses. Following are three approaches to quantifying brand associations:

1. **Naming Method** (open ended): You present consumers with attributes. You then ask them to list the brands that come to mind. With this, you can measure both the order and frequency of recall.
2. **Latency Method** (close ended): You show consumers attributes (or category names) followed by brand names. The consumer

clicks "yes" or "no" for each brand indicating whether it is associated with each attribute or product category. The computer records the time it took the consumer to respond for each answer. This is particularly effective with broader and more abstract category labels, such as "healthy foods," "outdoor products," or "products to help you manage your relationships."

3. **Scaled Questions:** You can complement the two previous techniques with scaled questions, such as agree/disagree, or opposite pairs on statements regarding attributes, benefits, personality, etc. Include other brands to mask the brand in question. Choose brands that are key players in categories into which you are considering extending your brand.

Brand Extension Research: Final Steps

After the brand asset study is complete and you have measured brand associations, the next step in brand extension work typically is developing the most promising product concepts and then quantitatively screening them against the following criteria: need/need intensity, uniqueness, market gap/dissatisfaction with current alternatives, and purchase intent. It is best when the results can be compared to a normative database for the brand and other companies in other industries. The final step, for those concepts that make it through the previous hurdles, is to create one or more test markets (taking the research in phases to reduce investment risk).

Successful brand extensions tend to have three characteristics[2]:

1. **Perceptual Fit:** The consumer must perceive the new item to be consistent with the parent brand.
2. **Benefit Transfer:** A benefit offered by the parent brand must be desired by consumers of products in the new category.
3. **Competitive Leverage:** The new items must stack up favorably to established items in the new category.

Therefore, actionable quantitative brand extension research test should incorporate all three components. In particular, incorporating the competitive set for each concept is critical. Consumers evaluate new products in the real world in a competitive context, so they need to do the same in a research test.

Other Useful Research Approaches

At a minimum, in order to understand how consumers perceive your brand, you need to probe in depth their first, most powerful and most recent experiences with the brand. Following are some useful research approaches.

Customer Service Testing

Customer service has a huge impact on brand perceptions. Don't take someone else's word that it is working. As a brand marketer, you should test your customer service approaches at least a couple times a year by testing Web, telephone, and in-person customer and technical support (as applicable). Look for these things:

- ✓ How quickly and easily were you able to get your question answered or problem solved?
- ✓ Is customer service available 24/7?
- ✓ How long you were put on hold, if at all?
- ✓ How many steps did you have to go through to get your answer?
- ✓ Did you have to communicate the same information more than once (name, account number, telephone number, etc.)?
- ✓ How friendly and helpful was the human interaction?
- ✓ Were you treated like an intelligent adult?

Brand Inundation/Deprivation Testing

Do you want to better understand the benefits your brand's product or service delivers? Do you want to discover ways to increase use of your brand's products and services? Try this: Identify a group of very light users and ask them to use your product or service as frequently as your heaviest users do for an extended period of time (at least through several usage cycles). Identify a group of heavy users and ask them to refrain from using your product or service for the same period of time. Ask the latter group to articulate what they used in lieu of your product or service to accomplish the same result. Ask both groups to keep a journal of their thoughts and feelings as they use or refrain from using your product or service. Follow up with in-depth one-on-one interviews to better understand the role your brand's products and services play in their lives. I guarantee you that this exercise will provide profound insight into the full potential for your brand's products and services.

Archetype Discoveries Worldwide

Archetype Discoveries Worldwide (www.archetypediscoveriesworldwide.com) was founded by Dr. C.G. Rapaille, the author of *The Seven Secrets of Marketing*. It offers the "best current approach to uncovering the unspoken needs of the customer or employees," according to Procter & Gamble, which has commissioned more than thirty-two Archetype Discoveries in recent years. In contrast to traditional marketing research firms, Archetype Discoveries does not rely on what people say. Instead these studies use a unique blend of biology, cultural anthropology, psychology, and learning theories to discover the hidden cultural forces that preorganize the way people behave toward a product, service or concept. Unlike opinions that can change in a minute, cultural archetypes are deeply imprinted in people's minds and strongly rooted in cultural codes. If these "mental highways" and cultural forces change, it is at a glacial pace. The results form a permanent platform for marketing, new product design, innovation, and improvement of products or processes, and for more effective communication strategies. Therefore they are particularly useful for marketing managers, planners, product designers, change agents, advertisers, and public policy makers. Archetype Discoveries has conducted over 200 discoveries, in more than twenty countries, for such diverse products, services, and concepts as: perfume, toys, cheese, security, quality improvement, nuclear power, automotive industry, credit cards, mergers, coffee, teenage pregnancy, and forests.

The Zaltman Metaphor Elicitation Technique

An interesting technique for discovering how consumers think about brands is the Zaltman Metaphor Elicitation Technique (ZMET)—developed by Jerry Zaltman of Harvard Business School and Robin Higie Coulter of the University of Connecticut. The technique is largely informed by "neuroscience, semiotics, and the ideas of Carl Jung,"[3] and it combines neurobiology, psychoanalysis, linguistics, and art theory to try to uncover the mental models that guide brand purchase behavior. This research recognizes that consumers can't easily access or articulate the underlying motivations to their behaviors. They must be drawn out in other ways. It taps into unconscious thoughts that are believed to be largely visual. Study participants are asked to take photographs or collect pictures that say something about the brand in question. They return for one-on-one personal interviews that include story telling, sorting the pictures into what will become mental maps, answering a series of probing questions, creating collages that summarize their thoughts, and creating a vignette that highlights important brand issues (among other possible exercises).

Other Approaches

Other approaches to better understanding consumer behavior include purchase diaries; spending time in participants' homes with them; shopping with participants; asking participants to spend a few weeks collecting photographs of whatever they would like, and later discussing the pictures in interviews; checking participants' closets, pantries, and cabinets; and even analyzing their household trash. Another approach is to create detailed identities for each of your target consumers and role-play each one for a day, including shopping for or using products in your category. Much of this is *ethnography*: putting yourself in the consumers' shoes by observing their brand shopping and usage patterns in real life situations.

Using the Internet

Most companies devote substantial marketing research resources to keeping in touch with their consumers. And yet, the Internet provides for a 24/7 interaction with consumers through chat, message boards, discussion forums, and other mechanisms (usenets or newsgroups and listservs). Smart companies will embrace these methods to keep in close contact with their consumers. These mechanisms are superior to most traditional research methods in the following ways:

- ✓ They provide for ongoing interactive dialog
- ✓ They allow the company to become aware of and address issues as they emerge
- ✓ They can become a mechanism for creating a stronger bond between the consumer and the company

Projective Techniques

Projective techniques overcome some of the limitations of direct questioning.[4] Here is why:

- ✓ People are not always conscious of their underlying motivations
- ✓ People tell you what they think you want to hear.
- ✓ People are sometimes embarrassed to admit their real motivations, thinking that divulging them would reflect negatively on them.
- ✓ Most people think of themselves as being completely rational in their decision making, so they discount or dismiss nonrational reasons for their behaviors.
- ✓ Some people fear how marketers might use the information "if they were to learn the truth about me," and so they withhold that information to avoid being manipulated.

Projective techniques can help you better understand brand personality. For instance, "if the brand was an animal/car/person/sports team/occupation, what animal/car/person/sports team/occupation would it be and why?"

Other projective research techniques that help you get below the surface include:

- ✓ Sentence completion
- ✓ Brand sorting (on a wide variety of dimensions)
- ✓ Word association
- ✓ Collages
- ✓ Brand obituary/epitaph
- ✓ Brand press release/headline
- ✓ Consumer letters
- ✓ Brand time capsule
- ✓ Stereotypes
- ✓ Thought balloons
- ✓ Psychodrawing/modeling
- ✓ Role-playing and reenactment

I also have used the technique of providing participants with numerous pictures of a wide variety of people in a wide variety of settings. I then ask which of those people would buy, receive as a gift, and use the brand, and which wouldn't. I then ask them to explain their answers.

Another technique explores perceived differences between brands. Ask people to sort products (competitors' products and your products intermixed) into two piles—the "brand in question" and "not the brand in question." (One version of this disguises the brand mark; the other one doesn't.) Once all of the products have been sorted, probe why they thought the product either was or wasn't the brand in question. (As with the previous technique, if this exercise is done in focus groups, ask participants to write their answers down first so they are not biased by each other's answers. Collect all of the answer sheets and compare the written responses to the group discussion.)

While at Hallmark, I worked with Dr. Sharon Livingston of The Looking Glass (www.researchonresearch.com) and Executive Solutions (www.executive-solutions.com). She and Dr. Glenn Livingston have compiled a list of "37 of the most common emotional self statements, based upon statistical analyses (factor analyses) of emotional purchase motivation revealed in focus groups." They have created a projective quantitative technique that:

- ✓ Rank orders the importance of the emotional drivers in your category
- ✓ Shows the direct link of features and functional benefits to the (emotional drivers)
- ✓ Graphically displays the position of your product or service, each of its features, your competition, the ideal company, and ANY additional advertising stimulus
- ✓ Assigns a single number to each product feature [that] represents the extent to which that feature is associated with all of the most important emotional benefits

You can learn more about this technique at: http://interface.executive-solu tions.com/.

Logo Research

When exploring new logo executions, the research may include any or all of the following components:

✔ **Logo Imagery:** Imagery evoked by various logo alternatives versus that evoked by the current logo (this usually includes the intended brand personality attributes and attributes such as "boring").

✔ **Logo Recognition:** Each variation of the logo is "mocked up" in its most likely usage environments (store marquees, product packaging, etc.) and then people at various distances are asked about what they see. This measures visibility, recognition and the ability to break through visual clutter at various distances.

✔ **Logo Recall:** One at a time, different logo alternatives and the current logo are mixed in with other companies' logos on a panel. People are allowed to view the panel for a few seconds. After that, the panel is covered or taken away and they must write down all of the brands that they remember seeing. Results are compared for each variation of the logo.

✔ **Logo Preference:** Each variation of the logo is featured on a card. People are given the deck of cards and asked to sort the logos/cards in order of preference. They are then asked to comment on why they ranked each logo variation the way they did.

Other Research Techniques

Another useful research technique is *eye-tracking research,* which is used to assess and enhance packaging, advertising, merchandising, brand identity and signage, direct marketing, and Web design. By tracking eye movements, one can determine which messages or products a person saw and which ones he or she ignored.

A technique to better understand brand price premium includes exposing different groups of participants to a wide variety of products and brands within the category in question, each time with your brand mark and your competitors' brand marks applied to the products in different combinations. We compare the quality perceptions, associations, intent to purchase, and price they would be willing to pay for the same products with different brand marks. A variation of this is to do the same with the products but without any brand marks, which highlights product (versus brand) preference.

Additional useful research techniques are conjoint analysis, corporate image tracking, and electronic real time research. For a list of online research resources go to www.brandforward.com.

Conjoint Analysis

Traditionally used for pricing research, conjoint analysis is very applicable for brand research as well. Respondents rate their buying intent for products comprised of various combinations of attributes (including product, service, sales terms, price and brand attributes). Brand name is one of the attributes. Not only is this an excellent approach to measure the overall equity of your brand name vis-à-vis competitors, but it also allows you to measure the inter-actions/relationships of your brand name with other attributes. Simulation exercises also allow you to project the impact on share of preference for various attribute combinations (what-if exercises).

Corporate Image Tracking

Corporate image tracking is an offshoot of brand image tracking, which measures changes in overall brand image on a variety of attributes.

- ✔ Its premise is that consumers have experiences with your company and brands in a variety of ways, and it is important to quantify the frequency and impact of those different experiences on the overall brand/corporate image.

- ✔ For example, consumer interact with and experience the Hallmark name in many ways: shopping in Hallmark stores, buying and using Hallmark products, seeing television advertising, visiting their website, sponsorships and other public relations efforts, and most recently, viewing the Hallmark Channel on cable/satellite TV.

- ✔ A research-tracking program can measure the frequency of these various points of contact, as well as the satisfaction of those experiences and the subsequent impact on overall brand image.

Electronic Real Time Research

Electronic Real Time Research (ERT) is qualitative research with some quantification of results. It is most often used for product research, but is adaptable to brand research. (Perception Analyzer is one company that conducts this research.) ERT is used to:

- ✔ Get immediate quantitative feedback on specific benefits or concepts
- ✔ Be able to instantaneously see that feedback by any chosen segmentation of the respondents

   ✔ Be able to ask the respondents questions based upon that feedback (for additional insights)

Research Mandatories

To ensure that your research is actionable and provides the highest return on investment possible, the first step in any research project should be to define the following:

   ✔ Objectives (both business and research)

   ✔ Hypotheses

   ✔ Action standards

   ✔ A predetermined feedback loop to identify whether the actions resulted in the intended outcome

Use the checklist in Exhibit 17-1 to assess the efficacy of your brand management practices in the area covered by this chapter. The more questions to which you can answer "yes," the better you are doing. The checklist also provides a brief summary of the material covered in the chapter.

EXHIBIT 17-1. BRAND MANAGEMENT CHECKLIST.

BRAND RESEARCH

	YES	NO
Do you conduct research other than focus groups, satisfaction studies, and attitude & usage studies?	_____	_____
Have you conducted brand asset research? Have you been able to successfully extend your brand into new products or services based upon this research?	_____	_____
Have you conducted brand equity research? Have you changed aspects of the brand based upon this research? Has this increased your brand's equity?	_____	_____
Do you use online methods (chat rooms, discussion boards, etc.) to stay in touch with your customers?	_____	_____
Have you used a variety of projective research techniques to better understand your brand's associations and those of your competitors' brands? Have you ever used ethnographic research to better understand your customers?	_____	_____

Do you measure the effectiveness of your advertising?
Have you improved your advertising based upon this
research?   _____ _____

Do you conduct ongoing ad/brand tracker and
corporate image studies?   _____ _____

Have you researched the effectiveness of your brand's
logo?   _____ _____

Do you measure the effectiveness of your direct
marketing? Do you measure the effectiveness of your
online marketing? Have you been able to improve on
both based upon this feedback?   _____ _____

Do you keep track of the degree of commoditization
within the categories in which your brand operates?
(This is determined by increased importance of price
in the purchase decision, decreased perceptions of
brand differentiation—including increased
congruence between competitive brands' perceptual
maps—and decreased preference for any brand in the
category. Other supporting indicators are lower
perceived brand innovation and vitality and higher
perceived brand "boringness" in general for all
brands across the category.)   _____ _____

Do you create objectives, hypotheses, action
standards, and a feedback loop for all of your
research?   _____ _____

Do you believe your brand is winning in the
marketplace based upon your brand research?   _____ _____

Notes

1. This section is largely based on the work of Dan Vandenberg, president of ConsumerVision, Inc. "Naming Method" and "Latency Method" are terms first used by Peter Farquhar.

2. Dan Vandenberg, referencing Peter Farquhar's characterization of brand extension.

3. Emily Eakin, "Penetrating the Mind by Metaphor," *New York Times*, January 22, 2002, p. B11.

4. Sources are Sharon Livingston's February 2, 2002 e-newsletter, *Quantifying Emotional End Benefits,* and my experience in conducting hundreds of focus groups and other qualitative research.

CHAPTER 18

Brand Equity Measurement

ACCORDING TO A well-known axiom, *you can't manage what you don't measure*. This is true of brand equity as well. Any strong brand equity measurement system will accomplish the following objectives:

- ✓ Measure the brand's equity across a variety of dimensions at different points in time over time.
- ✓ Provide diagnostic information on the reasons for the changes in brand equity.
- ✓ Gauge and evaluate the brand's progress against goals.
- ✓ Provide direction on how to improve brand equity.
- ✓ Provide insight into the brand's positioning vis-à-vis its major competitors including its strengths, weaknesses, opportunities, and threats.
- ✓ Provide direction on how to reposition the brand for maximum effect

When I was named director of brand management and marketing at Hallmark, I was given two primary objectives: (1) to increase Hallmark market share and (2) to increase Hallmark brand equity.

Market share is a relatively straightforward objective for which we already had metrics. Brand equity was much less well defined. I spent the better part of the next three years drawing upon the knowledge of various consultants, researchers and scholars and dozens of different brand equity models to define brand equity in a way that was useful to Hallmark. To be useful to Hallmark, it had to show how to move people from high brand awareness to brand insistence. Since then, this has resulted in a validated and refined measurement system with scores of organizations across dozens of industries.

▨ Brand Equity Measurement System Components

Here are the components that a brand equity measurement system should measure:

- ✓ Brand awareness (first mention [top-of-mind unaided recall], total un-aided recall)
- ✓ Brand preference
- ✓ Brand importance/rank in consideration set
- ✓ Brand accessibility
- ✓ Brand value (quality and value perceptions and price sensitivity)
- ✓ Brand relevant differentiation (open-ended question and perceptions on key attributes)
- ✓ Brand emotional connection
- ✓ Brand vitality
- ✓ Brand loyalty (multiple behavioral and attitudinal measures including share of requirements/wallet)
- ✓ Brand usage
- ✓ Brand imagery (against a standard battery of category-independent brand personality attributes [proven to drive brand insistence] and a customized battery of brand personality attributes for the particular organization and its product/service category)

Most Important Brand Equity Measures

The most important brand equity measures are:

- ✓ Unaided brand awareness, especially first recall
- ✓ Remembered/recalled brand experience
- ✓ Knowledge of the brand's promise
- ✓ Brand's position in the purchase consideration set
- ✓ Brand's delivery against key benefits. (We have found two separate approaches to this to be insightful: mapping benefit importance against brand benefit delivery (scaled response) and an open-ended question, "What makes brand XX different from other brands in the YY category?")
- ✓ Emotional connection to the brand
- ✓ Price sensitivity
- ✓ Relative accessibility

Specific Brand Equity Measures

Specific questions and measures that help you manage a brand's equity consist of the following:

✔ **Brand Awareness**

  ✔ What is the first brand that comes to mind when thinking about the xxx category?

  ✔ What other brands come to mind for the xxx category?

✔ **Brand Preference**

  ✔ Which brand of [product category] do you prefer? (The incidence of those with no brand preference can also provide insights into the importance of brand in the category.)

✔ **Brand Usage**

  ✔ Which brand of [product category] do you most often use?

✔ **Brand Accessibility**

  ✔ Widely available

  ✔ Easy to find and purchase

✔ **Brand Value**

  ✔ Quality perception

  ✔ Value perception

  ✔ Price sensitivity

✔ **Brand Relevant Differentiation**

  ✔ What makes brand xxx different from other brands in the yyy category?

  ✔ What one or two things make (category) brands different from one another?

  ✔ Which brand or brands of (product/service category) do you prefer when you are looking for the (relevant differentiated benefit)?

  ✔ Which brand of (category) best meets your needs? Why?

  ✔ How well does the xxx brand deliver against the yyy benefit? (5 point scale)

✔ **Brand Emotional Connection**

  ✔ Your brand is almost like a friend to your customers.

  ✔ It stands for something important to them.

  ✔ It says something about who they are.

  ✔ It has never disappointed them (see Figure 18-1).

✔ **Brand Loyalty**

  ✔ Share of requirements/share of wallet.

  ✔ Share of last ten purchases. (Constant sum questioning works best. Questions such as "brand most often purchased" or "brands bought in the past six months" almost always overstate purchases for well-known brands and understate purchases for low-price brands.)

FIGURE 18-1. EMOTIONAL CONNECTION.

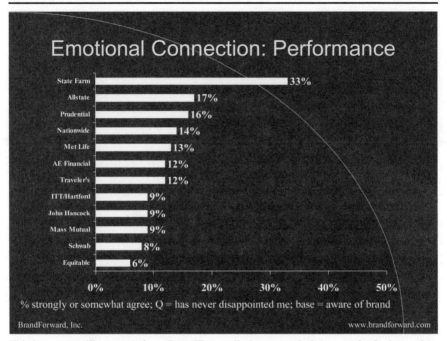

This is a very telling graph from BrandForward's insurance industry study. It shows that, other than State Farm, all of the top insurance companies have disappointed at least 83% of their customers at one time or another. Most have disappointed more than 90% of their customers. A company cannot create trust or emotional connection with that record.

   ✔ Satisfaction.
   ✔ Repurchase intent.
   ✔ Willingness to recommend to a friend.
   ✔ Deal sensitivity.
   ✔ Switching propensity.

   A particularly telling question is "Describe your most memorable recent interaction with [brand]." Such an open-ended question provides insight regarding source of interaction (touch point), quality of interaction, and intensity of interaction.

✔ **Brand Vitality**
   Design marketing campaigns to build perceived brand momentum:
   ✔ Do you hear more about the brand lately?
   ✔ Is the brand changing for the better?
   ✔ Which brand is reinventing the category?
   ✔ Which brand, in your opinion, will lead the industry four years from now?

Ladder of the Mind (Consideration Set Continuum: 7 point scale)

✔ I would never choose to buy this brand

✔ I've never heard of this brand

✔ I've heard of this brand but don't know much about it

✔ Not one of my preferred brands but I'd try it under certain circumstances

✔ Not one of my preferred brands but from what I've heard about it recently I'd like to try it/try it again

✔ This is one of my preferred brands

✔ This is the only brand I would ever consider buying

(*Source*: Transcript Proceedings: "Tracking the Obvious: New Ways of Looking at Old Problems" by Martin Stolzenberg, president, Stolzenberg Consulting, and Peggy Lebenson, senior vice president, Data Development Corporation. "Advertising and Brand Tracking: The Power of Today's Advertising and Brand Tracking Studies: An Advertising Research Foundation Key Issues Workshop," November 12–13, 1996, New York, Grand Hyatt Hotel, copyright 1997 by Advertising Research Foundation.)

✔ *Brand Consideration Set*

  ✔ How many other brands in consideration set?

✔ *Brand Personality*

  ✔ Popular

  ✔ Trustworthy

  ✔ Unique

  ✔ Others: innovative, dependable, contemporary, old-fashioned, practical, boring, fun

What a Robust Brand Equity Measurement System Must Have

A robust brand equity system should include all of the measures listed above. It should be tailored to a particular company and industry. (At a minimum, the competitive set, personality attributes, and category benefit structure will

A Sad Day

It is a sad day when a previously meaningful and vibrant brand is taken over by or combined with a new entity that does not share the brand's essence, promise, and values. This happens quite often, with mergers, acquisitions, when a company is taken private or public, or with other changes in ownership or leadership. Sometimes this happens when a financial owner (such as a venture capital firm) replaces the previous management team with its own new team. This is particularly true when people who only understand one thing, ROI (or, more specifically, their personal financial gain), replace the leadership team that had the original brand vision. This is akin to a person's spirit exiting his or her body to allow a new spirit to inhabit it. While the newly combined physical/spiritual entity may seem to be the same entity as before, new attitudes and behaviors will eventually betray the new spirit, but not until after the huge reservoir of brand equity is traded for short-term financial gains for the new owners. This is one reason previously strong brands seem to "lose their way."

vary by industry. Ways of measuring value and loyalty typically also vary by industry.) The measurement system should also include behavioral and attitudinal measures, especially for brand loyalty. Through regression analysis and other techniques, the system should determine attitudinal measures that best predict brand loyalty and other desired behaviors (predictive modeling). The system should be capable of analyzing brand equity by category or customer segment if required. Comparing results of frequent users, occasional users, and nonusers also provides useful insights. It is important to measure brand vitality because purchase intent is almost always overstated for well-known, well-regarded older brands with waning differentiation (i.e., declining brands) and understated for newer brands with low awareness but high relevance and differentiation (i.e., emerging brands). Brand vitality can help adjust for this.

Robust brand equity systems also deliver these beneficial features:

- ✔ A visual portrayal of positioning opportunities and vulnerabilities, such as mapping attribute/benefit importance against brand delivery (see Figure 18-2)
- ✔ Comparisons to other industries (from a normative database) to identify additional opportunities and vulnerabilities

FIGURE 18-2. PERCEPTUAL MAP.

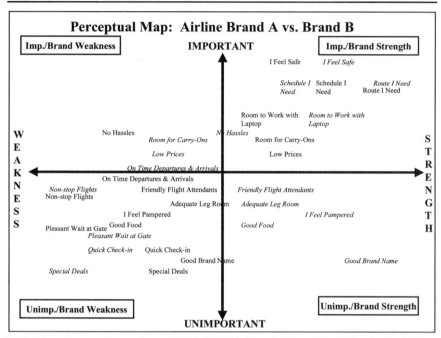

Which benefits are "cost-of-entry" benefits? If you were brand A (attributes in italics), which benefits would you emphasize? Against which benefits would you make improvements? Are there areas on which you would spend fewer resources? Are there benefits for which you would like to develop more proof points? What are your brand's greatest vulnerabilities? Which data points do you find hard to believe? Why? Why is "Good Brand Name" so low in importance? What would you like to research in greater depth? How would you position the brand? [The same questions apply to brand B.]

This chart is for illustrative purposes only. It contains fictionalized data and should not be taken to represent real companies or real brand positionings.

✔ Identification of natural customer clusters

✔ Demographic/lifestyle analysis and profiling

Common Brand Equity Measurement System Problems

The most common brand equity measurement problems include the following:

✔ The system from which to manage brand equity is too simplistic. For instance, those omnibus studies that measure only two to four dimensions of brand equity, such as awareness or favorability.

✓ No competitive comparisons are included in the measurement. (Many companies measure against themselves by, for instance, measuring customer satisfaction improvements. A brand equity measurement system must include competitive comparisons. By definition, brands are positioned against other brands. And few customers compare you against yourself. Most customers compare you to other companies and brands. Competitive context is critical to managing your brand's equity.)

✓ The sample size is too small to provide for valid subgroup analysis.

✓ The sample size is too small to detect small changes in brand equity in the shorter term.

✓ Surveying customers too frequently. Typically, it is sufficient to measure brand equity once a year unless one of the following conditions exist:

  ✓ The brand is new

  ✓ You have repositioned the brand or otherwise altered the brand communication or delivery in a major way

✓ Use of the organization's own customer and/or prospect list so that brand awareness, usage, and other measures are not projectable to the general population.

✓ Design of the survey in a way that biases the unaided brand awareness question—rendering the results of that question invalid.

✓ Organizations are unable to identify a primary product category or set of competitors due to the uniqueness of their brand or the lack of a brand unifying principle. This eliminates some of the most important brand equity measures (top-of-mind awareness, brand differentiation, etc.) from the measurement system.

✓ A tailored set of brand/category benefit statements is not included in the study. These statements must come from a rigorous understanding of the category benefit structure, typically identified by prior qualitative customer research dedicated to the purpose of identifying that structure.

✓ Confusion of other studies with a brand equity measurement system. Mostly typically, people believe the following to be brand equity measurement systems (or viable substitutes for them): customer satisfaction studies, attitude and usage studies, and corporate image studies.

Assessing the Effectiveness of an Organization's Brand Equity Measurement System

Brand equity measurement systems are the most effective when clients can answer each of the following questions affirmatively:

✓ Do you have a profound understanding of your brand's consumers?

✓ Do you know what drives your brand's equity?

✓ Have you established and validated equity measures for your brand?

✓ Have you set objectives against these measures?

✓ Do key decision makers regularly see results against these objectives?

✓ Are people held accountable for achieving brand objectives?

Brand Equity Should Not Be Measured Just for Customers

Businesses should also monitor their brand equity with the following groups (in addition to their customers):

✓ Industry analysts

✓ Financial analysts

✓ Employees

✓ Business partners

A brand's power comes not just from the loyalty that it creates in its customers, but also from the loyalty that it creates in its employees and its investors.

Brand Building and Marketing are Investments with a Tangible Return

I am tired of hearing some business people say that there is no way to correlate business results with marketing expenditures, implying that marketing is an expense with no corresponding return. Others are slightly more charitable, and say that there is no way to measure *direct* results. This is wrong—at least for direct response marketing, including direct response marketing via the Internet. (Many direct marketing Web sites even offer free direct-marketing ROI calculators.) For other types of marketing—this is partially wrong.

There are a few important components to measuring the results of marketing programs: (1) being clear about the program's objectives upfront, (2) being sure that there are ways to measure results against the objectives, (3) measuring those results, and (4) evaluating the program's results against the objectives. This is a closed loop system.

It is also important to keep in mind that there are marketing programs with long-term results, such as brand building, and there are marketing programs with short-term results, such as direct response marketing and sales promotion. You must be clear about which ones each marketing investment is intended to achieve (see Exhibit 18-1).

EXHIBIT 18-1. LONG-TERM VS. SHORT-TERM MARKETING INVESTMENTS.

	Long-term Investment	Short-term Investment
Type of Marketing Investment	Brand Building	Direct response marketing, sales promotion, and other shorter-term marketing expenditures
Primary Result	Creation of leverageable asset	Short-term increase in sales
Indirect Impact on Business	Decreased price sensitivity, increased customer loyalty, increased revenues, increased share of market, increased ability to hire and retain quality employees, increased stock price, increased company value, increased ability to grow into new product and service categories, increased ability to mobilize the organization around a vision	NA
Measurement	*Financial:* asset value *Nonfinancial:* awareness, relevant differentiation, preference, loyalty	Program ROI

Measuring Marketing ROI

There are many useful models for estimating the impact of various revenue drivers on total revenues. One of the more widely used models is as follows:

➤

The total customer base (number of people)
× (multiplied times) the average number of purchase transactions per person (per time period)
× (multiplied times) the average unit sales per transaction
× (multiplied times) the average price per unit
× (multiplied times) the percent of those transactions received by your brand
= (equals) your sales (per time period).

You can design your marketing programs to affect any combination of these factors, and you can measure the level of investment required to get the results through each of these levers.

- ✔ You can introduce your products to new audiences.
- ✔ You can encourage customers to upgrade their products or services or to purchases additional products and services.

✓ You can entice them to make more frequent purchases.

✓ You can increase the amount that they pay for the products and services.

✓ Your can encourage them to rely upon your brand for a greater proportion of their purchases.

Given the right data, it becomes trivial to estimate the return to your company from increasing your market share by one share point, gaining one more customer, or retaining a current customer's business for another year.

Take another example: lead generation. If you code ads and direct mail pieces, you will be able to determine which marketing programs resulted in leads, which of those leads were qualified, which of those qualified leads were translated into sales by your sales force, and how much revenue each of those successful leads returned. You can relate this to the marketing investment required to generate those leads. Now you have calculated return on marketing investment.

Many marketing tactics achieve numerous objectives. For instance, banner ads have been shown to increase brand awareness and reinforce a brand's positioning while also generating sales leads or transactions (depending on what is on the other side of the "click-through"). Trade shows also achieve multiple ends. Through our post-show research, Element K has found that shows increase brand awareness and preference and the prospect's propensity to purchase our products. They also increase current customer attitudinal loyalty. They generate qualified sales leads as well. Be careful to evaluate marketing tactics that achieve multiple ends against all of those ends—not just one.

On a macro basis, one can measure the effectiveness of marketing expenditures by comparing increases in total marketing expenditures to increases in sales for a specified period of time (quarter-over-quarter, year-over-year, etc.). Two cautions with this approach, however. First, a complex combination of variables affects sales. Not all of the credit (positive or negative) can be attributed to marketing actions. The general economy, sales tactics and other executive level decisions can also impact sales in significant ways. Second, remember that some of your marketing programs, including most brand building programs, are designed to affect a longer-term cumulative result not measurable in the short-term.

Importance of Investing in the Brand Asset

A number of recent studies have shown that the percentage of a company's value that is unaccounted for by tangible assets has increased significantly. From 50 percent to 90 percent of a company's total value is now attributable to factors other than tangible assets. In a 1996 study, the Cap Gemini Ernst &

Young Center for Business Innovation (CGI) discovered that nonfinancial assets account for 35 percent of institutional investor's valuation of a company. In its 2000 "Measuring the Future: The Value Creation Index" report, CGI reported that, after rigorous research, they discovered that 50 percent of a traditional company's value and 90 percent of an e-commerce company's value result from nine factors. The following value drivers seem to be common across most industries.[1]

- ✓ Innovation/R&D
- ✓ Quality of management
- ✓ Employee quality/satisfaction
- ✓ Alliances
- ✓ Brand investment
- ✓ Product/service quality

► **Neel Foster,** a board member at the Financial Accounting Standards Board [said], "As we move into more of an information age and service-based economy, the importance of soft assets is becoming more relevant to valuing some companies than brick and mortar. A lot of companies don't even have brick and mortar."[2]

An increasing number of methods have emerged to measure nonfinancial business drivers, from the Balanced Scorecard to Value-Based Management and the more recent Value Creation Index (from CGI). Wharton accounting professors recently conducted a study across 317 companies and discovered that 36 percent of the companies sampled used nonfinancial measures to determine executive incentive compensation.[3]

Building brand awareness, differentiation, and emotional connection together with the appropriate pricing and distribution strategies results in brand preference, purchase, repeat purchase, and, eventually, loyalty. Also, an increasing body of evidence links brand-building activities with a wide range of long-term benefits, from decreased price sensitivity and increased customer loyalty to increased stock price and shareholder value.

Sometimes, the results of brand-building programs are obvious, especially for new brands. When I arrived at Element K, Element K was a newly created brand. People in the e-learning industry had not heard of Element K. Our sales force found it difficult to gain the attention of potential buyers, we were not on industry analysts' "radars," we did not receive coverage in trade magazine articles, people passed by our trade show booth, and we got few calls from conference companies. After a year of focused and relentless brand-building efforts, prospects come to us (we are on their "short lists"), we are in all of the industry analysts' reports, our president writes a column for one of the major trade publications, we sponsor a major user conference in parallel with one of the most important industry trade shows, we receive a continuous stream of invitations to participate in conferences and other industry events, companies approach us about business partnerships, our employees are sought after as industry experts, and our competitors talk about us. In this case, the results of our brand-building efforts were obvious and didn't require the validation of formal brand equity measures or the corresponding revenue increases (both of which we also have).

You can measure and manage the non-financial impact of your brand through a brand equity measurement system (covered earlier in this chapter). You can also measure the financial value of your brand as an asset.

Brand valuation has been made possible by the following more recently developed financial approaches—Activity Based Costing (ABC), Discounted Cash Flow (DCF), and Economic Value Added (EVA)—and by a myriad of more recent customer purchase tracking techniques.[4] Interbrand (www.interbrand.com) has a depth of experience in brand valuation. Also, Don E. Schultz, Ph.D., professor of integrated marketing communications at Northwestern University and president of Agora, Inc., has studied and applied the concepts of brand valuation *and* return on marketing investment in depth. Both would be good resources for people with a further interest on this topic.

Brand Building and Marketing as Investments: A Summary

1. Brand building is an investment that results in a significant leverageable asset.
2. Other shorter-term marketing actions exist for the sole purpose of increasing sales.
3. You can measure the asset value of brands.
4. You can also measure the nonfinancial aspects of brands that drive positive financial consequences in the long term—awareness, relevant differentiation, loyalty, etc.
5. You can and should measure ROI for other shorter-term marketing programs.
6. Brands are a primary source of value creation for organizations.
7. Although some business people (typically finance and operations types) may view marketing as an expense without significant corresponding benefits, this is untrue. Marketing is one of the most important investments a company can make.

Implication: Don't look first to marketing (and employee training, for that matter) when expenses need to be trimmed to achieve short-term goals. This will only hamper value creation and revenue growth in the long term.

Marketing is a fundamental driver of organizational success. Together, brand building, marketing and sales strategies and tactics create, build, *and* sustain a company's revenues. To ensure positive results, you must understand and track how each marketing program impacts sales in the short-term and the long-term. In many instances, you will be able to track and measure the specific short-term impact of specific programs. In others, especially for longer-term brand building programs, you will have to track and measure indirect business drivers—brand awareness, attitudinal loyalty, etc., and validate how each of these affects revenue gains in the long run. Formal marketing (and brand) plans and metrics will help you achieve this end. And don't forget—a brand is an asset, and one of the most important assets in creating long-term value for organizations. Build the brand, sustain it, *and* leverage it.

Use the checklist in Exhibit 18-2 to assess the efficacy of your brand management practices in the area covered by this chapter. The more questions to which you can answer "yes," the better you are doing. The checklist also provides a brief summary of the material covered in the chapter.

EXHIBIT 18-2. BRAND MANAGEMENT CHECKLIST.

BRAND EQUITY MEASUREMENT

	YES	NO
Do you know what drives your brand's equity?	_____	_____
Have you established and validated equity measures for your brand?	_____	_____
Are your measures projective and actionable?	_____	_____
Have you established targets against those brand equity measures? Do you actively manage against those targets?	_____	_____
Do you measure your brand's equity at least once a year?	_____	_____
Are people held accountable for achieving brand equity objectives and targets?	_____	_____
Is senior management regularly updated on performance against brand equity objectives and targets?	_____	_____
Do you measure each of the following brand equity dimensions: awareness, accessibility/convenience, value, relevant differentiation, emotional connection, preference, usage, vitality, loyalty, and key associations?	_____	_____

Do you also measure your primary competitors against the same brand equity dimensions? ⎯⎯⎯ ⎯⎯⎯

Do you know if competitors are making inroads on key associations that you intend your brand to own? ⎯⎯⎯ ⎯⎯⎯

Do you measure behavioral *and* attitudinal aspects of brand loyalty? ⎯⎯⎯ ⎯⎯⎯

Do you measure repeat purchase rates? Do you measure consumer brand advocacy? ⎯⎯⎯ ⎯⎯⎯

Can you translate consumer loyalty to purchase probability? ⎯⎯⎯ ⎯⎯⎯

Do you measure your brand's price premium (with consumers and the trade)? ⎯⎯⎯ ⎯⎯⎯

Do you measure its time/convenience premium? ⎯⎯⎯ ⎯⎯⎯

Do you measure "intent to purchase?" ⎯⎯⎯ ⎯⎯⎯

Do you measure your brand's rank in the consideration set? ⎯⎯⎯ ⎯⎯⎯

Do you measure your brand's "share of dollar"/"share of requirements?" ⎯⎯⎯ ⎯⎯⎯

Do you measure your brand's share of market? ⎯⎯⎯ ⎯⎯⎯

For products sold at retail: Do you measure retail sales productivity/turns for your brand versus competitive brands? ⎯⎯⎯ ⎯⎯⎯

Is your brand equity system sensitive enough to measure changes in your brand's equity over time? ⎯⎯⎯ ⎯⎯⎯

Does the system provide diagnostics on why the equity is increasing or decreasing? ⎯⎯⎯ ⎯⎯⎯

Does the system provide insights into positioning threats and opportunities? ⎯⎯⎯ ⎯⎯⎯

Do you track changes in consumers' ability to accurately play back key brand positioning points? ⎯⎯⎯ ⎯⎯⎯

Do you have a plan (and measurement targets) for the brand associations you want to increase and decrease? ⎯⎯⎯ ⎯⎯⎯

Do you use the system to actively manage your brand's equity? ⎯⎯⎯ ⎯⎯⎯

Has your brand's equity been increasing over time? ⎯⎯⎯ ⎯⎯⎯

(continues)

EXHIBIT 18-2. (CONTINUED).

Is your brand perceived to be authentic? Is it perceived to have integrity?	_____	_____
Is your brand likable? Is it confident?	_____	_____
Do you know if your brand is perceived to be an up-and-comer (rather than on the decline)? Do you measure brand vitality?	_____	_____
If your brand is venerated and dominant in the market, would you be able to tell if it was in danger of becoming generic? If it was, are you aware of the steps that can be taken to avoid that outcome?	_____	_____
Have you measured the financial value of your brand asset? Have you shared that with your organization to reinforce that your brand is an asset that should be actively managed and leveraged? (Interbrand does this well and still features "The World's Most Valuable Brands" on its site at http://www.interbrand.com/features_effect.asp?id = 48. *Business Week* features top public companies' brand asset values.)	_____	_____

▨ Notes

1. "Measuring the Future: The Value Creation Index," Cap Gemini Ernst & Young Center for Business Innovation, 2000.
2. Michael Baltes, "Measuring Non-Financial Assets." *Wharton Alumni Magazine*, Winter 1997. http://www.cfigroup.com/nonfinl.html.
3. Ibid.
4. Don E. Schultz, Ph.D., "Managing and Measuring Brand Value," white paper.

PART SIX

OTHER BRAND MANAGEMENT CONSIDERATIONS

How Organization Age and Size Affect Brand Management Issues

BRAND MANAGEMENT ISSUES differ significantly based on the age and size of the organization. A key role of brand management is to create and reinforce an identity that promises relevant points of difference to consumers.

According to Al Reis and Laura Reis' book, *The 22 Immutable Laws of BRANDING*, the first two laws of branding are as follows:

1. *The Law of Expansion:* The power of a brand is inversely proportional to its scope
2. *The Law of Contradiction:* A brand becomes stronger when you narrow its focus

Clearly these first two laws favor smaller, younger organizations.

Brand identity firms will tell you that often they can create much stronger brand identities for smaller, younger companies because those companies have fewer constraints (existing logos, store décor, and signing), more focused businesses, and stronger business visions. They also have a more coordinated marketing function (often a single department with just a few people). Conversely, large organizations usually have separate product development, advertising, promotion, public relations, sales, and marketing research departments (to name a few).

Some people will tell you that the best promise a large organization's brand can make is to be "the quality, innovation leader in (insert the company's business category)." They say that organizational brands of large enterprises offer authority and assurance *period*. Yet some of the most successful organizational brands have more focused (consumer benefit-based) brand essences. For instance, Disney promises *fun family entertainment*, Nike promises *authentic athletic performance,* and Hallmark promises *caring shared.* All three are distinctive yet broad enough to make multiple product categories possible. Consider all the businesses that Disney is in. And, Hallmark, too, has much growth left (despite a mature greeting card category) and could offer gift candy, flowers, and even "love boat" cruises.

Brand Problems: Small vs. Large Companies

Exhibit 19-1 is a summary of the most likely brand problems of small and large organizations.

For smaller, younger organizations, key brand activities include developing a strong brand identity, building brand awareness through publicity and other less expensive means, and sometimes developing a better understanding of their consumers through marketing research (such as attitude and usage studies, and focus groups). Building "trust" through consultative selling, legendary service, customer testimonials, guarantees, and other approaches is also very important.

Because younger organizations must build their brands quickly with limited funds, they often resort to breakthrough ideas, redefining their categories, out-of-the-box marketing tactics, strong differentiation, thought leadership, taking bold stands, and the element of surprise to pierce the marketplace clutter (versus the steady, consistent leadership messages and other brand-building tactics more typically employed by larger, more established brands).[1] In taking these risks, smaller, younger organizations have much more to gain and far less to lose than their larger, older counterparts.

For larger, older organizations, the brand management job is much more complex. The most important task is to get the senior leadership team to agree to a distinctive, compelling marketplace positioning for the brand. Often the brand needs to be repositioned. Often, too, the brand identity standards and systems need to be overhauled (and the brand hierarchy simplified). Frequently, major organizational design changes are required. The necessary changes may be as wide reaching as rethinking the business portfolio itself.

The Value of Publicity

At the Institute for International Research's *The Branding Trilogy* conference in Santa Barbara, CA, Jill Vollmer, vice president of brand marketing for Mondera.com, said, "Publicity has helped us achieve five times the ad value of media placement for every $1 spent. If you consider that the message is coming from a third party (not paid, but endorsed), the additional credibility may result in ten times the value."

EXHIBIT 19-1. MOST LIKELY BRAND PROBLEMS IN LARGER VS. SMALLER ORGANIZATIONS.

	Smaller, Younger Organizations	Larger, Older Organizations
Leadership	An entrepreneur with a vision and passion	A seasoned executive with experience in running large, complex enterprises
Size	A small number of people who work closely together and often share the entrepreneur's vision and passion	A large number of people in different divisions and departments with different functional backgrounds and allegiances, often very much decentralized
Business Scope	Usually focused on one core product or product category	Usually offering a wide variety of products and product lines, many times in multiple business categories and even in different industries
Brand Structure	Usually one brand	Often very complex including multiple brands, subbrands, endorsed brands, etc.
Organization Infrastructure	Rapidly being built to support the entrepreneur's vision	Many assets, systems, processes, organizational levels, etc. Very difficult to change.
Corporate Culture	Usually strong based upon the entrepreneur's personality. May evolve as new top managers are added.	May be very strong based upon the legacy of a strong founder or a current strong leader. Companies that have long and rich histories often have entrenched cultures.
Marketplace	The business category is often in its infancy with many positioning possibilities for a new company.	Industry is often mature or maturing. Sometimes declining. Competitors are much more entrenched with few, if any, viable marketplace positions not taken. (Recently deregulated industries provide notable exceptions.)
Decision Making	Usually very quick with fewer decision-makers.	Depending on the organization design, the decision-making process can be very cumbersome.
Financial Resources	Often scarce as the organization is growing rapidly and reinvesting all available cash flow. May be less scarce after an IPO.	Usually substantial including cash flow and borrowing capacity.
Primary Marketing Method	Publicity	Advertising

(continues)

EXHIBIT 19-1. (CONTINUED).

	Smaller, Younger Organizations	Larger, Older Organizations
Brand Identity	Often evolving, but easier to encode in standards and systems (because the organization is starting with "a clean slate").	Often strong and entrenched, but more difficult to codify due to the scope and complexity of the enterprise and the inconsistencies that have arisen over time.
Brand Awareness and Esteem	Usually low or nonexistent	Often high
Brand Differentiation	Often very high, but not always (If its differentiation is not high, the organization may go out of business or be a takeover target.)	Usually declines over time as more and more competitors enter the market or achieve parity on what were differentiating benefits

Clearly, brand management needs to vary with organization age and size. Use the checklist in Exhibit 19-2 to assess the efficacy of your brand management practices in the area covered by this chapter. The more questions to which you can answer "yes," the better you are doing. The checklist also provides a brief summary of the material covered in the chapter.

EXHIBIT 19-2. BRAND MANAGEMENT CHECKLIST.

HOW ORGANIZATION AGE AND SIZE AFFECT BRAND MANAGEMENT ISSUES

	YES	NO
Do you know what your organization's number one brand management priority is?	_____	_____
Given your organization's age and size, do you know what its most likely brand management issues are?	_____	_____
If you work for a smaller organization with a relatively young brand, have you addressed the following: (a) building brand awareness quickly and aggressively, (b) pursuing breakthrough ideas, strategies and tactics to do so, (c) fully understanding your customer's attitudes, needs and behaviors, (d) identifying relevant and compelling points of difference to break through the market place clutter, and (e) establishing "trust" through outstanding service, guarantees, customer testimonials, and other vehicles?	_____	_____

If you work for a larger organization with an older and more established brand, have you addressed the following: (a) lack of unifying brand vision, (b) lack of innovation, (c) lack of compelling differentiating benefits, (d) overly complicated brand architecture, and (e) inconsistent brand identity and communication?   _____ _____

▨ Note

1. Tom Birk, "Small Wonder: Joining CP&B from Arnold Changed More than My Wardrobe," *Adweek*, December 3, 2001, p.14; and my personal experience in working at both Hallmark and Element K.

CHAPTER 20

Legal Issues in Brand Management

▨ Trademark Law

As a brand steward, you must be aware of the laws under which legal protection is available. First, trademark law protects a brand's identity. That is, it protects names, titles, taglines, slogans, logos, other designs, product shapes, sounds, smells, colors, or any other features that distinguish one source of products or services from another. Trademarks that protect services are often called service marks ("SM"). There are also "collective membership marks" (Boy Scouts of America) and "certification marks" (UL approved).

Did you know?

"TM" indicates an unregistered trademark.
"SM" indicates an unregistered service mark.
® indicates a registered trademark.
© represents copyrighted material.

Harley-Davidson filed to federally register the sound of its motorcycle engines.
Dirt Devil vacuum cleaners are strongly associated with the color red.
Taco Bell owns the Chihuahua icon.

I am not a lawyer and this chapter is not legal advice but rather is meant merely to consider legal issues in brand management. When actually dealing with any specific issues in this area, please consult with lawyers who have an expertise in intellectual property law.

Although the best defense against copycat competitors is to stay ahead of them with a continuous stream of innovative, highly differentiated, and superior products and services, it is equally important to seek as much legal protection as possible for your brand.

Trademarks, like brands, build in strength over time. The test for trademark infringement is "confusing similarity." Put another way, if the average consumer believes both products to have come from the same source, there is infringement. Obviously, the more a consumer is familiar with a particular brand, the more defendable its mark. That's why it behooves a company to do the following:

✔ Choose a distinctive mark, including a "coined" name. (As I mentioned in the brand identity chapter, brand names range from generic and descriptive to suggestive and arbitrary or fanciful ("coined"). Obviously it takes longer to build meaning for *coined* names, but they are also more distinctive and easiest to protect legally. Kodak, Xerox, and Exxon fall in that category. *Suggestive* marks are the next most protectable. Examples include Coppertone, Duracell, and Lestoil. Even common words can be used as trademarks as long as they are not used descriptively. These common words/phrases are also suggestive marks: Amazon (big), Road Runner (fast), and Apple (different, offbeat). *Descriptive* marks are not protectable unless the brand creates a secondary meaning for the word, such as Weight Watchers, Rollerblade, or Wite-out. *Generic* marks, such as Shredded Wheat and Super Glue, are not protectable at all.)

✔ Avoid geographic names as a part of your mark—they can be the basis of trademark refusal.

✔ Register the mark.

✔ Be consistent in the use of the mark.

✔ Create strong trade dress (mentioned below).

✔ Widely advertise and distribute its trademarked products.

✔ Do all of this over a long period of time.

Because the strength of a mark is dependent upon consumers' familiarity with it, it is much easier for a competitor to neutralize your mark soon after it has been introduced than after it has been in use for a long period of time.

Courts use the following tests to determine infringement:

✔ Strength of the trademark claiming infringement.

✔ Similarity of the two marks.

✔ Evidence of consumer confusion.

✔ Care a consumer takes in comparing products.

✔ Intent of the organization in using the potentially infringing mark. (Some drug and grocery stores have used generic brands that emulate a leading brand's package shape, colors, typestyle, formulation, etc., and display the product side-by-side with the leading brand to imply that there are no differences between the two, encouraging consumers to purchase the lower priced generic item. In this situation, there is clearly intent to emulate the leading brand and reduce the perceived differentiation and value advantage of that brand, but it is not clear that there is intent to deliberately cause confusion as to source.)

✔ Relatedness of the two businesses.

✔ Overlap between communication and distribution channels.

By using the mark in association with your products and services over time, you gain trademark protection. Registering your mark (marks can be registered at the state and federal levels) provides additional protection. Although common law and federal trademark statute protect an unregistered mark, registering your mark transfers the burden of proof to the second comer in challenging a mark's registration. With federal registration, you can sue infringers in Federal court. Also, after five years of registration, the mark becomes incontestable. Federal trademark registrations last ten years and can be renewed every ten years ad infinitum.

You can acquire trademark rights in one of two ways. To acquire trademark rights based on use in commerce, you must be the first person or organization that uses the mark in conjunction with the products or services for which trademark protection is sought. To acquire the mark base upon intent to use, you must apply to register the mark through the United States Patent and Trademark office.

Before choosing a trademark, first conduct a simple search to weed out marks that are not available. This search can be done online for free (for a list of online resources go to www.brandforward.com). After that, for the remaining candidates, conduct a full search through a law firm specializing in trademark law or through an experienced trademark search firm.

Strong brands run the danger of becoming category descriptors. Always use trademarks as adjectives, not verbs or nouns. If your brand is in danger of becoming a category descriptor, consider talking about your brand in the following way: "Jell-O® gelatin," "Kleenex® facial tissue" and "Xerox® photocopier" to differentiate the brand from the category.

Trade Dress

Trade dress is a second form of legal protection for a brand. Trade dress is a brand's distinctive aesthetic design features (package or product design). To be protectable, trade dress must be nonfunctional and distinctive (or, have acquired a "secondary meaning," that is, source identifying characteristics). The more nonfunctional differentiating features one can build into a product and its packaging, the more likely it will be that infringement can be proved.

It is easy for a competitor to say, "I developed this very similar product independently" when it is fairly generic (such as a birthday card with a floral design that says simply "happy birthday"). It is more difficult to convince a courtroom of that when your product has many of the same random non-functional elements that a competitor's product has (e.g., a line of greeting cards of an unusual size that open from the top with rounded edges printed on green tinted recycled paper, all at 99 cents, and all addressing the theme of friendship). For a competitor to develop a similar line of cards with similar features independently is highly unlikely. It points to copying.

To protect its trademarks and trade dress, a company must constantly be watchful for and strenuously defend against infringement. For instance, Apple has filed several lawsuits to defend its iMac against knock-offs. Trademark rights can be enforced through lawsuits at a state or federal level. Proving infringement requires proof that the infringer had second use of the mark and that the second user's mark is confusingly similar to the senior party's mark.

When launching brand extensions, companies should be careful to main-tain the same brand identity and trade dress in those new items. If the brand's name and logo are the only common elements across all of a brand's prod-ucts, it weakens the power of the other trade dress elements to differentiate and legally protect the mark.

Copyright Law

Although organizations don't often pursue this protection, logos are typically protectable by copyright law. Make sure your organization, and not an out-side person or agency, owns the copyright to your brand's logo. Advertising/marketing agencies will often include an assignment of rights, titles, and inter-ests (including copyright interests) to their clients in their letters of agreement. While trademark infringement requires proof of "confusing similarity," copy-right infringement requires proof of "substantial similarity."

Online legal interpretation is evolving, but in general, organizations whose brands are strong and well known ("famous brands") can legally defend their names and other marks against unauthorized use in domain names and metatags. For example, Playboy (unsuccessfully) and Estee Lauder (success-fully) sued other sites for using their brand's names or slogans in their site's metatags.

Other online legal issues include the following:

✓ Cybersquatting: people who register and warehouse domain names that are other party's marks

✓ For-pay search engines selling marks as keywords to businesses that don't own the marks

✓ Spammers who use other mark's e-mail addresses as return addresses for their solicitations

Special Problems

Organizations that license and franchise their marks encounter added challenges to protecting their marks. License and franchise agreements should be drafted to provide maximum control over the mark and to minimize the mark owner's exposure to liability. Further, every effort should be made to establish processes to review, approve and monitor use of the mark by licensees and franchisees.

Trade Secrets

Don't overlook trade secrets as a form of protection. Trade secrets are simply information, techniques, procedures, codes, patterns, plans, processes, formula, and prototypes that are developed confidentially and that are kept confidential. This even includes customer lists and instructional methods. The Coca-Cola syrup formulation is an example of a trade secret. (The added value of this approach from a brand perspective is that it often creates a mystique that has its own cachet.)

Sometimes it is better to keep something a trade secret than to patent it. In some industries, companies routinely watch for competitors' new patents and then try to design around them. Noncompete and nondisclosure agreements are important, but not infallible, in protecting trade secrets. The Economic Espionage Act of 1996 protects trade secrets against theft. Information is legally considered to be a trade secret if an organization can show that it took reasonable measures to keep the information secret and that there is economic value to the information not being made public.

Did You Know?

Coca-Cola's syrup formula is kept in a bank vault in Atlanta, and only Coca-Cola's board of directors has the power to request the vault to be opened. Only two anonymous employees know the formula, they have signed nondisclosure agreements and they are not allowed to fly together on the same plane.

(*Source:* Stephen Fishman and Rich Stim, *Trade Secret Basics,* www.nolo.com.)

A business can protect its trade secrets in the following ways:

- Share confidential information only on a "need to know" basis.
- Limit the number of employees exposed to trade secrets. Always inform employees exposed to those trade secrets (a) that they are being exposed to secrets, and (b) of the importance of keeping the secrets secret.

✔ Mark all confidential documents "confidential—no copies allowed." For added security, number each copy and keep a log of which numbered copy was given to which employee.

✔ Use access logs for trade secrets.

✔ Require anyone (employees, suppliers, customers, consultants, and other business partners) who might come in contact with trade secrets to sign confidentiality and nondisclosure agreements *before* the relationship begins.

✔ In consultant contracts, be clear about what intellectual property the consultant is to assign to your company during his or her assignment.

✔ Require employees to sign noncompete agreements, prohibiting them from working for competitors for a period of time after their employment with you ends. If this is done within an employment contract, present this to prospective employees well before they commence their employment with you so that the "consideration" is employment.

✔ Employment contracts can also prohibit moonlighting or consulting for companies in similar lines of business while employed at your company, or, less restrictively, while on company time or using company equipment (including computers).

✔ Educate employees about the treatment of proprietary information during and after their employment with you.

✔ Carefully orchestrate employee terminations so that employees are not able to take proprietary information with them.

✔ Schedule exit interviews with departing employees. Use those interviews to remind departing employees of their confidentiality obligations.

✔ Develop, communicate, and enforce security processes—from building security to paper document and computer security. Secure confidential information with electronic and mechanical locks. (Passwords or codes should be changed regularly.)

✔ Never store or allow transfer of confidential information outside of your company's firewall.

✔ Make extensive use of shredders.

✔ Be especially careful of contract workers. Provide them with a company computer so they don't have to use their own on the job.

✔ Conduct trade secret audits.

✔ Most importantly, identify all trade secrets and develop formal protection plans for those secrets.

False or Deceptive Advertising

False or deceptive advertising is another legal consideration in brand management. Advertising is considered to be false or misleading if it *could* mislead

Did You Know?

Perceptions of your product or service's performance have a significant impact on your brand's equity. (*Source:*"They Said My Brand Was Popular—So What?," Nigel S. Hollis, group research & development director, Millward Brown International. Validated by several other sources.)

consumers about a product's place of origin, nature, quality, or maker. (It is not necessary to prove actual deception.) Advertisers must be accurate about material aspects of their products or services and those of their competitors (in comparative advertising) to avoid prosecution.[1] The Federal Trade Commission looks for the following when investigating complaints:[2]

- ✓ What are the expressed or implied claims? What was said and what was not said?
- ✓ Are the claims material? That is, do they say something about the product's functions, features, performance, effectiveness, maker, price, safety, etc.?
- ✓ Does the advertiser have evidence to support the claims?
- ✓ Could the ad as a whole mislead a consumer acting reasonably under the circumstances?

Note that claims such as "best in the world" or "the world's leader" are considered to be puffery (not false advertising), and that the average consumer is believed to process such claims with some degree of skepticism. False advertising claims can be brought before the following entities for resolution:[3]

- ✓ The organization against which the claim is made
- ✓ State or local consumer protection offices
- ✓ The National Advertising Division of the Better Business Bureau
- ✓ The Federal Trade Commission
- ✓ Industry self-regulating bodies
- ✓ Advertising regulatory bodies

Use the checklist in Exhibit 20-1 to assess the efficacy of your brand management practices in the area covered by this chapter. The more questions to which you can answer "yes," the better you are doing. The checklist also provides a brief summary of the material covered in the chapter.

EXHIBIT 20-1. BRAND MANAGEMENT CHECKLIST.

LEGAL ISSUES IN BRAND MANAGEMENT

	YES	NO
Do you know that coined names and fanciful or arbitrary marks are the most protectable by law?	____	____
Is your trademark distinctive?	____	____
Have you completed a full trademark search for any new brand name you are considering using? Have you completed this search in all countries in which the brand might operate?	____	____
Have you registered your trademark at a federal level and in all countries in which your brand will operate?	____	____
Have you marketed your brand in all fifty states? (The first organization to use a particular name in a specific geographic area has "priority of use" protection in that area under common law.)	____	____
Have you searched to ensure that the brand name you are considering is available as an Internet domain name? Have you registered that domain name? Have you registered typical variations of that domain name? Have you registered that domain name as ".com," .org," ".net," etc.?	____	____
Do you know the difference between trademarks with a "TM" and an ®?	____	____
Do you use the TM and ® symbols when appropriate?	____	____
Do you always use your brand name as an adjective (versus as a noun)? If you are concerned that your brand name may become a category generic descriptor, are you using the following wording in all of your brand communication: "[brand name] brand [product category descriptor]?"	____	____
Do you design your brand's trade dress to have as many arbitrary design elements as possible so that you are more likely to win a trademark infringement legal battle with your competitors?	____	____
Does your brand identity system include as many elements as possible (beyond name and logo)? (Examples: visual style, brand voice, colors, icons, typography, slogan, mnemonic devices, etc.)	____	____

(continues)

EXHIBIT 20-1. (CONTINUED).

Do you retain experts to help you protect your brand mark online? _____ _____

Did you know that trademark protection is enhanced through proper use and can be lost through improper use? _____ _____

Did you know you can sue another company for using your brand's name or slogan in their site's meta-tags? _____ _____

Did you know that using another organization's well-known mark as a domain name is also illegal, even if used associated with an unrelated product or service category? _____ _____

Do you aggressively pursue those who are using your brand mark improperly or illegally? _____ _____

Do you have strong brand identity standards and systems that are available to all employees and vendors? Have you trained all people who might use the trademark in its proper use? _____ _____

Are you very careful to whom you license your trademark? Do you have processes in place to monitor their use of your mark and to immediately stop (or correct) their use of your mark if they are using it improperly? _____ _____

Are you very cautious about creating registered users of your mark internationally? (They will have rights to your mark forever, even after you have severed a business relationship with them.) _____ _____

Are you also protecting your intellectual properties through patents, copyrights and trade secrets? _____ _____

Have you maintained thorough records of trademark development and use? _____ _____

Have you kept your Web site's log files to validate that your brand has been operating in all fifty states and in many foreign countries? _____ _____

Did you know that people can legally use your brand mark if the following three conditions are met: (1) it is a necessary use, (2) the use is limiting, and (3) there was no consumer deception? (For instance, a watch repairman who only repairs Timex watches can say in advertising copy (or on the side of his building) that "I repair Timex watches" even if he is not employed or licensed by Timex to do so. This, however, does not give him the right to use the Timex logo improperly.) ____ ____

Did you know that under the Trademark Dilution Act of 1995, you can now stop others from using your trademark if it weakens, blurs, or tarnishes the mark? ____ ____

Did you know that you can take action against a competitor for false or misleading advertising claims? Do you know the process you must follow and what you must prove? ____ ____

Did you know that, as a manufacturer, you can lawfully set resale prices? Saturn and Coach both do this. (While possible, this is a very complex area of law that should not be pursued without thoughtful legal advice.) ____ ____

Do you know a successful intellectual property attorney? Is that person available to help you with your legal issues? ____ ____

Notes

1. American Bar Association, "False Advertising," http://nbc-2.findlaw.com/newcontent/consumerlaw/chp5_a.html. 6/21/01.
2. "False Advertising Under the FTC Act," http://www.producersconference.com/law/legal_principles/false_ftc.html. 1/21/02.
3. American Bar Association, "False Advertising."

PART SEVEN

BRAND
MANAGEMENT:
A SUMMARY

CHAPTER 21

Common Brand Problems

AWARENESS OF THE problems and pitfalls brands can encounter is an important step in maintaining a strong, healthy brand.

Problem Number 1: *The cumulative result of gradually and incrementally decreasing product or service quality to reduce costs*
   Analysis: There is the old story about each new brand manager of a coffee brand improving brand profitability and his or her promotion potential by slightly reducing the ratio of premium Brazilian coffee beans to the less expensive African beans. Each time, consumer research indicates no discernable difference in taste or preference, but one day the company discovers that their coffee brand share has significantly eroded. Brand quality erosion may not be discernable in the short term, but over time it will negatively affect a brand's market share. Focus cost-cutting on things that are truly invisible to your customers, and most importantly, manage brands for the long term.

Problem Number 2: *The cumulative effect of raising product or service prices at a rate greater than inflation over time (inviting low-end market segments and competitors)*
   Analysis: This is the other side of a brand's value equation: price. Consider what has happened in several industries in which companies have raised prices faster than inflation over time. Remember Marlboro's Black Friday? Would Malt-o-Meal still exist if cereal companies had not raised their prices as much as they had? And would discount card stores like Factory Card Outlet have grown from zero share of the greeting card market to over 20 percent within a few years if greeting card companies hadn't raised card prices to well over two or three dollars in the same time period? Make sure your brand delivers a good value to the consumer. Even if price sensitivity studies show you can raise prices more, consider the long-term consequences. If you "push the envelope" on price, you will invite two outcomes: (1) consumers leaving your category and (2) new competition.

Problem Number 3: *Focusing on short-term profitability at the expense of long-term revenue growth*

Analysis: This may be the underlying cause of the previous two problems. This problem is driven by the organization's reward systems. If brand managers and general managers are compensated and promoted on delivering quarterly or annual financial results without a focus on longer-term business growth, this is sure to occur. This problem is most acute in publicly held companies that are pressured to deliver quarterly financial results. The solution is to create a balanced scorecard that integrates growth objectives into common and individual performance measures.

Problem Number 4: *Limiting the brand to one channel of distribution or aligning the brand too closely with a declining channel of trade*

Analysis: Have you heard much about Tupperware lately? Although that brand was one of the pioneers of the network marketing approach, it hasn't extended its distribution much beyond that. In contrast, Rubbermaid-branded products are available in many popular distribution channels. Don't ever become too dependent on one channel of trade. Always look for the best new opportunities for distributing your products or services.

Problem Number 5: *Reducing or eliminating brand advertising*

Analysis: When it is time to "tighten the organizational belt," advertising is always a likely source of savings. The budget is usually big enough to contribute significantly to cost savings, and it is often difficult to tell advertising's return on investment. Finally, even if there is an ill effect, the brand won't immediately suffer from an equity withdrawal (or so goes the all too common logic). But, actually, recent studies have shown there is a positive correlation between advertising spending and revenues, earnings, market share, and stock price. Tod Johnson of the NPD Group (which has studied customer purchase behavior since 1978) indicates that a decline in brand loyalty has two causes. One is erratic advertising or advertising that does not keep pace with the competition. The other is cannibalization caused by brand extensions.[1] Set specific objectives for your advertising and track results against those objectives. Copy test all of your ads to make sure they are effective. And, finally, constantly and vigilantly sell the importance of advertising to key internal decision makers.

Problem Number 6: *Applying branding decisions at the end of the product development process ("Now, what will we name this?") versus treating brand management as the key driver of all of your enterprise's activities*

Analysis: You are probably working for a manufacturing company that really doesn't understand brand management and marketing. They design, manufacture, and sell products and services. They don't market brands, or if they do, they leave that function to the advertising or communications department or to the advertising agency. A brand is a source of a promise to the consumer. Everything a company does should support that promise. Start with the target consumer and the brand design (essence, promise, personality and positioning) and then decide what the products and services will be. (This may be an organization design and staffing competency issue.)

Problem Number 7: *Confusing brand management with product management*

Analysis: These are not the same. Brands, if well managed, should have a much longer life than individual products and even product categories. Brand management is much more holistic than product management, encompassing all of the marketing elements and many of an organization's other functions. Consumers do not develop relationships with products nor are they loyal to products. Brands and what they stand for establish the emotional connection with consumers. As Jim Speros of Ernst & Young put it, "Products are manufactured in factories . . . brands are created in the mind of the consumer." (If need be, pass this book around to those who are most in need of enlightenment!)

Problem Number 8: *Defining your brand too narrowly, especially as a product category (for instance, "greeting cards" versus "caring shared")*

Analysis: One of the key advantages of a strong brand is its ability to be extended into new product and service categories. It is a growth engine for your organization. It helps you transcend specific product categories and formats that may become obsolete. Define your brand's essence and promise in terms of what key benefits your brand delivers to consumers (independent of the specific product or service). Then continue to find new ways to deliver against that essence and promise. GE successfully broadened its frame of reference by moving from "General Electric: Better living through electricity" to "GE: We brings good things to life." (GE just adopted a new slogan: "Imagination at work.")

I consider one of my most important successes as the "brand guy" at Hallmark was to change our leaders' perceptions of Hallmark from a greeting card company/brand to a "caring shared" company/brand, paving the way for us to launch gift candy, flowers, and other products to sustain our growth into the next decade. I did not want to see us make the same mistake that Smith-Corona did (defining itself as a product, typewriters, versus a consumer benefit, word processing).

Problem Number 9: *Failure to extend the brand into new product categories when the core category is in decline*

Analysis: "It is our core category. It is our *cash cow*. We must focus all of our resources on preserving it." Sound familiar? It is one thing to prematurely walk away from your core category. It is yet another to myopically focus all of your organizational resources on a flat or declining category in the misguided hope that you may be able to revive it, especially if you are not trying to radically redefine or re-engineer it. Try and try again, but also know when it is time to "quit" (that is, when it is time to do no more than maintain and "milk" the core category and reinvest the profits in new, more promising ventures.) Often, realistic financial projections are the best wake-up call in these situations.

One Reason Great Brands Get Off Track

It has been my experience that brand decline often stems from the "change of guard" at the top of the brand's organization. I have witnessed this first hand more than once (and have heard many other stories of it from friends who have led other brands). The original top manager knew what the brand stood for "in his gut," perhaps because he was the organization's founder with the original vision or perhaps because he was a visionary leader by nature. Then someone else took over the helm (to mix metaphors), someone with little vision. Perhaps someone who only understands business models or numbers or operational excellence, but not the brand's customers and not the brand's essence and key point(s) of difference. Costs are cut in "unnecessary" areas of employee and customer satisfaction. Actions that preserve the "soft stuff" (such as corporate culture, brand vitality and emotional connection, "unnecessary" services, relationship building "gestures" and experiential elements) are eliminated in the name of "efficiency" and "cost effectiveness." How does one get through to individuals who only see the world as cash flow, balance sheets and income statements? Who can only think linearly? Who do not seem to exercise their "right brains"? Who are only interested in their own personal power and wealth? Who are unable to empathize with their employees or their customers? Who do not seem to be in touch with their own "souls"? *Strong, intuitive, visionary, service-based leadership seems to lie at the core of strong brands.*

Problem Number 10: Overextending your brand into different categories and markets so as to completely blur the brand's meaning and points of distinction

Analysis: You can always make more money in the short term by licensing your brand out for use on a variety of products or by extending your brand into a myriad of new categories. The long-term effect of this, however, is detrimental. People no longer will be able to tell what your brand stands for. It will lose its meaning and its point of difference. Extend your brand based on a clear understanding of its essence, promise and personality. And make sure your consumers "get it."

Problem Number 11: *Frequently changing your brand's positioning and message*

Analysis: New brand managers and marketing executives often feel as though they need to make a name for themselves to continue the climb up the corporate ladder. Don't succumb to the temptation of doing this by changing the advertising campaign or the brand slogan, especially if the current ones are working well or haven't been in place long enough to assess their effectiveness. Consistent communication over time is what builds a brand. After all, Hallmark has used its "When You Care Enough to Send the Very Best" slogan since 1944; the Marlboro Man has been Marlboro's icon since 1955; Absolut Vodka has featured its bottle's shape in consumer communication since 1978; and GE has been using its "We Bring Good Things to Life" slogan since 1979. If you do make changes, make them gradually in an integrated fashion based on sound consumer research.

Problem Number 12: *Creating brands or subbrands for internal or trade reasons, rather than to address distinct consumer needs*

Analysis: There is nothing more inefficient or wasteful than creating a new brand or subbrand for a purpose other than meeting a different consumer need. Brands and subbrands should exist to address different consumers and consumer-need segments. It is expensive to launch a new brand (and very expensive to maintain multiple brands that meet similar consumer needs; it also adds unnecessary complexity to your organization). Worst of all, it dilutes the position of your original brand. This problem often results from egos and organization structure. People head up divisions or business units that deliver specific products or services. They create a name and identity to put on business cards and to rally their employees around, whether the products or services are similar to products or services other divisions create or not. (This has resulted in the following printer lines for Hewlett Packard: DeskJet, OfficeJet, OfficeJet Pro, LaserJet, DesignJet, DeskWriter, and PhotoSmart. It is unlikely that consumers understand many of these distinctions. They are likely to think of them all as Hewlett Packard printers.)

Sometimes, companies create separate brands or subbrands for trade reasons—for instance, to offer something different to specialty stores versus mass channels of distribution. (Hallmark created the "Expressions from Hallmark" brand to offer mass channel stores while specialty stores continued to carry the Hallmark brand. These two brands don't meet different consumer needs and I'm not sure consumers perceive differences between the two.) This problem can also result from mergers and acquisitions in which the brands are neither rationalized nor strategically managed after the enterprises are combined. (WorldCom runs this risk with its MCI, 10-10-321, 1-800-Collect, 10-10-220, Skytel, and other brands.)

Problem Number 13: *Launching subbrands that inadvertently reposition the parent brand in a negative light*

Analysis: What does Miller Lite say about Miller High Life? What do Bayer aspirin-free products say about Bayer aspirin? What do Fat-Free Fig Newtons say about Fig Newtons? Make sure you know what you are doing when you create a new subbrand, and be sure to test its impact on the parent brand.

Problem Number 14: *Overexposing the brand to the point that it becomes uncool*

Analysis: Occasionally, a brand can become so ubiquitous through aggressive marketing and distribution that it seems to be everywhere. While brand awareness soars, the brand loses any uniqueness or mystique that it once had. The brand seems to no longer make a unique statement about the individual who uses it. It becomes common. People tire of it. This is particularly true if the brand is mostly hype, logo, and identity, with no strong underlying idea or compelling point of difference. Nike has struggled with this. Its abundant success has also been its downfall: While Nike does stand for something, the brand's overexposure made it too common. The lesson here: *Focus more on the core consumer and maintaining relevant product/service differentiation and less on brand and logo ubiquity.*

Problem Number 15: *Well-known, high-profile brands are often targeted by special interest groups who want to make public statements about their causes*

Analysis: High-profile brands are prone to being knocked off their pedestals by environmental, human rights, equal rights, and other activists and by anti-big business groups. Nike, Wal-Mart, McDonald's, as well as the Boy Scouts of America have all struggled with this issue. Nike has had to deal with opposition to its campus sponsorships and concerns about its alleged use of third world "sweat shops." Wal-Mart is seen as all-powerful and monolithic, and is often accused of putting long-standing local "mom & pop" stores out of business through monopolistic practices. People are concerned about Wal-Mart's alleged use of third world "sweat shops," too. McDonald's is now facing a number of revelations from the recently published book *Fast Food Nation: The Dark Side of the All-American Meal*. The Boy Scouts of America is a target because of its squeaky clean, wholesome image, and its recently highlighted position on homosexuality.

Lesson: If your brand is well known, (a) identify possible exposures (through internal muckraking) and rectify them if at all possible, and (b) develop public relations and crisis management plans to address the exposures.

Problem Number 16: *Treating brand management primarily as "logo cops"*

Analysis: Often the current power structure within an organization will try to put a new brand management function in this "box," either out of ignorance or as a way to minimize or negate a power shift. As I hope you have discovered by now, the brand management function has responsibilities far beyond brand identity management. It is multifaceted, affecting all of marketing and much of the rest of the enterprise. For this reason, it is important that the brand management function exist at a high level in the organization structure. It is also important that the organization's senior executives understand and support this scope of responsibility.

Problem Number 17: *Viewing brand equity management as a communications exercise, but ignoring it in other business processes and points of contact with the consumer*

Analysis: Too often, organizations relegate brand management to a specific department (advertising, marketing, brand management, etc.) or agency. Brand management is an organization-wide process, especially when the brand is a corporate brand. The brand promise must be delivered at each point of contact with the consumer, including customer service lines, retail sales associates, etc. For the brand promise to be clear to your consumers, it must be well understood by everyone in your organization, from the CEO to the receptionist. It must be manifest not only in consumer communication, but also when and wherever the brand name and logo are used. There is a recent trend to design the total enterprise in support of the brand promise, including putting mechanisms in place to develop a brand-building culture.

Problem Number 18: *Not delivering against the communicated brand promise*

Analysis: Again, this is a symptom of viewing brand management as a communications exercise. As mentioned earlier, United Airlines' 1997 advertising campaign, "United Airlines Rising" backfired on them. While they were trying to communicate that their service was rising to meet consumers' expectations, their flight attendants were involved in a labor dispute, and threatening CHAOS ("Creating Havoc Around Our System"). Their customer relations department was so unresponsive to complaints that it prompted a disgruntled customer to create the Web site www.untied.com, featuring United Airlines passenger complaints.

The lesson here: The communicated promise must be delivered in product, service, and the total customer experience. Internal brand strategy education and communication may be necessary to ensure all employees are helping the brand deliver its promise. Tying employee compensation to delivery against the brand promise also will help ensure the promise is delivered.

Problem Number 19: *Not linking brand planning to the business' strategic planning process*

Analysis: A brand plan is useless if it is not an integral part of the organization's business planning process. And, if you aspire to be a market-driven organization, the brand plan should drive the business planning process. Redesign your processes to ensure these two are integrally linked.

Problem Number 20: *If you are the market leader, following challengers because it's easier and produces more immediate results, rather than creating new ways to meet consumer needs*

Analysis: This is an easy trap to fall into: If you are ahead, just match the competition to stay ahead—that way they can never catch up. That is a fairly common sailboat-racing tactic. The problem with this strategy is that you begin to play by your competitor's rules. It is easier to win at your own game than at someone else's. It may be a more natural reaction to match competitive moves, but, as you are doing that, you are distracted from doing what you do best—playing your own game. And, remember, other competitors that *are* playing by different rules may not be far behind.

Problem Number 21: *Not applying the latest product and service innovations to your flagship brand because it is getting too old and stodgy (a self-fulfilling prophecy)*

Analysis: It is a tragedy to walk away from a brand into which you may have invested millions of dollars, over time. It is better to reposition, revitalize, and extend an aging brand than to ignore it. You should carefully monitor consumer opinion to ensure the brand is perceived as relevant and vital. Also, track the brand's consumers to make sure they are not a shrinking or aging group. Often, new subbrands can make the parent brand more relevant to new consumer segments.

Problem Number 22: *Defining your target consumer too broadly (for instance, women ages 18 to 65)*

Analysis: By definition, a brand cannot be all things to all people. A brand promises relevant differentiated benefits to a *target* consumer. Increasingly, companies are focusing on brand usage over penetration. That is, they are getting a larger portion of a smaller group's business by offering more products and services that deliver against the brand promise. This helps to build loyalty. This is in lieu of trying to attract additional consumers to the brand. It is a well-known fact that it costs seven times more to gain a new consumer that it does to get a current consumer to make an incremental purchase. Corporate parent brands can achieve increased targeting through well-targeted subbrands.

Note

1. David N. Martin, *Be the Brand* (Richmond, Va.: New Marketplace, 2000), p. 44.

Twenty Keys to Success in Brand Building: A Summary

As you think about the most important things that can be said about brand management, keep in mind the following:

1. ***The Bottom Line: Why Brand Management Is Essential.*** Brands deliver the following key benefits to organizations:
   - ✓ Increased revenues and market share
   - ✓ Decreased price sensitivity (or the ability to charge price premiums to consumers and the trade)
   - ✓ Increased customer loyalty
   - ✓ For manufacturers, additional leverage over retailers
   - ✓ Increased profitability
   - ✓ Increased stock price and shareholder value
   - ✓ Increased clarity of vision
   - ✓ Increased ability to mobilize an organization's people and focus its activities
   - ✓ Ability to attract and retain high quality employees

A strong, well-positioned brand extends the life of your organization indefinitely by providing independence from a particular product category, increasing flexibility for future growth (through extension), and therefore, increasing the ability to expand into new product and service categories and alter the product and service mix to keep up with marketplace demands. Without a strong brand, your organization's life span will be tied to the life span of the products it manufactures or the services it provides.

2. ***Brand Positioning and Design Are Extremely Important.***
   - ✓ You must define the target consumer, essence, promise, personality, and positioning for your brand.

Did You Know?

✔ Generating trial is frequently the focus of smaller brands while large brands tend to focus on maintaining (and building) loyalty. (*Source*: Allan L. Baldinger and Joel Robinson, "Brand Loyalty: The Link Between Attitude and Behavior," The NPD Group.)

✔ For a new brand, it is important to track the number of stores deciding to sell the product, while for a mature brand, it is more important to look at the number of stores delisting the product. Source: Lars Finskud, "Bringing Discipline to Brand Value Management," *Financial Times Retail & Consumer Publishing, Brand Valuations* 1998.)

✔ "For a fast-growing brand, the number of *new loyal* customers is important, but for an established brand it is the number of *lost loyal* customers that is the telling indicator." (Source: Finskud, "Bringing Discipline to Brand Value Management.")

✔ In a major brand loyalty study, the researchers found that two thirds of the time, when people who were more attitudinally loyal than behaviorally loyal to the brand ("prospects") outnumbered those who were less attitudinally loyal than behaviorally loyal to the brand ("vulnerables"), the brand's market share increased. Market share decreased when the opposite was true. That is why it is important to measure both attitudinal and behavioral loyalty. (*Source*: "Brand Loyalty: The Link Between Attitude and Behavior," http://www.npd.com/corp/newsletters/product_brandbbldrjar.htm 3/27/99.)

3. *Brand Insistence Drivers.*

✔ The goal of brand equity building is to move consumers from brand awareness to brand insistence (see Figure 22-1).

✔ Awareness, relevant differentiation, emotional connection, value, and accessibility drive brand insistence.

✔ Creating awareness is the first step in building a strong brand.

✔ Strive to maximize brand impressions and accessibility.

✔ Overexposing a brand will accelerate its death.

FIGURE 22-1. BRAND INSISTENCE DRIVERS.

Brand Equity Drivers

- Awareness
- Relevant Differentiation
- Emotional Connection
- Value
- Accessibility

Business Results

- Decreased price sensitivity
- Increased consumer loyalty
- (For manufacturers) increased bargaining power with retailers
- Independence from a particular product category
- Increased flexibility for future growth (through extension)
- Increased ability to hire and retain talented employees
- Increased ability to focus the organization's activities & resources
- Increased market share
- Increased stock price
- Increased shareholder value

4. ***Focus and Differentiation.*** Focus and differentiation are the two most important concepts in brand design.

   ✔ By definition, a brand is not for everyone—therein lies its power.

   ✔ The more specific your brand's promise is, the stronger your brand's equity will be.

   ✔ Ideally, the brand tells a story that is unique to its organization.

   ✔ Differentiate your brand in ways that are relevant and compelling to your target consumer.

   ✔ Number 2 brands must never try to emulate market leaders. Their power (as is true of all brands) lies in relevant differentiation.

   ✔ Whenever possible, a brand should try to own the "next big thing" (the emerging key relevant differentiating benefit).

5. ***Common Mistakes Made by Those Who Don't Understand Branding***

   ✔ A brand is not a product or service and a product or service is not a brand.

   ✔ Brand management is not product management.

   ✔ Brand management is much more than advertising or brand identity management.

6. ***A Brand Is the Personification of a Product, Service, or Organization.*** It is also the source of a relationship with customers. Like a person, it must have human qualities and possess a soul.

- ✔ Think of a brand as a person—possessing core values and a personality.
- ✔ The brand is the source of the organization's relationship with people.
- ✔ Strive to create an emotional connection with your consumer.
- ✔ The most successful brands tap into deeply felt human needs.
- ✔ A brand must have a heart and a soul.
- ✔ A brand must be trustworthy. It must earn people's trust.
- ✔ A brand must be courageous. It must unwaveringly stand for something.
- ✔ A brand must possess integrity, that is, it must deliver what it promises— always.
- ✔ A brand must be authentic, not manufactured.
- ✔ A brand must win people's hearts. It must endear itself to consumers.
- ✔ A brand is more likeable if it is vulnerable, laughs at itself and admits to its mistakes.
- ✔ A brand gets credit for attempting to do what is right.

7. *A Brand Must Deliver a Good Value.*

8. *A Brand Must Be Accessible and Convenient.*

9. *Focus on Delivering the Brand Promise.* You must focus the organization on delivering the brand promise—brand management is much more than marketing (a.k.a., making the brand promise real).
   - ✔ Branding is not an afterthought; rather it is the core value of the organization.
   - ✔ Have a singular focus on delivering the brand promise.
   - ✔ The brand's products and services must deliver upon the brand's promise.
   - ✔ Focus everything your organization does on delivering the brand promise.
   - ✔ An organization must manifest its brand's essence, promise, and personality at each point of contact it makes with people.
   - ✔ Carefully manage all the points of contact you make with the consumer.
   - ✔ An organization's culture must reinforce its brand's essence, promise, and personality.
   - ✔ To be truly successful, a brand must be based upon the enlightened vision of a strong leader and a relentless employee passion to better meet the needs of the customer.

On Relationships

People develop relationships with other people. Brands exist so that organizations can do the same. So, what maximizes a brand's appeal? The same things that maximize a person's appeal—authenticity, honesty, integrity (that is, a congruence between thoughts, words and deeds), charisma, warmth, assertiveness, approachability, passion, reliability, originality, etc. And here is the thing that makes people and brands the most interesting. Each possesses a different combination of qualities that appeals to different people at different times.

The best brands will challenge and comfort and inspire and draw out one's best and help one grow, just as the best human relationships do.

Branding, at its best, transforms organizations so that they are capable of creating, nurturing and sustaining mutually profitable relationships with people. And *that is* a very good thing.

✓ Don't forget to hire, train, motivate, and compensate frontline employees to deliver the brand's essence, promise, and personality.

✓ The brand's essence, promise, and personality must drive organization decision-making and resource allocation.

✓ Ultimately, you want to use brand identity systems, advertising, packaging, retail environment, services, the Internet, and other delivery mechanisms to "bring your brand to life."

10. *Brand Management Starts with Understanding the Customer.*

✓ A brand must be based upon a profound understanding of the target consumer and the marketplace in which he or she lives.

✓ You must have a profound understanding of your consumers and their values, attitudes, motivations, and behaviors (purchase and usage).

✓ Understanding the target consumer's hopes and fears is essential to designing a strong brand.

11. *The Importance of Choosing the Right Brand Benefits.*

✓ Ideally, a brand should own benefits that are (1) highly important to the target consumer, (2) a core competency of the delivering organization, and (3) not being addressed by the brand's competitors.

The Quick Brand Health Assessment

You know your brand is winning in the marketplace when:

✔ The brand is mentioned to customers and potential customers, and they brim with enthusiasm in their response.

✔ Your brand's external messages "ring true" with all employees.

✔ Employees are enthusiastic and consistent in recounting what makes their brand special.

✔ The brand's market share is increasing.

✔ Competitors always mention your brand as a point of reference.

✔ The press can't seem to write enough about your brand.

✔ Your CEO has a strong vision for the organization and its brand. He or she talks more about the vision than financial targets.

✔ Your organization's leaders always seem to "talk the brand" *and* "walk the brand talk."

✔ A brand must engage people on an emotional and sensory level.

✔ It is much more powerful and sustainable for a brand to own emotional, experiential, and self-expressive benefits than it is for it to own functional benefits.

✔ Competitors cannot easily emulate brand benefits that are based upon your organization's core values.

12. ***A brand must be based upon the leader's vision and the employees' passion.*** To be truly successful, a brand must be based upon the enlightened vision of a strong leader and a relentless employee passion to better meet the needs of the customer (or, Brand as an Internal Rallying Cry).

✔ Strategic vision is an essential component of strong brands.

✔ Brand management must be owned at the highest level of the organization—and throughout the organization.

✔ Brand management is a much less difficult task when the CEO has internalized the brand's essence, promise, and vision.

✓ It is certainly as important (if not more so) to indoctrinate employees about what the brand stands for as it is to do so for external audiences.

✓ The brand can become the mobilizing influence and rallying cry within an organization.

✓ The brand's vision should inspire and empower people.

✓ The most successful brands possess passion. Its leaders are "hungry" with "fire in their bellies."

✓ Everyone in the organization must truly believe in and "live" the brand.

✓ Convert everyone in your organization (and suppliers and retailers) into evangelists for your brand.

✓ Storytelling is an important part of brand building.

✓ Your organization must have a clear vision of how your brand uniquely adds value in the marketplace. People in the organization must share a vision of what the brand stands for.

✓ When employees sincerely believe that their brand stands for something that makes a difference in the world, the brand becomes unstoppable.

13. *Use a Wide Array of Brand Identity Elements for Maximum Effect.*

✓ In today's multimedia environment, an organization must use all of the components of a brand identity system for greatest effect—brand name, logo, icon, typography, colors, tag lines, attitude, voice, visual style, scent, sound, motion/animation, etc.

✓ Your brand's identity system should be multifaceted, going well beyond name, logo, and slogan to include personality, voice, and visual style, among other elements.

✓ Consistent execution of brand identity is crucial. Think of your brand as a person. It should exhibit consistent behaviors, not multiple personalities.

14. *The Importance of Superior Products and Services to Strong Brands.*

✓ Brands are meaningless if their products and services are not superior.

✓ Find a way to have your brand redefine quality within its product category.

✓ A brand must be kept vital and relevant. It requires constant innovation, communication and promotion.

✓ Understand all the compromises your brand (and every brand in your category) makes with consumers. Break those compromises to "leapfrog" the competition.

✓ Value-generating innovation may be the most powerful engine for brand growth. Products, services, innovation, and the customer experience are all integral elements of a strong brand.

15. ***Create a Total Brand Experience for Your Customers.***

✓ Always give your customers something new to discover about your brand.

16. ***Cocreating Products, Services, and Experiences with Customers Is the Future of Brands.***

✓ Communicate with the consumer whenever and wherever you can.

✓ Maintain a constant and intimate dialog with your consumer.

✓ The most powerful brands in the long run are those that are cocreated by the consumer and the marketer—those that are a result of ongoing dialogue.

✓ Brands that align themselves with communities, and, more powerfully, brands that create communities, will thrive.

✓ Brands that share values with consumers will survive.

✓ The most successful brands will create experiences, evoke emotions, and celebrate and elevate the human spirit.

17. ***Celebrate the Brand Manager.*** Brand manager is an underrated, difficult, but intrinsically rewarding job.

✓ Brand management is an art and a science. It requires in-depth consumer research, thorough analysis, creativity, sound judgment, and strategic vision.

✓ Due to its complexity and its need to touch all aspects of the business, brand management is not easy. Often, few people in the organization understand the full scope and complexity of brand management. Nevertheless, and perhaps because of all of its challenges, brand management can be very rewarding.

18. ***Use Direct Marketing, the Internet, and Direct Experiential Interaction with Consumers.*** They will become increasingly important in building strong brands.

19. ***Recognize that your people and brands are your most important assets.*** Organizations that do will be more successful than those that do not.

20. ***Determining How Fast and in What Ways to Grow the Brand Is a Key Brand Manager Role.*** This decision should be informed by an intimate knowledge of the customer, and by intuition and common sense.

The Future of Brand Management: My Prognostications

- ✔ Building emotional connection will be key

- ✔ Brands will focus more on creating/engineering the total customer experience

- ✔ Customer-relevant innovation will be a key success factor

- ✔ Outstanding customer service will also be a key success factor

- ✔ Hiring the right employees and creating the appropriate culture will be essential

- ✔ More and more, brands will co-create the customer experience with the customer

- ✔ More and more, brands will need to "stand for something" to survive

- ✔ Strong brands will not only "stand for something," they will also provide forums for people who believe in what the brands stand for

- ✔ Organizations whose employees become consultants to and friends and partners with their customers will be the most successful

- ✔ One-on-one marketing will become more and more important

- ✔ The Internet will also become increasingly important as a brand-building vehicle

- ✔ For larger organizations, customer relationship management (CRM) will become a critical success factor

- ✔ Fast, flexible and agile organizations will increasingly "win" in the digital age

- ✔ With the explosion of virtual and morphing organizations and ever-changing business alliances, the brand essence and promise and the organizational culture may increasingly be the only elements that create a sense of "entity" for organizations

> ✔ **The viral spread of information will increasingly expose organizations for what they really are—integrity and consistency will be key**
>
> ✔ **Managing "buzz" will be an essential brand management activity**

▪ Waning Philosophical—Brand Management at its Best

At its worst, the organizational brand is a name and a logo that is inconsistently applied to an unrelated set of products and services. It is overused and means nothing, and it reminds people of the worst of an overly commercial society. It feels cold and seems exploitative. It is perceived to be a vestige of a past era.

At its best, brand management aligns organizations with value-adding activities. It keeps organizations focused on meeting real human needs in compelling new ways. And, at its best, the organizational brand defines how the organization best meets its customers' needs in unique and compelling ways. It serves as the organization's unifying principle and rallying cry, it infuses the organization with a set of values and a personality, and it holds an organization's employees to a consistent set of behaviors. The organizational brand stands for something. It establishes trust and a certain level of assurance, it makes it possible for people to establish relationships with the organization, and it creates expectations that must be fulfilled. The brand can bring an organization to life in a very real way.

In the end, brand management is all about meeting people's physical, emotional, spiritual, intellectual, and other needs in unique ways. It is the application of free enterprise to the timely and timeless needs of mankind.

I wish you a brand at its best. May you unleash your brand's power and transform your organization through branding.

PART EIGHT

APPENDIXES

APPENDIX A

Brand Audits

A **BRAND AUDIT** provides an analysis of an organization's brand and its brand management and marketing effectiveness. It assesses a brand's strengths, weaknesses, opportunities, and threats. It identifies brand growth opportunities, including those achieved by brand repositioning and brand extension. The audit should result in recommendations to improve brand equity, brand positioning, and brand management and marketing effectiveness.

Brand Audit Components

The following are typical components of a brand audit:

- *Strategy Review*
  - Business plans
  - Marketing plans
  - Brand positioning statement
  - Brand plans
  - Creative (or agency) briefs
  - Media plans
- *Marketing Research Review*
  - Brand positioning research
  - Brand asset studies
  - Brand equity measurement system (awareness, preference, usage, value, accessibility, relevance, differentiation, vitality, emotional connection, loyalty, associations, personality)
  - Brand extension research
  - Product/service concept testing
  - Logo recall and recognition testing

✓ *Communications Review*
  - ✓ Advertising and promotion materials
  - ✓ Other brand marketing elements, including pricing, packaging, merchandising, distribution, direct marketing, sponsorships, and flagship stores
  - ✓ Press kit
  - ✓ Press releases
  - ✓ Sales collateral materials
  - ✓ Internal communications
  - ✓ Business cards, letterheads, etc.
  - ✓ Web site
  - ✓ Intranet site
  - ✓ Employee training programs
  - ✓ Employee orientation
  - ✓ Manager training
  - ✓ Sales force training

✓ *External Information Source Review*
  - ✓ Competitors' press releases, advertising, and promotion
  - ✓ Industry analyst reports
  - ✓ Customer comments
  - ✓ Business partner comments
  - ✓ Marketing vendor interviews

✓ *Employee Interviews*
  - ✓ Corporate officer interviews
  - ✓ Marketing employee interviews
  - ✓ Sales force interviews
  - ✓ Customer service employee interviews
  - ✓ Frontline customer contact interviews
  - ✓ General employee interviews

✓ *Human Resource Systems Review*
  - ✓ Organization charts
  - ✓ Department mission/vision statements
  - ✓ Department objectives
  - ✓ Common objectives
  - ✓ Recruiting criteria
  - ✓ Individual competency dictionary
  - ✓ Succession planning criteria
  - ✓ Planning and resource allocation systems/processes

✓ *Proprietary Brand Research (performed by the auditing company, if required)*

✓ Brand asset research

✓ Brand equity research

✓ Brand positioning research (qualitative and quantitative)

Brand Management Audit

A qualified brand audit company will investigate the following areas of brand management:

✓ **Brand Research**

  ✓ Does this company have a deep understanding of its consumers' values, attitudes, needs, desires, hopes, aspirations, fears, and concerns?

  ✓ Has this company rigorously analyzed its competition?

  ✓ Which of the following types of brand research has the company conducted: brand positioning qualitative and quantitative, brand asset studies, brand equity measurement and monitoring, brand extension, logo recall, and recognition?

  ✓ How robust is each of these research studies?

  ✓ How are the company and each of its competitors positioned in the marketplace?

✓ **Brand Strategy**

  ✓ Is there a marketing plan?

  ✓ Is there a brand plan?

  ✓ Are those plans aligned with and integrated into company business plans?

  ✓ Does the company have a future vision and a well-thought out plan to get there?

  ✓ Is it clear which marketing objectives, actions, and vehicles will provide the greatest leverage in achieving the long-term vision?

✓ **Brand Positioning**

  ✓ Is there a brand positioning statement? Does it include the following: target consumer, differentiating brand benefit, brand essence, brand personality?

  ✓ Do most employees know the brand's positioning (verbatim or paraphrased)?

  ✓ Was the brand's key differentiating benefit based on an analysis of consumer needs, organizational strengths (core competencies), and competitive weaknesses?

- ✔ Does the brand own a benefit that is highly differentiated, compelling, and believable?
- ✔ What are the brand's strengths, weaknesses, opportunities, and threats?

✔ *Brand Identity Standards and Systems*

- ✔ How robust is the company's brand identity system?
- ✔ How easy is it for the company's employees and business partners to use?
- ✔ What brand identity controls does the company have in place?
- ✔ Is the company's brand architecture simple and understandable?
- ✔ Which of the following brand identity components does the company use in its system: name, logo, icon, tag line, type style, colors, shapes, symbols, visual style, mnemonic (sound) device, brand voice, music, animation, etc.?
- ✔ Does the company have cobranding standards?
- ✔ How accurately and consistently have these standards been applied across all internal and external communications?

✔ *Brand Advertising*

- ✔ Do the ads break through the marketplace clutter?
- ✔ Do they powerfully communicate the brand's promise and personality?
- ✔ Do they include the "reasons why" (differentiating benefit proof points)?
- ✔ Do they connect with the target consumer on an emotional level?
- ✔ Do they tap into the consumers' beliefs, values, aspirations, hopes and fears?
- ✔ Do they include components that are "ownable"?

✔ *Organization Design and Internal Brand Building*

- ✔ Is the company market driven or does it have a traditional manufacturing company design?
- ✔ Does the company's culture support the brand's essence, promise, and personality?
- ✔ Is the company's marketing function centralized or distributed?
- ✔ What mechanisms has the company put in place to integrate its marketing?
- ✔ Are all of the required marketing functions present?
- ✔ Are brand objectives integrated into company and common objectives?
- ✔ Do the company's recruiting, training, performance management, compensation, succession planning, business planning, budgeting,

resource allocation, and other systems support brand building? Are they designed to help the company deliver upon its brand's promise?

✓ Does the company screen job applicants for their alignment with the brand's essence, promise, and personality?

✓ Is the organization a "learning organization"?

✓ **Brand Extension**

✓ What are the brand's assets?

✓ Is the brand over- or underextended (or both)?

✓ What are the most promising areas for brand extension?

✓ What processes does the organization have in place for brand extension? How does it safeguard against inappropriate extension?

✓ **Marketing Employee Competency**

✓ How competent are the company's marketers?

✓ Which skill sets do they possess and which ones are missing?

✓ Has the company augmented missing internal skill sets by augmenting them with external sources?

✓ What are its external marketing vendors' strengths and weaknesses?

✓ Do the company's marketing employees (and also its senior managers and the rest of its employees) exhibit a marketing mindset? That is, do they profoundly understand its customers and sincerely and passionately strive to meet their wants and needs?

Brand Positioning Investigation

Brand auditors should assess the strength of an organization's mission and vision and the strength of its brand's essence, promise, and personality (especially in relationship to the organization's stakeholders' perceptions of the organization). As part of the process, the auditor should investigate how congruently each of the following groups or sources articulate or manifest these organizational and brand attributes:

✓ Its leaders

✓ Its official documents

✓ Its internal and external communications

✓ Its marketers

✓ Its salespeople

✓ Its customer service employees

✓ Its other employees

- ✓ Its business partners
- ✓ Each and every point of contact the brand makes with its clients/customers

Who Performs the Audit?

Brand Auditor Skill Set

Ideally, the company performing the audit has broad and deep experience (as line managers and as consultants) in each of the following areas:

- ✓ Brand research
- ✓ Brand strategy and positioning
- ✓ Brand identity standards and systems
- ✓ Brand advertising
- ✓ Organization design

Size of Audit Team

Audits will vary from company to company based upon the company's unique needs, organizational complexity, marketing competency, and other factors. Given the large amount of work required to complete the audit in a reasonable period of time, the audit team should consist of at least three people. The more marketing experience each team member has, the better.

A Caution

Weaknesses to look out for in self-proclaimed brand auditors are:

- ✓ Strength in other areas of marketing (advertising, promotion, etc.), but not in brand management
- ✓ Primary foci on brand research, strategy, and positioning, but little knowledge of how to design an organization to deliver upon the brand promise
- ✓ Strong knowledge of brand management but little understanding of organization design
- ✓ Lack of brand research experience

Cost and Duration of a Brand Audit

Audit Cost

Audit costs may vary from a low of $150,000 to more than $1,000,000 depending on the global reach of the business, complexity of the brand and product structure, amount of proprietary research required, project's duration, number of people assigned, audit firm's profit margin and billing rate, etc. If an audit company provides an estimate much lower than that, it indicates a lack of understanding of the scope and complexity of this type of project.

Audit Duration

The project may last anywhere from a month (fast track with concentrated interviews and little to no additional research) to six months.

Areas Investigated in a Brand Audit

A brand audit should identify strengths, weaknesses, opportunities, and threats in the following areas:

- ✔ Brand strategy and positioning
- ✔ Brand equity
- ✔ Leveraging the brand for business growth
- ✔ Capacity of the organization to manage and market the brand effectively
- ✔ Alignment of the organization's structure and systems to deliver upon the brand's promise

Bottom Line Questions

Here are some questions that a strong brand auditor will attempt to answer:

- ✔ Does this company have a profound understanding of its consumers?
- ✔ Is the brand well positioned in its marketplace? Does it own a relevant and compelling point of difference?

✔ Do the leaders of this company have a vision for their brand(s)?

✔ Is this company's marketing staff competent?

✔ Is the organization mobilized to deliver upon its brand's promise?

✔ Does the corporate culture reinforce the brand essence, promise, and personality?

✔ Are the brand identity standards and systems simple, robust, and powerful?

✔ Does this organization accurately and consistently reinforce its brand's identity and positioning in internal and external communication?

✔ Does the brand create an emotional connection with its consumers?

APPENDIX B

→ Online Brand Management and Advertising Resources

▪ Online Brand Management Resources

http://www.brandera.com/—BrandEra.com, the Marketer's Marketplace, serves as the business-to-business destination for the marketing communications industry. It brings professionals with marketing needs together with suppliers of creative solutions, offering timely news articles, a Request for Proposals exchange, and searchable online portfolios for freelancers (photographers, illustrators, graphic designers, multimedia artist, art directors, and copywriters). There are also comprehensive ad agency listings, a fully searchable resource center and industry directory, job classified ads, an online collaborative tool, and more.

http://www.clickz.com/—Comprehensive archive of articles on all aspects of marketing.

http://www.webmarketingtoday.com/webmarket/branding.htm—Web Marketing Info Center. Its "Branding on the Web" features a comprehensive archive of articles.

http://marketing.about.com/?once = true&pid = 2737& cob = home—About Marketing: articles, forums, chat, and more.

http://www.marketingprofs.com—MarketingProfs.com: Marketing knowhow from professors and professionals.

http://www.marketingsherpa.com—MarketingSherpa, Inc. is a media company publishing useful news, case studies, and best practices data about Internet and integrated marketing for advertising, marketing, and PR professionals.

http://www.mad.co.uk/bs/—mad.co.uk is an invaluable resource for marketing, media, new media, advertising, and design professionals.

http://www.allaboutbranding.com/—allaboutbranding.com is dedicated to examining the nature of branding and the issues encountered in shaping and managing brands.

http://www.admedia.org/internet/home.html—Internet Advertising Resource Guide.

http://www.iab.net/—Founded in 1996, The Interactive Advertising Bureau is the industry's leading interactive advertising association. Its activities include evaluating and recommending guidelines and best practices, fielding research to document the effectiveness of interactive media, and educating the advertising industry about the use of interactive advertising and marketing. Membership includes companies that are actively engaged in the sale of interactive advertising and marketing.

Online Brand-Related Publications

http://bubl.ac.uk/journals/bus/—Abstracts from marketing journals.

www.adage.com—*AdvertisingAge*.

www.marketingpower.com—American Marketing Association.

http://brandmarketing.com—*Brand Marketing*.

http://www.mad.co.uk/bs/—*Brand Strategy*.

www.brandweek.com—*Brand Week*.

www.arfsite.org/Webpages/JAR_pages/jarhome.htm—*Journal of Advertising Research*.

www.mcb.co.uk/forums/market.htm—Links to several (mostly European) marketing journals.

www.mcb.co.uk/jpbm.htm—*The Journal of Product & Brand Management*.

www.salesandmarketing.com—*Sales and Marketing Management*.

Online Advertising Resources

Here is a list of online advertising resources, including brief descriptions (including some taken straight from the Web sites themselves).

http://www.adforum.com/—AdForum is the Internet's leading portal to the advertising, marketing, and communications industry, with direct links to more than 16,796 agencies in 134 countries.

http://www.warc.com/—The World Advertising Research Center (WARC) provides knowledge and data to the global advertising, marketing and media industries, through its Web sites, hard copy publications, and conferences.

http://www.oneclub.com/OneShow—The One Show is an annual advertising competition judged by a group of the advertising industry's most reputable creative directors. Every year, a different team of top creative directors judges ads sent in from all over the world.

http://www.commarts.com/CA/—Founded in 1959, Communication Arts is the leading trade journal for visual communications. It's the largest design magazine in the world and showcases the top work in graphic design, advertising, illustration, photography, and interactive design. The magazine has an audited paid circulation of 74,834.

http://www.shots.net/—shots.net is a dedicated site for professionals involved in the advertising and production industry. Collected over the past ten years, shots.net presents the finest archive of creative talent: over 4000 of the most original spots—with credits—to search and view on your computer.

http://www.adcritic.com—AdCritic.com is a business-to-business and business-to-consumer knowledge resource for the advertising industry and related industries. Peter Beckman, founder, CEO, and chief technology officer of AdCritic.com, developed the concept of AdCritic.com to be a premiere screening service for television commercials using broadband video in 1999. AdCritic.com serves a need for agencies seeking creative talent, for creative talent to be found, and for consumers to give valuable feedback, survey data and rating of advertising collateral.

http://www.ecreativesearch.com—A comprehensive database of directors, production, and post-production services from around the world, plus thousands of spots and credits. eCreativeSearch is a subscription-based Internet service for the commercial broadcast production industry. It provides access to a searchable and comprehensive database of directors, production companies, music and other talent, and support services, as well as commercials.

http://www.clioawards.com/—Welcome to the Clio Awards Web site, the first stop for news about Clio and its 41-year history, and eventually for all relevant news about the world of creative advertising.

http://www.effie.org/—Introduced by the New York American Marketing Association in 1968, EFFIE has since become recognized by agencies and advertisers as the pre-eminent award in the advertising industry. It is the only national award that honors creative achievement in meeting and exceeding advertising objectives. In short, it focuses on effective advertising, advertising that works in the marketplace.

http://www.aaaa.org/—Founded in 1917, the American Association of Advertising Agencies (AAAA) is the national trade association representing the advertising agency business in the United States. Its membership produces approximately 75 percent of the total advertising volume placed by agencies nationwide. Although virtually all of the large, multi-national agencies are members of the AAAA, more than 60 percent of its members bill less than $10 million per year.

http://www.aaf.org/—The American Advertising Federation protects and promotes the well-being of advertising through a unique, nationally coordinated grassroots network of advertisers, agencies, media companies, local advertising clubs, and college chapters. To accomplish its objectives, AAF initiatives include the following:

- ✓ Advertising Hall of Fame
- ✓ Advertising Hall of Achievement
- ✓ ADDY® Awards
- ✓ American Advertising Conference
- ✓ American Advertising Federation's Executive Summit
- ✓ Government Affairs Conference
- ✓ Great Brands Campaign
- ✓ Most Promising Minority Students Program
- ✓ NSAC: College World Series of Advertising
- ✓ Principles & Recommended Practices for Effective Advertising in the American Multicultural Marketplace

http://www.ana.net/—The Association of National Advertisers, Inc. (ANA) is the industry's premier trade association dedicated exclusively to marketing and brand building. Representing more than 300 companies with 8,000 brands that collectively spend over $100 billion in marketing communications and advertising, the Association's members market products and services to consumers and businesses.

http://www.arfsite.org/—Founded in 1936 by the Association of National Advertisers and the American Association of Advertising Agencies, the Advertising Research Foundation (ARF) is a nonprofit corporate-membership association, which is today the preeminent professional organization in the field of advertising, marketing, and media research. Its combined membership represents more than 400 advertisers, advertising agencies, research firms, media companies, educational institutions, and international organizations. The principal mission of the ARF is to improve the practice of advertising, marketing, and media research in pursuit of more effective marketing and advertising communications.

http://www.iaaglobal.org/—The IAA is the only global partnership of advertisers, agencies, the media, and related services. Its mission is to:

- ✓ Promote the critical role and benefits of advertising as the vital force behind all healthy economies and the foundation of diverse, independent media in an open society

✓ Protect and advance freedom of commercial speech and consumer choice

✓ Encourage greater practice and acceptance of advertising self-regulation

✓ Provide a forum to debate emerging professional marketing communications issues and their consequences in a fast-changing world environment

✓ Take the lead in state-of-the-art professional development, education, and training for the marketing communications industry of tomorrow

http://www.cahners.com—Cahners is a leading provider of critical information and marketing solutions to business professionals in targeted industry sectors. Its properties include more than 135 business-to-business publications, over 125 Web sites, and a range of services, including Web development, custom publishing, research, business lists, and industry events. Cahners is a member of the Reed Elsevier plc group—a world-leading provider of information-driven services and solutions. CARR (Cahners Advertising Research) Reports—found under the Research/CARR Reports tab— provides a wide variety of free downloadable reports on specialized business publications, advertising effectiveness, and other advertising-related business results.

www.adage.com—For more than 65 years, Advertising Age has been the preeminent source of marketing, advertising, and media news, information, and analysis.

http://www.ciadvertising.org/—The site for the Center for Interactive Advertising at the University of Texas at Austin contains research and resources in the areas of Internet advertising, electronic commerce, and advertising education.

http://www.magazinescanada.com/—Magazines Canada is the source for the Canadian magazine industry, including research summaries and archives.

http://www.ahaa.org/— The mission of the Association of Hispanic Advertising Agencies (AHAA) is to promote the growth, strength and professionalism of the Hispanic marketing and advertising industry to a diverse audience of business, government, and educational institutions.

http://www.adslogans.co.uk/index.html—ADSlogans Unlimited, home of the Advertising Slogan Hall of Fame, runs the world's most comprehensive advertising slogans database. A unique global resource for advertisers and ad agencies, comprising many thousands of English-language advertising slogans, taglines, claims, straplines, theme lines, endlines, payoffs, base lines, slogos (the slogan by the logo), and catchphrases.

APPENDIX C

Brand Management Quiz

Questions

1. Can you name three individuals who have successfully branded themselves?
2. Can you describe their brands' essences?
3. Can you identify their target audiences?
4. Can you name three commodities that have been successfully branded?
5. What created the perceived differences between each of those brands and the commodity?
6. What industry is currently trying to transform itself from commodity status through branding?
7. What are some of the ways that electric utility companies can differentiate themselves?
8. What major brands built their businesses with little or no advertising?
9. Of twenty-five top brands in twenty-five different product categories in 1923, how many are still category leaders today?
10. As consumer satisfaction increases in a product category, (a) does consumer loyalty increase or decrease? (b) Why? (c) If you could only use one of the two measures (consumer satisfaction or consumer loyalty), which would you use?
11. If a consumer has a high repeat purchase rate, is he or she necessarily a loyal consumer?
12. Are the heaviest purchasers the most loyal?
13. Can you give a few examples of "ingredient branding," branded components of other brands' products or services?
14. Can you name four or more brands that have become (or run the risk of becoming) category generic descriptors?

15. Which is the most predictive of brand market share: (a) brand loyalty, (b) brand value, (c) brand penetration, (d) brand awareness, or (e) brand differentiation?

Answers

1. Madonna, Dennis Rodman, Martha Stewart, Stephen King, Isaac Asimov, Deepak Chopra, M.D., and Marilyn Manson, to name a few.

2. Hint: Create a two-to-three word phrase that captures the "heart and soul" of each individual.

3. Hint: Create a two-sentence description of the type of person who would most appreciate (that is, derive functional, emotional, experiential, or self-expressive benefits from) each individual.

4. Bottled water, vodka, chicken, bananas.

5. Hints: What makes you choose one brand over another in the category: consistent quality, taste, health concerns, making a personal statement? What communicates these attributes: brand name, packaging, label, advertising?

6. Electric utilities.

7. Bundled services, environmental/social responsibility, customer service, energy reduction consulting, add-on services, etc. (Nicor has chosen "unconditional primal warmth" as its point of difference.)

8. Harley-Davidson, Body Shop, Starbucks, Gateway, Compaq, Wal-Mart, Haagen-Dazs, Palm Pilot, Hotmail, Trivial Pursuit, ICQ.

9. Twenty.

10. (a) Decrease. (b) As satisfaction increases, most options eventually exceed consumer's requirements; when that happens, consumers become indifferent to brands. (c) Consumer loyalty.

11. No, not necessarily. The behavior could be driven by a purchaser frequency program that does not create sustained (or attitudinal) loyalty. The reverse, however, is true. Loyalty should result in high repeat purchase rates.

12. Not necessarily. Often, the most enthusiastic category purchasers buy the product—regardless of brand—whenever and wherever they find it.

13. Dolby, NutraSweet, Intel, Kevlar, Lycra, Nylon, Gore-Tex, and Culligan (Culligan water filtration systems are sold within GE appliances).

14. Aspirin, Cellophane, Escalator, Styrofoam, Kleenex, Shredded Wheat, Thermos, Band-Aid, Scotch Tape, Super Glue, Chap Stick, Wite-out, Beer Nuts, Q-tips, Jell-o, Rollerblade, Bungee, Xerox, and Palm Pilot.

15. (c) Brand penetration. Although brand penetration is the most predictive of brand market share, it does not guarantee profitable market share. For instance, if it is achieved by "buying" distribution (by paying retailers high sales terms), it will result in high market share at reduced profit margins. For profitable market share gains, one must focus on all of the drivers of customer brand insistence: awareness, accessibility, value, relevant differentiation, and emotional connection.

Index

common problems with, 201
concepts, 199–200
definition of, 12–13
evaluation matrix for, 201, 202
key considerations in, 198
risks of, 197
steps in, 199
successful *vs.* unsuccessful, 200–201
types of, 195–196
brand goals, 174
brand health assessment, 276
brand identity
audit of, 286
color used for, 69
components of, 10, 61
cross-divisional council used for, 70
definition of, 10
effect of organization size on, 245
ensuring consistency of, 69–70
multifaceted elements of, 277
legal protection of, 250–252
standards, 69
brand identity manager, creation of, 70
brand image, 7
brand insistence
drivers, 78, 80–87, 272, 273
hierarchy of effects, 86
loyalty-inducing approaches, 86
model, 77
brand inundation testing, 218
brand logos, 65
brand loyalty, 229–230
brand management
as organization-wide process, 269
audit of, 285–287
future of, 279–280
importance of, 278
intranet sites, 70
key benefits of, 271
online resources, 291–292
paradigm, 175–176
quiz, 296–298
as logo cops, 268

brand management function, 18
brand management process
flowchart, 17
overview of, 15–18
research in support of, 18–19
brand mantra, 8
brand marketing, 173
as investment, 239
budget allocation, 126
budget components of, 181
cause-related, 119
direct, *see* direct marketing
employee competency audit, 287
ideation techniques in, 129
integration across organization,
182–184
long-term *vs.* short-term investments
in, 235, 236
measuring effectiveness of, 237
outrageous breakthroughs, 120
ROI measurement, 236–237
use of trade shows for, 181–182
brand message guidelines, 69
brand names
associative descriptive, 63, 64
coined, 63, 64, 251
decision tree used for, 65, 66
descriptive, 251
desirable characteristics of, 64
generic, 63–64
suggestive, 251
tips for, 62–64
brand ownership, larger-than-life, 119
brand personality
as component of brand design, 15
attributes, 44
definition of, 9
brand plan
components of, 14
linked to business plan, 269
objectives of, 13
brand portfolio, 11
brand positioning
audit of, 285–286